ARCHAEOLOGICAL SURVEY OF INDIA, NEW IMPERIAL SERIES, VOL. XXXIX

COORG INSCRIPTIONS

(REVISED EDITION)

ARCHAEOLOGICAL SURVEY OF INDIA, NEW IMPERIAL SERIES, VOL. XXXIX

COORG INSCRIPTIONS

(REVISED EDITION)

BY

B. LEWIS RICE, I.C.E.

MEMBER OF THE ROYAL ASIATIC SOCIETY, FORMER DIRECTOR OF PUBLIC INSTRUCTION IN MYSORE AND COORG, LATE DIRECTOR OF ARCHAEOLOGICAL RESEARCHES, EDITOR OF THE GAZETTEERS OF MYSORE AND COONG FOR THE IMPERIAL GAZETTEER OF INDIA

EPIGRAPHIA CARNATICA

VOL. I

GYAN

Published by

Gyan Publishing House
5, Ansari Road
Daryaganj, New Delhi-110002
Phone: 011-47034999, 9811692060
E-mail: books@gyanbooks.com

Distribution Network
gyanbooks.com
India, USA, Canada, UK, Australia, France

ISBN : 978-81-212-2200-6 (HB)
First Published, 1914

2nd Impression 2021

Printed at: Gyan Press, Delhi.

Coorg Inscriptions Vol. I
Author: B. Lewis Rice

ARCHÆOLOGICAL SURVEY OF INDIA, NEW IMPERIAL SERIES, VOL. XXXIX.

COORG INSCRIPTIONS

(REVISED EDITION)

BY

B. LEWIS RICE, C.I.E.,

MEMBER OF THE ROYAL ASIATIC SOCIETY, FORMER DIRECTOR OF PUBLIC INSTRUCTION
IN MYSORE AND COORG, LATE DIRECTOR OF ARCHÆOLOGICAL RESEARCHES,
EDITOR OF THE GAZETTEERS OF MYSORE AND COORG
FOR THE IMPERIAL GAZETTEER OF INDIA.

EPIGRAPHIA CARNATICA.

VOL. I.

MADRAS:
PRINTED BY THE SUPERINTENDENT, GOVERNMENT PRESS.

1914.

CONTENTS

WORKS REFERRED TO

AQR	Asiatic Quarterly Review.
DKD	Dynasties of the Kanarese Districts by Dr. Fleet.
EC	Epigraphia Carnatica.
EI	Epigraphia Indica.
IA	Indian Antiquary.
IGI	Imperial Gazetteer of India.
Ind Pal	(Grundriss of) Indo-Aryan Palæography by Dr. Bühler.
JRAS	Journal of the Royal Asiatic Society.
MAR	Mysore Archæological Report.
Mad AR	Madras Archæological Report.
Mad EpR	Madras Epigraphical Report.
MCI	Mysore and Coorg from the Inscriptions.
SBE	Sacred Books of the East, ed. by Prof. Max Müller.

PREFACE

Following on my decipherment and publication of the Mercara plates in 1872, I discovered the Ganga inscriptions Nos. 4 and 5, and some copies, mostly imperfect, of various inscriptions in Coorg were furnished to me by Government in the time of Colonel Hill with a view to their being translated. But owing to all my spare time being taken up with numerous other important engagements and absence on duty in Calcutta, it was not till 1886 that the first edition of this work was issued. Though the light thus thrown upon the early history of the country was valuable as far as it went, I could not but regret, when recently called upon to compile the Gazetteer of Coorg for the new Imperial Gazetteer of India, the absence of fuller and more satisfactory information on the subject. Under the conviction that something additional might probably be found in the way of epigraphic records, I deputed two of my Archæological Assistants, with the approval of the Commissioner (Mr. Lionel Davidson), to make inquiries. The result fully justified my expectation. For copies of a number of inscriptions previously unknown were obtained, which enabled the filling up of the blanks hitherto existing in the past history. These were published as supplements to the Tumkūr and Bangalore volumes (xii and ix) of my Epigraphia Carnatica. Four more have now been added of which notice was received from Mr. L. T. Harris.

But the Government of India having been pleased, on the application of the Chief Commissioner, the Hon'ble Mr. S M. Fraser, to sanction the issue of a revised edition of the work, brought up to date, the opportunity has been taken of collecting all belonging to Coorg, now more than trebled in number, into one volume in this edition, and publishing them on the same plan as in the remaining volumes of the series, of which this forms the first. For the present edition I have received much assistance from the impressions procured for me by Rao Sāhib Krishna Śāstri, Assistant Superintendent for Epigraphy, Southern Circle.

Harrow-on-the-Hill,
Easter 1913.

LIST OF ILLUSTRATIONS

KEY TO ABBREVIATIONS FOR THE NAMES OF TĀLUQS, USED IN THE EPIGRAPHIA CARNATICA

Sign	Tāluq	District	Volume	Sign	Tāluq	District	Volume
An	Ānekal	Bn	IX	Kp	Koppa	Kd	VI
Ag	Arkalgūḍ	Hn	V	Kr	Krishṇarājpēṭ	My	IV
Ak	Arsikere	Hn	V	Kg	Kuṇigal	Tm	XII
Bg	Bāgepaḷḷi	Kl	X	Mi	Maddagiri	Tm	XII
Bn	Bangalore	Bn	IX	Ma	Māgaḍi	Bn	IX
Bl	Bēlūr	Hn	V	Ml	Malavaḷḷi	My	III
Bp	Bowringpēṭ	Kl	X	Mr	Mālūr	Kl	X
Cl	Chaḷḷakere	Cd	XI	Md	Maṇḍya	My	III
Ch	Chāmrājnagar	My	IV	Mj	Manjarābād	Hn	V
Ci	Channagiri	Sh	VII	Mk	Moḷakālmuru	Cd	XI
Cp	Channapaṭṇa	Bn	IX	Mg	Mūḍgere	Kd	VI
Cn	Channarāyapaṭṇa	Hn	V	Mb	Mulbāgal	Kl	X
CB	Chik-Ballāpur	Kl	X	My	Mysore	My	III
Cm	Chikmugaḷūr	Kd	VI	Ng	Nāgamaṅgala	My	IV
Ck	Chiknāyakanhaḷḷi	Tm	XII	Nr	Nagar	Sh	VIII
Ct	Chintāmaṇi	Kl	X	Nj	Nanjangūḍ	My	III
Cd	Chitaldroog	Cd	XI	Nl	Nelamaṅgala	Bn	IX
Cg	Coorg	Cg	I	Pg	Pāvugaḍa	Tm	XII
Dg	Dāvaṇgere	Cd	XI	Sa	Sāgar	Sh	VIII
Dv	Dēvanhaḷḷi	Bn	IX	Sr	Seringapatam	My	III
DB	Doḍ-Ballāpur	Bn	IX	Sk	Shikārpur	Sh	VII
Gd	Gōribidnūr	Kl	X	Sh	Shimoga	Sh	VII
Gb	Gubbi	Tm	XII	Sd	Siḍlaghaṭṭa	Kl	X
Gu	Guṇḍalpēṭ	My	IV	Si	Sira	Tm	XII
Hn	Hassan	Hn	V	Sb	Sorab	Sh	VIII
Hg	Heggaḍadēvankōṭe	My	IV	SB	Śravaṇa-Beḷgoḷa	Hn	II
Hr	Hiriyūr	Cd	XI	Sg	Śṛiṅgēri	Kd	VI
Hk	Hoḷalkere	Cd	XI	Sp	Śrīnivāspur	Kl	X
HN	Hoḷe-Narsipur	Hn	V	Tk	Tarikere	Kd	VI
Hl	Honnāḷi	Sh	VII	Tp	Tipṭūr	Tm	XII
Ht	Hoskōṭe	Bn	IX	Tl	Tīrthahaḷḷi	Sh	VIII
Hs	Huṇsūr	My	IV	TN	Tirumakūḍal-Narsipur	My	II
Jl	Jagalūr	Cd	XI	Tm	Tumkūr	Tm	XII
Kd	Kaḍūr	Kd	VI	Yd	Yeḍatore	My	IV
Kn	Kānkānhaḷḷi	Bn	IX	Yl	Yelandūr	My	IV
Kl	Kōlār	Kl	X				

LIST OF NĀḌS IN THE TĀLUQS OF COORG

Maḍikēri or Mercāra Tāluq—
- Horamale-nāḍ
- Hālēri-nāḍ
- Horūr-Nūrokkal-nāḍ
- Uluguli-Muḍikēri-nāḍ
- Huḍikēri-Mandapa-nāḍ
- Kāntamūr-nāḍ
- Kaggoḍlu-nāḍ

Pāḍinālknāḍ Tāluq—
- Pāḍinālk-nāḍ
- Kāḍiyat-nāḍ
- Kuyaṅgēri-nāḍ
- Benga-nāḍ
- Tavu-nāḍ

Yeḍenālknāḍ Tāluq—
- Yeḍenālk-nāḍ
- Beppu-nāḍ
- Ammatti-nāḍ

Kiggaṭnāḍ Tāluq—
- Anchikēri-nāḍ
- Tavalakēri-nāḍ
- Hatgaṭ-nāḍ
- Beṭṭiyatt-nāḍ

Nanjarājpaṭna Tāluq—
- Ramasvāmi-Kanave-hōbli
- Nanjarājpaṭṇa-hōbli
- Yeḍava-nāḍ
- Gaḍi-nāḍ
- Surlabimuttu-nāḍ

(*Old Yēḷusāvira-sīme*)
- Koḍli-hōbli
- Bilaha-nāḍ
- Niḍuta-nāḍ

COORG INSCRIPTIONS

INTRODUCTION

The inscriptions of Coorg, though few in number, are of importance, especially the earlier ones. It is true they tell us little about the Koḍagas, or Coorgs, themselves. Nor was this to be expected, for the Coorgs are naturally an unlettered race, their very language having no written characters[1]; and although the predominant class, they form no more than one-fifth of the population. The earliest express mention of the Koḍagas that has been met with in inscriptions is in 1174, in the time of the Hoysaḷa king Vīra-Ballāḷa (Hs 20). They are also mentioned in 1722, in the time of Chikka Dēva-Rāja of Mysore (Sr 64). But the name Kuḍakam (Coorg) apparently occurs in Tamil literature so far back as the 2nd century[2]; and the Seven Kombu of Sk 136 may have reference to Coorg in 1068.

Nevertheless, some idea may be formed of ancient divisions of the country. Thus, in 887, under the Gangas, we have mention (Cg 2) of the Male Thousand (the hill country to the west). This was apparently ruled in 977 by four Malepas or hill chiefs (Cg 4). In 1013, Kuḍa-malaināḍ in Tamil (TN 35), Koḍaga-malenāḍ in Kannaḍa (TN 122), is included in the conquests of the Chōḷa king Rājarāja. In 1095 the Kadamba Duddharasa is described (Cg 57) as 'a pleasure-garden of the Malepas,' meaning perhaps that they found with him a safe retreat. In 1124 we find (Bl 178) the Changāḷvas coming to the aid of the Malepas against the Hoysaḷas. And in 1174 two Coorg chiefs (? Malepas) and the Koḍagas of all the nāḍs assisted the Changāḷva king in his final struggle against the Hoysaḷas (Hs 20). From the mention here of Kuruche, this may have been a chief place of the Malepas. In 1275 and 1281 the Hoysaḷa king Nārasimha III signs himself (Md 79, TN 100) *Malaparoḷ-gaṇḍa*, 'champion among the Malapas or Malepas,' but this may have been a Hoysaḷa title from the beginning.

In the south-east, also under the Gangas, in 888 and 978 (Cg 2, 4) there was a district called the Peddoṟegare or Beddoṟegare Seventy (the banks, *gare*, of the Ped-doṟe or big river, the existing Doḍḍa-hoḷe or Lakshmantīrtha). At the latter date the king's younger brother was its governor. North from the above were the Changāḷvas, who filled a large space in the history of the country. Their later capital was at Nañjarājapaṭṭaṇa, which still gives its name to the northern tāluq of Coorg. North from them, again, were the Kongāḷvas, who were established in the Yeḷusāvira or Seven Thousand country by the Chōḷas in 1004 (Cg 46), and who disappeared soon after the expulsion of the Chōḷas from Mysore by the Hoysaḷas in 1116. Muḷḷūr seems to have been an important place in their territory. In 1390 Muḷḷūr-nāḍ was given as a grant by the Vijayanagar king Harihara II to an officer named Gonka-Raḍḍi-nāyaka, serving under his general Guṇḍappa-daṇḍanāyaka (Cg 39).

Firishta says that at the end of the 16th century Coorg proper was governed by its own chiefs, called Nāyaks, who admitted the supremacy of Vijayanagar. According to tradition the country was divided into twelve Kombus and thirty-five Nāḍs. The Changāḷvas fell

[1] For writing they employ the Kannaḍa (or Kanarese) letters.

[2] Kanakasabhai Pillai, in *The Tamils 1800 years ago*, p. 10.

before the Mysoreans in 1644, and the Coorg Rājas next established themselves as masters of the whole country, until it was annexed to British India in 1834. The close connection of the province with Mysore throughout the greater part of its history is made clear by these records, a connection which has been perpetuated to the present day in the arrangements for its administration by the British Government.

The earlier inscriptions show that the Jain faith was exclusively the State or court religion at first. Then followed the Śaiva and Vaishṇava creeds; and lastly the Vīra-Śaiva or Lingāyit form of Śaivism. All this while the Coorgs no doubt, as now, kept to their own Ancestor and Demon worship. The former is one of the most widely extended in the world[1]. No. 5, dated in 1000, possibly furnishes evidence of the antiquity of the Coorg houses. A Coorg *kaḍaṅga* is named in No. 2, even in 888.

Kadambas

The inscriptions which have now been discovered enable us to trace the history of Coorg as far back as early in the Christian era. But the puranic account of the foundation of the State and monarchy, given in the *Kāvērī-Māhātmya*, connects it with a prince named Chandravarmmā, the son of a king of the Matsya country, who was succeeded by his son Dēvakānta. Now Matsya (Virāṭa's capital) has been identified with Hāngal in Dharwar (called Virāṭan-kōṭe), and there is ground for the conclusion that Chandravarmmā was a Kadamba prince. The Kadambas were a line of independent kings ruling in the west of Mysore, in North and South Kanara, and other parts, between the 3rd and 6th centuries. They were Mysorean in origin, and are identified with Banavāsi as their capital. This is situated on the river Varadā, on the north-west frontier of Mysore, in North Kanara. It had the Brāhman name Jayanti or Vaijayanti. Banavāsi was a very ancient city, being one of the places to which Buddhist missionaries are said to have been sent in the time of the Maurya emperor Aśōka, the 3rd century B.C.; and it is also mentioned by Ptolemy in the 2nd century A.D.

The origin and rise of the Kadambas is described in the fine old inscription on a pillar at Tālagunda in the Shikārpur tāluq of Mysore (Sk 176). According to this, a Brāhman student in the agrahāra of Sthānakundūr (Tālagunda) was the progenitor of the royal line. He went to the Pallava capital (Kānchī, or Conjeeveram, near Madras) in order to complete his studies, but owing to a violent quarrel there with Pallava horsemen, he resolved, for the purpose of revenging the insults he had received as a Brāhman, to become a Kshattriya. Training himself in the use of arms, he escaped to the forests leading to Śrīparvata (Karnūl District), where he became so powerful, levying tribute from the great Bāṇa (or Bṛihad-Bāṇa) and other kings, that the Pallavas found it impossible to put him down. They therefore resolved to recognize him as a king, and installed him in a territory extending to the Western Ocean. He is known as Mayūravarmmā. Of his successors, one of the most distinguished was Kākustha, whose daughters were given in marriage to the Gupta and other kings. The reference is probably to Samudra-Gupta, who made an expedition throughout the South, as recorded on the pillar at Allahabad. Another daughter was apparently given to the Ganga king of Mysore. The Kadambas were subdued by the Chālukyas from the North in the 6th century, but held subordinate positions for several centuries later. We

[1] See Tylor's *Primitive Culture*, vol. ii, ch. 18; and Sir Monier Williams' *Religious Thought and Life in India*, p. 24.

know from inscriptions that Kadamba states existed in the 11th century in the country now called Manjarābād, in the north of Coorg; and in the 10th to the 12th century in Bayalnāḍ, now called Wainād, to the south of Coorg; as well as in Hāngal and Goa.

Of the Kadambas of Manjarābād we have an inscription in Coorg itself (No. 57), dated in 1095. It relates to a king named Duddharasa, and is a *vīra-śāsana* erected to his memory by his brother Jūjarasa. Duddha is described as a mahā-maṇḍalēśvara, lord of Tripura, sun to the Balīndra-kula,[1] a pleasure-garden of the Malepas (or hill chiefs), his father's warrior (*ayyan-aṅkakāra* , and has other titles. He protected Maleya (Malabar), and was governing Samhatha-nāḍ, Pākuvāḍi and other places; having 15 horses, 50 male servants, 250 strong men (*ekkaṭigaru*), 45 retainers of good family, and a retinue of many subjects, guards, relatives, and landholders. He was the son of Hiṭṭeyarasa and Junjala-Dēvi. At the request of his wife Chikkala-Dēvi, he had a tank made. He also endowed Brāhmans, and formed rice-fields at the river. The inscription was apparently composed by Moḷate-Duddhamalla, his minister for peace and war, and written by the *sēnabōva's* son Bamma-dēva.

Of this Duddharasa we have a record in Mj 18, of the same year, when his son Dayasimha was on the throne. Here Duddha is styled a mahārāja, and is said to be the son of Chāgi-mahārāja, which must have been the titular name of his father. By his wife Mēchalarasi he had three sons—Sārtthiga-nṛipa, Chāgi-mahārāja, and Dayasimha-nṛipa. The last is described as a crest-jewel of the Kadamba-vamśa, and lord of Banavāsi-pura. He slew an enemy named Śrīpāla, who had an immense army. His court resounded with the mingled notes of songs, drums, dances, flutes and guitars; he was a critical examiner of poems and dramas; and proficient in logic, grammar, painting, music and many others of the sixty-four branches of learning. Why have another Bhārata story (says the inscription); is not Dayasimha's history enough ?[2] We also have a notice of Duddha in Sk 151, where Chāmuṇḍa-Rāyarasa, the governor of the Banavase Twelve Thousand under the Chālukyas in 1047, has, among other epithets, that of 'a grindstone to Duddha.'

If Duddha-mahārāja was preceded on the throne by his father Chāgi-mahārāja, as we must suppose was the case, they connect with the Kadamba king Nīti-mahārāja, of whom there is a series of seven inscriptions in Manjarābād. The dates range from 1026 (Mj 53) to about 1035 (Mj 55), the latter recording his death with the performance of the Jaina rite of *sannyasanam*. The inscriptions are very short and much effaced. In Mj 51 only , . . . *loḷe* remains of the name of his residence, and Mj 55 contained the name of his father, which is gone.

GANGAS

But the earliest of the inscriptions in Coorg show that this country formed part of the territory of the Gangas, a line of kings who ruled over Mysore from about the 2nd to the 11th century. Their kingdom was called Gangavāḍi, described as a Ninety-six Thousand country, and their capital, at first Kuvalāla or Kovalāla (Kolār), was removed in the 3rd century to Talakāḍ on the Kāvērī, in the south-east of the Mysore District. The dynasty was founded by two Jain princes of the Ikshvāku (Solar) race, who came from the North, and were aided

---

[1] While he is here said to be of the Balīndra-kula, his son, in the Manjarābād record of the same date, is said to be of the Kadamba-vamśa. But the Duddha in both must be the same person, as Coorg in this part and Manjarābād adjoin one another and are really one territory.

[2] The same question is asked (Hn 53) with reference to the Hoysaḷa king Vishṇuvarddhana—A Duddarasa is mentioned as associated with the Hoysaḷa royal family in 1176 (Cg 33).

by the Jain *āchārya* Simhanandi,[1] whom they met at Pērūr, still distinguished as Ganga-Pērūr (in the Kaḍapa District). By name, the Gangas seem to be connected with the Gangaridæ or tribes of the Ganges valley who, according to Greek and Roman accounts of the times of Alexander the Great and Seleucus Nicator, were subjects of Chandra-Gupta, the founder of the Maurya dynasty of Pāṭalīputra (now Patna on the Ganges). Jain traditions represent him as ending his life at Śravaṇa-Belgoḷa in Mysore. The Gangaridæ are mentioned by Ptolemy, and the Latin authors Virgil, Valerius Flaccus, and Curtius also make reference to them. Pliny writes of the Gangaridæ Calingæ or Gangas of Kalinga (Orissa and neighbouring parts), where there was an important line of Ganga kings in the 7th and 8th centuries, and where Ganga kings ruled down to as late as the 16th century. But the Gangas of Mysore were the original line, and the Gangaḍikāras, who still form the largest section of the agricultural population of Mysore, represent their former subjects, this name being a contraction from Gangavāḍikāra.

Curiously enough, the first discovery of this important line of kings, who were the rulers of Mysore for nearly the whole of the first millennium of the Christian era, but whose very name had dropped into oblivion, was due to the copper plates (Cg 1) found in the treasury at Mercara[2]. As to when or by whom they were placed there no trace has been found, and they relate, not to any place in Coorg, but to one in Mysore. They were brought to the notice of Dr. Burgess by Mr. Graeter, and are now deposited in the Lutheran Mission Museum at Basle in Switzerland. Much controversy arose as to their date, the year 388 being given in the plates without mention of any era. By some they were accepted as one of the earliest unquestionable inscriptions discovered in India, whilst others imagined they might be forgeries. The full and abundant information that has since come to light in the inscriptions obtained by me from all parts of Mysore, some of which were published at the time in the *Indian Antiquary* or other works, and all of which appear in full in the volumes of my *Epigraphia Carnatica*, enables us to maintain the credibility of the Mercara plates. The date contained in them, as regards the year, is correct according to the Śaka era, nor is this belied by the palæography[3]. The language of the main portion is Sanskrit, but the details of the grant are in Haḷa Kannaḍa.

What the plates tell us is, that of a gift made by the Ganga king Koṅgaṇi-mahādhirāja, named Avinīta, whose pedigree is given, to a Jain priest, whose spiritual descent is also given, in the year three hundred and eighty-eight (in words), with other details of the month, day, etc.,[4] (but as usual at that early period with no name of the cyclic year), the minister

---

[1] He is named as a great poet by Indrabhūti in his *Samayabhūshaṇa*, along with Ēlāchārya (Padmanandi, the guru of Śākaṭāyana) and Pūjyapāda (*I.A.*, xii, 20); and in SB 54 is mentioned next to Samantabhadra, who belongs to the 2nd century.

[2] First deciphered by me and published in 1872 (*Ind. Ant.* i, 363; see also xii, 12).

[3] Objections to this were raised by Dr. Fleet, who said (EI, iii, 162) 'it is definitely betrayed by a character which furnishes a leading test in dealing with southern records' and which he said could not appear earlier than 804. In this he was shown to be mistaken (EC, iv, Int. 6), and Dr. Bühler (*Ind. Pal.* §29, B2) remarked to the same effect. Dr. F's reply (EI, vi, 79) was--'I concede that this instance adduced by Mr. Rice is to be referred probably to the 6th century A.D. But it has nothing to do with the matter that we have in hand. It is a Grantha character.' It was then pointed out (EC, vi, Int. 30) that even supposing it was Grantha, the letter was undoubtedly the same, as Tamil had no aspirated letters. Dr. Bühler also (*l.c.* §31, A B6) refers it to the Kanarese-Telugu script.

[4] Regarding a discrepancy in the week-day and *nakshatra*, Dr. Bhandarkar says (*Ind. Ant.* i, 363):—Finding that Māgh śuddha 5th S. 388 fell on Wednesday, I submitted the question to Prof. Keru Lakshman Chatre. He finds the day to fall on 'Wednesday, Budhavāra or Saumyavāra, nakshatra Uttara-Bhādrapada',

(*mantri*) of Akālavarsha Prithuvī-Vallabha (a Rāshṭrakūṭa king), having obtained from Avinīta-mahādhirāja by grant the village named Badaneguppe, situated in the Eḍenāḍ Seventy of the Pūnāḍ Six Thousand, gave it, together with the rights pertaining to six included villages, to the Śrīvijaya Jina temple of Talavana-nagara (Talakāḍ), along with certain other privileges and lands (adding considerably to the value of the donation).

The grant is thus ascribed to the time of Avinīta, and the date given, which is equivalent to 466 A.D., agrees with the history as we now know it, for Avinīta reigned from *c.* 430 to 482, this long reign being due to the fact, stated in many inscriptions, that he was crowned while an infant on his mother's lap.

But farther clear historical allusions in the plates require us to show that two other kings belonged to the same period, namely, Akālavarsha, undoubtedly a Rāshṭrakūṭa, and Kṛishṇavarmmā, a Kadamba. Of these, the former may be recognized as follows to have been contemporary with Avinīta. For, as I was the first to point out, the *varsha* titles of the Rāshṭrakūṭa kings were so constant that the title is a sufficient guide to the king's name. Akālavarsha is thus synonymous with a Kṛishṇa-Rāja.

Now it so happens that coins of a Kṛishṇa-Rāja have been found at Dēvalānā in the Nasik District and other parts of Bombay, which, as Professor Rapson says (*Indian Coins*, 27), have been attributed to a Rāshṭrakūṭa king of this name, *c.* 375–400 A.D. But he considers this date too early for the style of the coins, which are imitated from the latest Gupta coins current in this locality. For the same reason, he says, it is impossible to place them as late as the better known Kṛishṇa-Rāja Rāshṭrakūṭa, *c.* 750 A.D. Dr. Fleet suggested (DKD 296, 385) that they may be Kalachuri coins of Kṛishṇa-Rāja, the father of Śaṅkaragaṇa (apparently about 570 A.D.). But the Kalachuri coins have quite a different device. Accepting the coins, therefore, as Rāshṭrakūṭa, 466 as a date for the Kṛishṇa-Rāja of whom we are in search seems to satisfy the required conditions and supply the wanted intermediate figure. Sir Walter Elliot says (*Coins of So. Ind.* 149) 'General Cunningham's ascription of these coins to Kṛishṇa-Rāja Rāshṭrakūṭa is confirmed.'

As to the relations subsisting in this, the 5th century, between the Rāshṭrakūṭas and Gangas, and other contemporary powers, we have the following evidence. The Siragunda stone (Cm 50) says that Nirvvinīta's (*i.e.* Avinīta's) younger son was crowned with the Koṅgaṇi diadem by Kāḍuveṭṭi[1] (or the Pallava king) and the Vallava (Ballaha or Rāshṭrakūṭa) king[2]. This we may account for by the statement (in Bn 141, Mi 110, and DB 68) that Avinīta, acting on the advice of his own *guru*, had set aside Durvvinīta (from the succession) in favour of another son, but that Lakshmī (the goddess of sovereignty) of her own accord came and embraced his broad chest. Then, (in Nr 35) Durvvinīta is said to have captured Kāḍuveṭṭi on the field of battle and placed his own daughter's son Jayasimha-Vallabha on his hereditary throne.

---

and considers that the engraver, being careless, has written Sōma for Saumya. Nakshatra Svāti never falls near 5th Māgh śuddha, but the astrologer consulted, he thinks, may have carelessly taken Māgh vadha, and given Svāti, which falls only a day in advance of the 5th for S 388. Dr. Kielhorn's calculations (*id.* xxiv, 11) give the same results.

[1] Kāḍuveṭṭi or Kāḍava-Rāya is the common designation in Mysore inscriptions for the Pallava king. The former name survives in Kārvēṭi-nagara, in the North Arcot District.

[2] This rendering has been suggested by Mr. Narasimhachar (MAR, 1912), and he points out the interesting parallel occurrence, some centuries later, when the Ganga king Śivamāra-Saigoṭṭa, after his release from captivity, was crowned with their own hands by the Rāshṭrakūṭa king Gōvinda Prabhūtavarsha and the Pallava king Nandivarmmā, as related in Yd 60 and Nl 60. The proposed identification of Jayasimha is also due to him.

Now Jayasimha-Vallabha is the name given in the Aihoḷe inscription (EI, vi, 1) as that of the Chālukya prince who, in the Yewūr, Kauṭhem and other grants (IA, xii, 12; xvi, 15), is said to have gained a footing for the Chalukyas by subduing a Rāshṭrakūṭa king named Indra, the son of Kṛishṇa. If we may identify these two Jayasimhas as the same person, it follows that he had a Ganga mother and a Chalukya father. But it must be admitted that the Gangas (who were of the Solar race) nowhere claim such a connection with the Chalukyas (who were of the Lunar race), unless we are to uuderstand the solitary statement (MAR, 1912) that Durvvinīta was of the Kṛishṇa-*kula*[1] (and therefore Lunar race) as making such a claim at this particular period (perhaps through his mother). In any case, a Rāshṭrakūṭa Kṛishṇa here also appears in contact with the Gangas at this time.

Putting together the various coincident items, the following appears to have been the state of affairs. The Ganga king Avinīta (whose mother was a Kadamba princess, the sister of Kṛishṇavarmmā) married the Punnāḍ Rāja's daughter, and had by her his son Durvvinīta. This son he set aside (from the succession) in favour of another son (no doubt born of a different mother), and the latter obtained the Koṅgaṇi (or Ganga) crown from (or with the support of) the Pallava and Rāshṭrakūṭa kings. Nevertheless, Lakshmī (the goddess of sovereignty) came to Durvvinīta of her own accord, and he on his part entered into alliance with the Chalukya prince, giving him his daughter in marriage. The son born of this union was Jayasimha-Vallabha. Durvvinīta next seized Kāḍuveṭṭi (the Pallava king) on the field of battle and placed Jayasimha-Vallabha on his hereditary throne. And he in his turn made good the Chalukya supremacy for the time being by defeating the Rāshṭrakūṭa, the son of Kṛishṇa, but was eventually, it appears, slain in an encounter with Trilōchana-Pallava.

It is clear, as Dr. Bühler remarked, that Rāshṭrakūṭas ruled in the Dekhan in the 3rd to the 5th centuries. And I may add that although no other evidence has yet come to light that the Kṛishṇa-Rāja Rāshṭrakūṭa of that period was called Akālavarsha, the family custom was no doubt adhered to. This identification, if it could be accepted, Dr. Fleet admitted, would of course be a strong argument in favour of the genuine antiquity of the Mercara plates.

As regards the Kadamba king Kṛishṇavarmmā, we are introduced in Bl 121 to two so named in that family. The first was the great-grandfather of the second, the donor of the grant, which is dated only in the regnal year. The first Kṛishṇavarmmā is described as performer of the horse sacrifice, and as having married the daughter of Kaikeya, by whom he had a son Vishṇuvarmmā. The latter is the donor in Kd 162, which is also dated only in the regnal year. Here too his father is said to have performed the horse sacrifice, and besides to have had an elder brother Śāntivaravarmmā. This is another form of the name Śāntivarmmā, who was the son of Kākustha according to the Tālagunda pillar (Sk 176; EI, viii, 24). Kākustha is there said to have given his daughters in marriage to the Gupta and other kings. This there can be no doubt, as previously said, refers to Samudra-Gupta, who is the only Gupta known to have made an expedition to the South, as recorded on the pillar at Allahabad. Now Samudra-Gupta belongs to the latter part of the 4th century. Kākustha's younger son Kṛishṇavarmmā may therefore be placed in the first part of the 5th century, and his sister could naturally be the mother of Avinīta, who was ruling from about 430.

---

[1] Here, of course, the god Krishna. See also a similar claim for the Changālvas, p. xiii.

It has thus been shown that both Akālavarsha Rāshṭrakūṭa and Kṛishṇavarmmā Kadamba can be accounted for as belonging to the period of Avinīta Koṅgaṇi, the Ganga king. The direct and unaffected way in which they are mentioned in the plates, without any boast or demonstration, bears on the face of it the aspect of truth, and cannot have been intended in any way to deceive or mislead. The plates are consequently so far justified as valid and reliable records.

The first Kṛishṇa or Kannara Akālavarsha of the Rāshṭrakūṭa or Raṭṭa line previously known to us occupied the throne in about 760 A.D., and the earliest Rāshṭrakūṭa inscriptions that have been found in Mysore are of the time of his son, Jagattunga Prabhūtavarsha Śrīvallabha, or Gōvinda II (Cl. 33, 34). This is the king mentioned by Jinasēna as then ruling in the South in his Jain *Harivaṁśa*, composed in 783.

Akālavarsha's minister, the donor of our grant under consideration, does not give us his own name, nor any other particulars regarding himself. He may therefore have retired from public service, and taken up his residence in the Mysore country, possibly at Talakāḍ, the Ganga capital, where he made the grant. He may even have been a Mysorean, come back to end his days in his own country. Badaneguppe, the subject of the grant, still exists under the same name, and some of the other villages mentioned can be identified (see note to translation).

The plates were engraved by Viśvakarmma, which we know from other instances was a common official designation for the court engraver. It occurs as far back as the 3rd century as that of the engraver of the Kadamba grant on the Malavaḷḷi pillar (Sk 264), and the older Āndhra or Śātavāhana grant of Sātakarṇṇi which precedes it on the same pillar may also have been engraved by the same. Many of the Ganga grants on copper plates were engraved by a Viśvakarmma at various dates wide apart.

The Pūnāḍ Six Thousand was situated in the south-west of Mysore, adjoining Coorg, and is interesting on account of its antiquity. For it is the Punnāṭa to which the Jain immigrants from the north, under Bhadrabāhu, in the 4th century B.C., took their way when their leader remained behind at Śravaṇa-Beḷgoḷa (in the Hassan District) in expectation of his death, being waited on in his last moments by one single disciple, believed to be the distinguished Chandra-Gupta. Harishēṇa, in his *Bṛihatkathākōśa*, dated in 931, says that the whole Saṅgha went by the guru's direction to the Punnāṭa country, situated in the South.[1] It is further mentioned in the 2nd century A.D., by Ptolemy as Pounnata, 'where is beryl.' In the 5th century the Ganga king Avinīta married the Punnāḍ Rāja's daughter, and the province thus came to be annexed to Gangavāḍi under their son Durvvinīta. Jinasēna, before mentioned, was of the Bṛihat-Punnāṭa-saṅgha. An inscription of the Punnāḍ Rājas[2] gives Kitthipura as their capital, which is identified (Hs 56) with Kittūr on the Kabbani river in the Heggaḍadēvankōṭe tāluq.

It is strange that stone inscriptions of the time of Akālavarsha II, who ruled from 884 to 913, have been found in the Dēvanhaḷḷi tāluq (Dv 42, 43), relating to a local Punnāḍ, a village circle which, in a neighbouring inscription of the 14th century (DB 38), is described as the Punnāḍ Seventy. The correspondence in names is singular, but there is otherwise no apparent connection with the incidents in the Mercara plates.

The Ganga lineage, as first brought to our knowledge in these plates, begins with Koṅgaṇi-mahādhirāja, whose son was Mādhava-mahādhirāja, whose son was Harivarmma-

---

[1] *Saṅghō'pi samastō guru-vākyataḥ dakshiṇā-patha-dēśastha-Punnāṭa-vishayaṁ yayau.*

[2] *Ind. Ant.* xii, 13; xviii, 366.

mahādhirāja, whose son was Vishṇugōpa-mahādhirāja, whose son was Mādhava-mahādhirāja, whose son, by a princess who was the sister of the Kadamba king Krishṇavarmma-mahādhirāja (and probably a daughter of the Kadamba king Kākustha), was Koṅgaṇi-mahādhirāja, named Avinīta. The descriptive epithets applied to each of these kings, though novel at the time the plates were first deciphered by me, are now familiar enough from their repetition in so many Ganga inscriptions that have since been obtained.

The next three inscriptions, in order of date, are also Ganga and Jain, but on stone,[1] as are all the rest. The date of the first is 809 Śaka (888 A.D.), the 18th year of the reign of Satyavākya-Koṅguṇivarmma-dharmma-mahārājādhirāja, lord of Kovalālapura, lord of Nandagiri (Nandidroog). The king, who is described as the Permmanaḍi, gave to a Jain priest, for the Satyavākya-Jina temple of the Penne-kaḍaṅga, the twelve hamlets of Biliūr in Peddoṟegare, or the bank of the Peddoṟe or Beddoṟe. This name, meaning the big river, is generally the designation of the river Krishṇā in Kannaḍa inscriptions, but here it means the Lakshmaṇtīrtha, which is still called the Doḍḍa-hoḷe or big river in Coorg. Among the witnesses are named the officials of the Ninety-six Thousand, that is Gangavāḍi, and of the Beddoṟegare Seventy, the village circle aforesaid. Among the guardians or trustees we have those of the Male Thousand (the hill country), and the Five Hundred.[2] The grant was engraved by Sedōja.

The donor was the Ganga king Rājamalla or Rāchamalla Satyavākya II, who reigned from 870 to 907. His nephew Ereyappa was at one time governor of the Koṅgal-nāḍ Eight Thousand (Hs 92), which, as will be seen farther on, may have included the Yēḷusāvira or Seven Thousand country in the north of Coorg. The title Permmanaḍi or Permmānaḍi, also written Permmāḍi, was first assumed by the Ganga king Śrīpurusha, who reigned from 726 to 776, and is applied to all his successors. According to Nr 35 it previously belonged to the Pallavas, but on Śrīpurusha's crushing defeat of (the Pallava) Kāḍuveṭṭi of Kāñchī, he took away from him this title. After the Ganga power was overthrown in 1004, the Noḷambas, who represented the Pallavas, resumed the title (Dg 71).

The mention of the Penne-kaḍaṅga is of considerable interest, as shewing the antiquity of the *kaḍaṅgas* or war trenches found in a great part of Coorg. They are carried over hills, woods and comparatively flat country for miles and miles, at some places branching off in various directions or encircling hill-tops. Some are nearly 40 feet from summit to bottom of ditch, and often taken along hill sides with an angle of 80° to the horizon. In the Mendala-nāḍ they show great regularity and are broad and deep, the lower side of the ditch facing the open country, but in Kiggaṭ-nāḍ they are of smaller dimensions. There is no doubt that they were war trenches, and may have served as covered ways, but it is more than probable that at the same time they formed, at least to some extent, also the boundaries between the different nāḍs. Similar earthworks were constructed by the ancient Britons. Mr. Wilkins, in an article[3] headed "Were the Ancient Britons savages?" says—'They are extremely difficult of access from the steepness of the mountain heights on which they were formed. This difficulty the primitive engineer greatly increased by the most simple and natural means. He sunk one or more deep trenches round the summit of the hill and raised lofty banks with the excavated

---

[1] The versions of these published by the Rev. F. Kittel in *Ind. Ant.* vi, 99 ff. are not trustworthy, as they contain many errors (see xiv, 76).

[2] The Five Hundred, here and in No. 4, may be the Five Hundred *Svāmis* of Āryyāvale or Ayyāvale (now Aihoḷe. in the Bijapur District), regarded as the heads of the *vīra-Baṇanju-dharma*, or merchant class.

[3] *Fortnightly Review*, April 1875.

soil. Undoubtedly this is the most ancient species of rampart known ; it existed ages before the use of mural fortifications, and originated in all probability with the nations of the east.'

Then follows No. 3, which is of the time of the same king, but undated. It records the binding on of the *Permmāḍi-paṭṭa* (by euphony *vaṭṭa*) on the son of a *gāvuṇḍa* or farmer, and the fixing of the land rent and rice dues in permanence for the estate or *kalnāḍ* granted him. The inscription was engraved by Sōmayya. The *paṭṭa* was a golden band or ribbon to be worn on the forehead, inscribed with some title of honour, in this case that of the king. It was a symbol of royalty, but also conferred as a mark of royal favour. *Kalnāḍ* was the term generally applied to the portion of land granted for public services, or to the family of a man who fell in war.

Here intervene three fragmentary Ganga inscriptions, Nos. 60, 74 and 28. The first, which is without date, records the grant of a village to apparently Ereyarasa for an agrahāra, and also a grant by a man who, with other names, bore that of Koṅgaṇivarmmā. It may belong to about 900 A.D. The second, also without date, records the death of one of Eṛeyapa's followers. The third is dated in Śaka 866 (944 A.D.). It is a memorial of self-sacrifice, such as are recorded in several instances during the Ganga and later periods. A man named Būchaga had himself beheaded in fulfilment of a vow, and his mother set up this monument to him. These vows of self-immolation were taken with the object of securing the accomplishment of some cherished desire. Thus, Sb 479 informs us of a man who, in about 991, gave up his head to a goddess at Hayve in order that the king Śāntivarmmā might have a son. In 1050 a servant had his head cut off in order to die with the king Pompala (Ct 31). In 1123 a cowherd vowed his head to swing before the god at Koṇḍasa-bhāvi if the king should have a son (Sk 246). Other instances are mentioned in my *Mysore and Coorg from the Inscriptions*, ch. iv. The mode in which these decapitations took place was as follows, as represented in sculptured stones. The votary was seated with his back to a tall elastic rod fixed in the ground behind. This was forcibly bent down over the head of the victim and made fast by a hook to the top-knot of hair. On being severed from the body, the head flew up, carried with the rebound of the rod released from its tension.

No. 4 is another Ganga inscription, dated in Śaka 899 (978 A.D.). It is also of the time of a Satyavākya-Koṅgiṇivarmma-dharmma-mahārājādhirāja, lord of Kōlālapura, lord of Nandagiri, whose name was Rāchamalla-Permmanaḍi. But this was Satyavākya IV, and his younger brother Rakkasa, who, along with other epithets, has that of *aṇṇana-baṇṭa* (elder brother's warrior), was governor of Beddoṛegare (see No. 2 above). A Jain priest, whose spiritual descent is given, a resident of Śrī-Beḷgoḷa (Śravaṇa-Beḷgoḷa) acquired possession of Perggadūr (Peggūr where the inscription is), and the *posa-vādaga* or new trench, secure against obstruction. The witnesses include the officials of the Ninety-six Thousand and of the Peddoṛegare Seventy. Among the guardians or trustees are the four Malepas or hill chiefs, and the Five hundred[1]. The grant is apparently described as Śrīpurusha-mahārāja's gift[2]. If this be correct, the king must have reverted to the use of an ancestral popular name. It was engraved by Chandanandiyayya, and is called the *śāsana* of the *basadi* (or Jain temple) of Perggadūr.

---

[1] See note, p. 8.

[2] This name has come up in the most recent impression, and is well known as that of a Ganga king who ruled 726 to 776 A.D., but has not been hitherto met with subsequent to that period. In the impression in my first edition and in that given in *Ind. Ant.* vi, 102, it is clearly Śrīpurada mahārāja, the mahārāja of Śrīpura, perhaps the Sirivur mentioned in No. 65. A very slight change is required to turn *Śrīpurada* into *Śrīpurusha*.

The date of this inscription requires some explanation. It is given as the *Nandīśvara-talpa-devasam* of *Phālguṇa-śukla-paksha.* According to information from a Jain source, it appears that Nandīśvara is the name of an island in the Jain cosmography, the eighth from Jambu-dvīpa. A plan of it on stone or brass is kept in many Jina temples, and a Nandīśvara temple in conformity with the plan has, it is said, been lately erected by the Jains in Delhi. From the 8th of the bright fortnight in the months Āshāḍha, Kārttika and Phālguna, till full moon, is the time of the Nandīśvara-pūjā, or observance of the season when certain deified beings—Saudharmēndra, Īśānēndra, Chāmara and Vairōchana—assemble for worship at the island of Nandīśvara, which has fifty-two Jina temples on it. These are also the approved times for the commencement of any religious vows. The authorities for these statements may be found in *Trilōkasāra* and in *Nandīśvara-bhakti.* The date of our inscription must therefore be taken as Phālguna śukla 8, the beginning of the Nandīśvara days in that month.

The title of *aṇṇana-baṇṭa* given to the prince Rakkasa is also used with regard to him in SB 60. In Sp 59 we have an inscription of the same Rakkasa-Ganga Rāchamalla when on the throne, on which he succeeded his elder brother. He was the patron of the Kannaḍa poet Nāgavarmmā, the first of that name, author of the *Chhandōmbudhi,* who, in the introduction of his work, has verses relating to himself, beginning *arasam Rakkasa-Gangam,* found in the several palm leaf copies.[1]

The term *vādaga* is used in mentioning the new trench, instead of *kaḍaṅga,* but it refers to the same thing. From this inscription and No. 10 it is evident that a close connection existed between the Jains of Coorg and those of Śravaṇa-Beḷgoḷa in Mysore. The four Malepas or hill chiefs were no doubt at the head of the Male Thousand mentioned in No 2. The Hoysaḷa kings have the title Maleparoḷ-gaṇḍa or Malaparoḷ-gaṇḍa, meaning champion among the Malepas, but who in particular are intended does not appear. With regard to Śrīpura, this is the name of a place where a Jain temple is stated to have been erected in the Dēvarhaḷḷi plates (Ng 85). It also occurs in the Hosūr plates (Gb 47). From the latter it may be conjectured that it was near Gūḍalūr, which is at the western foot of the Nilgiris on the Wynaad boundary. But this is uncertain. A Sirivūr is mentioned in No. 65, which would be in Coorg.

The next inscription (No. 5) is dated in Śaka 921 (1000 A.D.) and is of the time of the last Gaṅga king, though no mention is made of any king. It refers to a man who had served his time with Kuṇindora, which may be the name of one of the Coorg houses, and thus furnish evidence of their antiquity. He then set up for himself, and to expiate any guilt in taking forcible possession of certain places (named), bathed in the stream, and worshipping Rāmēśvara, made a grant of land for *dharma* or charity.

As the Ganga inscriptions in Coorg end here, it may be useful for reference to give a table of the whole of the kings, based on the information that has now been obtained from a host of inscriptions in Mysore and surrounding countries, the Mercara plates (No. 1) having been the first that brought the dynasty to light. Further particulars will be found in my work *Mysore and Coorg from the Inscriptions*, published by Constable & Co., London, in 1909.

Of the Ikshvāku or Solar race, was Dhanañjaya
|
Hariśchandra, king of Ayōdhyā
⋮

[1] For reasons unknown the Rev. F. Kittel has omitted these in his edition called *Nāgavarma's Canarese Prosody*, published at Mangalore in 1875, but refers to them in his Kannaḍa-English Dictionary, under *Ganga* and *Ajitasēna.*

- Padmanābha
  - 1. Mādhava I, 103 Koṅguṇivarmmā [1]
  - Daḍiga
    - 2. Mādhava II, Kiriya-Mādhava
      - 3. Harivarmmā, 247—266 [2]
        - 4. Vishṇugōpa
          - Pṛithivi-Ganga
            - 5. Mādhava III, 357—370 [3] Taḍaṅgāla-Mādhava, m. Kadamba princess [4]
              - 6. Avinīta, c. 430—482 Nirvvinīta, Kali Ganga m. Punnāḍ princess
                - 7. a son
                - 8. Durvvinīta, c. 482—522 [5]
                  - 9. Mushkara, Mokkara, m. Sindhu princess
                    - 10. Śrīvikrama
                      - 11. Bhūvikrama,—679 Śrīvallabha
                      - 12. Śivamāra I, 679—713 Nava-Kāma, Śishṭa-priya, Pṛithivi-Koṅgaṇi I
                        - ? Ereganga
                          - 13. Śrīpurusha, 726—776 Muttarasa, Pṛithivi-Koṅgaṇi II, Permmānaḍi [6]
                            - 14. Śivamāra II,—816 Saigoṭṭa
                              - Mārasiṁha, 797 Mārasiṅg-Ereyappa, Lōka-Triṇētra
                              - Pṛithivīpati I, ? c. 815 Piḷduvipati ? Diṇḍika
                                - Mārasiṁha
                                  - Pṛithivīpati II, c. 910 Hastimalla
                            - Vijayāditya, Raṇavikrama
                              - 15. Rājamalla Satyavākya I [7], 817—828 m. Pallava princess
                                - 16. Nītimārgga I [8],—869 Ereyaṅga, Raṇavikramayya

[1] This name is applied to all the kings to the end. The Tamil chronicle *Koṅgudēśa-rājākkaḷ* says that he was ruling in 189 and reigned for 51 years.

[2] In the same Tamil chronicle 288 is given as a date in his reign.

[3] In addition to the grants of his reign mentioned in my *Mysore and Coorg from the Inscriptions*, one has since been discovered at Melekōṭe in the Tumkūr tāluq, which is unique in being made to a Buddhist (*MAR.* 1910). From the mention of the Avaniya-nadi among the boundaries, the site of the grant seems to have been in the neighbourhood of the old religious centre named Ávani, in the Mulbāgal tāluq of the Kolar district. Unfortunately one plate is missing, which may have contained the date.

[4] At this point, between Mādhava III and Avinīta, the Tamil chronicle inserts a Diṇḍikara-Rāja or Hariśchandra, who ruled for only a short time. An inscription containing the name of Diṇḍika-Rāja has lately been discovered at Śravaṇa-Beḷgoḷa, engraved in characters like those of the Bhadrabāhu inscription SB 1. (*MAR.* 1909).

[5] More recently a grant of his 40th year has been obtained, at Gummareḍḍipura, Śrīnivāspur tāluq (MAR. 1912), which contains fresh information of importance. It states that he was himself the author of a *Śabdāvatāra*, and of a version in Sanskrit of the *Vaḍḍakathā*, which, from the corresponding passage in Tm 23, apparently means the *Bṛihatkathā*.

[6] This title is used of all the subsequent kings, often alone, without any name.

[7] These names are used as titles by all the kings that come after.

[8] This name is used as a title by the kings that follow.

- 17. Rājamalla Satyavākya II, 870–907
- Būtugēndra, 870, Būtarasa, Guṇaduttaranga, m. Rāshṭrakūṭa princess
  - 18. Ereyappa, 886–913, Ereganga, Nītimārgga II, Satyavākya, Mahēndrāntaka
    - 19. Rāchamalla Satyavākya III, Kachcheya-Ganga, 920
    - Pāmbabbe, m. to Immaḍi Dhora, d. 971
    - 20. Būtuga, 938–953, Būtayya, Nanniya-Ganga, Ganga-Gāngēya, m. Rāshṭrakūṭa princess
      - Maruḷa-Dēva
      - ? Sōmi-Dēvi m. to Rāshṭrakūṭa prince
      - 21. Mārasimha, 961—974, Guttiya-Ganga, Noḷambakulāntaka
        - 22. Rāchamalla Satyavākya IV, 977
        - 23. Rakkasa-Ganga, 984, Rāchamalla
          - 24. Nītimārgga III, Rāchamalla ? 989, 999
        - Arumuli-Dēva
          - Rāja-Vidyādhara

Chōḷas

The Ganga sovereignty was overthrown by the Chōḷas, an ancient line of kings in the Tamil country, and they became the dominant power in the south and east of Mysore and in Coorg for a little more than a hundred years. Their early capital was Oreyūr (Warriore, near Trichinopoly). But the one with which they are chiefly identified is Tanjore, and they also took the capital city Kānchī from the Pallavas. In the course of the campaigns in which they subjected the Pallavas and the Eastern Chālukyas, the latter of whom were aided by the Rāshṭrakūṭas, the Chōḷa king Parāntaka had in 921 uprooted the Bāṇas, who ruled in the east of Mysore and claimed to be friends of the Rāshṭrakūṭa king Kṛishṇa II. He then conferred the title of Bāṇādhirāja on the Ganga prince Pṛithivīpati, giving him the name Hastimalla. But the Gangas being closely allied by intermarriages with the Rāshṭrakūṭas, the Ganga king Būtuga in 949 slew, at Takkōlam (near Arkōnam), the Chōḷa king Rājāditya, who was at war with the Rāshṭrakūṭa king Kṛishṇa III. The latter, who was Būtuga's brother-in-law, rewarded him with the Banavase Twelve Thousand (the Shimoga District), and claims to have captured Kānchī and Tanjore. In 997 the Chōḷa king Rājarāja had gained a footing in the east of Mysore (Ht 111). But in 1004 his son Rājēndra-Chōḷa, who was in command of the Chōḷa army, succeeded in capturing Talakāḍ, the Ganga capital, and brought the Ganga power to an end. The conquest of all the south and east of Mysore, in an arc extending from Arkalgūḍ in the west, through Seringapatam, and north by Nelamangala to Niḍugal, was speedily effected, and Rājēndra-Chōḷa gained the title Gangaikoṇḍa-Chōḷa.[1]

In their operations westwards the Chōḷas were opposed by the Changāḷvas, who were ruling in the Huṇsūr tāluq of Mysore and in Coorg. But these were defeated in a decisive battle at Panasoge or Hanasoge on the Kāvērī, and the Changāḷvas thus came under the

[1] There is a belief, I am informed by Mr. Krishna Sastri, that he obtained it through subduing various kings up to the Ganges and compelling them to bring the sacred water of the river to pour into the tank he had made at his capital Gangaigoṇḍachōḷapuram.

domination of the Chōḷas. The victory over them was due to a warrior named Manija under the general Panchavan-mahārāya. He was rewarded by the Chōḷa king Rājarāja with the title of Kshattriya-śikhāmaṇi Koṅgāḷva (Cg. 46) and granted an estate at Mālavvi (now Mālambi). The Kongāḷva territory extended over the Arkalgūḍ tāluq of Mysore and the Yēḷusāvira country in the north of Coorg. Both the Chaṅgāḷva and Koṅgāḷva kings from this time have Chōḷa prenomens, denoting their subordination, and the Chōḷas in the list of their conquests include Kuḍa-malainād, which indicates the Coorg hill country, Kuḍagu or Koḍagu-malenāḍ, as expressly stated in TN 122.

CHAṄGĀḶVAS

The Chaṅgāḷvas or Chaṅgāḷuvas are a line of kings of much interest, having ruled in the west of Mysore and in Coorg from the 10th to the 17th century. Their original territory was Chaṅga-nāḍ (Hs 97), corresponding chiefly with the Huṇsūr tāluq. They claim to be Yādavas and of the Lunar race (Hs 63, Yd 26), descended from a king named Chaṅgāḷva, who was in Dvārāvatī, and having defeated Bijjala, seized his titles. This Chaṅgāḷva cannot be traced, and there is nothing to show what Bijjala is meant. The kings are generally styled *mahā-maṇḍalika maṇḍalēśvara* or *mahā-maṇḍalēśvara*. They were originally Jains, and are first met with in connection with Panasoge or Hanasoge, on the south of the Kāvērī in the north-west of the Yeḍatore tāluq, where there are many ruined *basadis*. These, according to Yd 26, were set up by Rāma, the son of Daśaratha, the elder brother of Lakshmaṇa, and husband of Sītā. The Jain priests of the Hottage (or Pustaka)-gachchha claim exclusive jurisdiction over *basadis* at Panasoge and at Tale-Kāvērī in Coorg, which may perhaps have been the limits of the Chaṅgāḷva kingdom east and west.

One of the *basadis* or Jain temples at Panasoge set up by Rāma was endowed by the Ganga king Mārasimha, who reigned from 961 to 974; and was rebuilt by Nanni-Chaṅgāḷva (Yd 25). He is the first Chaṅgāḷva of whom we have any certain knowledge, and as he had the prefix Rājēndra-Chōḷa before his name he belongs to the beginning of the 11th century. But as their kingdom was subdued by the Chōḷas at the time when the Ganga power was overthrown in 1004, the Chaṅgāḷvas must have been an established line of kings prior to that. Their inscriptions are found mostly in the Huṇsūr and Yeḍatore tāluqs and in Coorg.

The subjugation of the Chaṅgāḷvas by the Chōḷas seems to have resulted from their defeat at Panasoge by the Chōḷa general Panchavan-mahārāya (Cg 46); and the subsequent kings for more than a century bore Chōḷa prenomens. When the Chōḷas were expelled from Mysore by the Hoysaḷas in 1116, the Chaṅgāḷvas strove to maintain independence. But they were compelled in the end to submit to the Hoysaḷas. And when the Hoysaḷa power was overthrown in the 14th century by Moslems from the North, the Chaṅgāḷvas passed under the dominion of the new Vijayanagar empire then established. At length they were conquered in 1644 by one of the Mysore kings,—these having risen to power after the fall of Vijayanagar—, and their dynasty was thus brought to an end.

It is difficult to draw up a consecutive table of the kings, as they are mostly mentioned only as Chaṅgāḷvas, without any individual names, down to the end of the 13th century. Nanni had the prenomen Rājēndra-Chōḷa, but his successors generally had that of Kulōttuṅga-Chōḷa, and when the Chōḷas disappeared from Mysore, seem to have used only Kulōttuṅga, without the Chōḷa. They had some time before this embraced the new Lingāyit religion and were devoted Śaivas. Their family god was now Mallikārjuna, whose temple was on the Beṭṭadpur hill in the Huṇsūr tāluq, and this they named Śrīgiri, no doubt after the famous Śaiva sacred hill Śrīparvata in the Karnūl District.

The following are some of the names that are met with in the earlier period, with their dates, and references to the inscriptions in which they occur :—

Nanni-Changāḷva	1034 (Yd 37), 1037 (Hg 104)
" "	c. 1060 (Yd 25, 26)
Mādēva	1090 (Ag 65)
Oḍeyāṭya	1097 (Hs 57)
Annadāni	1106 (Cg 51)
Mahadēva	1174 (Hs 20)
Pemma-Vīrappa	1175 (")
Sōma-Dēva, Boppa-Dēva	1245–52 (Ag 53)
Malli-Dēva	1280 (Bl 89)
Malli-Dēva, Harihara-Dēva	c. 1280 (Cg 54, 55)
" "	? 1296 (Cg 45)
Harihara-Dēva	1297 (Cg 59)

The inscriptions of 1034 and 1037 do not mention the name Nanni, but they no doubt belong to him, as in the latter, Panchavan-mārāya, the victor over the Changāḷvas, is said to have then bound *paṭṭas*, or badges of honour, on certain *gāruṇḍas*. Mādēva has various epithets applied to him. Besides being entitled to the *pañcha-mahā-śabda*, he is styled Nigalanka-malla. He may be the Tribhuvanamalla of Cg 61. But the Changāḷvas were apparently lifting their heads too high. So, in about 1104, the Hoysaḷa king Ballāḷa I led an expedition against Changāḷva (Hn 162). In 1106 Annadāni is mentioned (Cg 51), but shorn of titles. He is not said to be a Changāḷva, but as their family god was called Annadāni-Mallikārjuna, he was very likely one, who built the temple for it. In ? 1124 we find Changāḷva helping the hill chiefs against the Hoysaḷa army (Bl 178). But in 1130 Vishnuvarddhana is described as a submarine fire to the ocean the Changāḷva king (Cm 137), and in 1139 the Changāḷva *purāṇika* had to apply to the Hoysaḷa king for confirmation of a grant (Cn 199). In 1145 Nārasimha I is said to have slain Changāḷva in battle, and seized his elephants, horses, gold and new jewels (Ng 76). In 1155 Nārasimha's general Chōkimayya brought the Changa king's territory into subjection to his sovereign (Hn 69). An inscription of 1169 says of Gōvi-dēva, the younger brother of Biṭṭi-dēva, the chief of Huliyera under Nārasimha, that the wounds he inflicted with his spear on the face of the elephant on which the Changāḷuva king was seated resembled the characters of an inscription recording his own valour. In 1171 Sōvi-dēva, the Kadamba governor of Banavase, took Changāḷva prisoner and put him into irons, as he had vowed he would (Sb 345). When Nārasimha's son, the prince Ballāḷa, made a tour through the hill countries in the west, Changāḷva is named as one of the kings who was compelled to do homage to him (Bl 86). But after Ballāḷa had come to the throne, he had to send an expedition in 1174 under his general Beṭṭarasa against the Changāḷva king Mahadēva, who had retired to Coorg and fortified himself at Pālpare in Kiggaṭnāḍ. Beṭṭarasa marched there, and having destroyed him, made Pālpare the seat of his own government. But the Changāḷva Pemma-Vīrappa, perhaps Mahadēva's son, afterwards attacked him at Pālpare, aided by Bāḍagaṇḍa Nandi-dēva, Udeyāditya-dēva of Kuruche, and others 'the Koḍagas of all the nāḍs'. Beṭṭarasa was near being altogether worsted, but secured the victory through the devotion and bravery of one of his officers (Hs 20). This is the first express mention of the Koḍagas that has been met with in inscriptions. The Changāḷvas seem after this reverse to have submitted to the Hoysaḷas. For in 1175 we have grants made in Coorg by Ballāḷa II (Cg 65, 70).

In apparently about 1280 there is mention (Cg 27) of a Changālva in connection with a Munivarāditya, who seems to have been ruling in ? 1264 (Cg 75). A chief of this name is said (Cn 203) to have presented in 1223 an emerald to the Hoysaḷa king Nārasimha II, who, no doubt on account of its being of unique size and value. added it to his necklace and celebrated the event by a feast in Chūḍavāḍi (the Chūḍagrāma or Mudiyanūr in Muḷbāgal tāluq—see Mb 157), where he was at the time encamped during his campaign against Magara. This Munivarāditya must be a different person from the one in the present inscriptions, as the title in the other seems to have belonged to a chief of Mēlai (or western)-Mārāyapāḍi (in the Kaḍapa District) in 1124 (Ct 162); whereas the present Munivarāditya may more probably be connected with the Mulivarāditya-nāḍ or Munivarāditya-nāḍ mentioned in No. 45 in 1296, which was evidently in Coorg, and probably to the east of Merkara.

This last inscription was written by the *sēnabōva* of Kopaṇa-tīrtha, which is a place deserving of notice. It is in all probability the Kopal or Koppal, situated in Raichūr District, in the south-west of the Nizam's Dominions. It was a great sacred place or *tīrtha* of the Jains, and is mentioned in the 9th century by the Rāshṭrakūṭa king Nṛipatuṅga in his *Kavirājamārgga* as one of the four cities in which the pith of the Kannaḍa language was spoken. It is no doubt the Koppam where a sanguinary battle took place in 1052 between the Chōḷas and the Western Chālukyas. The Chōḷa king Rājādhirāja was slain, but his brother Rājēndra-Dēva took command and succeeded in putting to flight the Chāḷukya king Āhavamalla. Koppam in this connection is described as a *tīrtha* on the Pērār or big river, a designation generally applied to the Krishṇā, but here apparently referring to the Tuṅgabhadrā. In 1113 Ganga-Rāja, the victorious general of the Hoysaḷa king Vishṇuvarddhana, is said (SB 47), by his restoration of ruined Jina temples throughout Gangavāḍi, to have made it shine like Kopaṇa. In modern times its hill fort was occupied by Ṭīpu Sultān in 1786, and rebuilt by him with the assistance of his French engineers. Sir John Malcolm pronounced it the strongest fort he had seen in India. It is now the chief place in the *jāgīr* of the first Sir Sālār Jung, the eminent Haidarabad minister.

In 1252, the Hoysaḷa king Sōmēśvara, who had taken up his residence at Kaṇṇanūr or Vikramapura, near Śrīraṅgam and Trichinopoly, in the Chōḷa country which he had subdued, on the death there of his Tamil wife, resolved to revisit the capital Dōrasamudra (Halebīḍ in the Hassan District). Sōma-Dēva and Boppa-Dēva, the two Changālvas who were jointly ruling then, came to receive him at Rāmanāthpur, which they had rebuilt in 1245 (Ag 53). This was probably the boundary of their kingdom, and the place where the king had to ford the river Kāvērī, as perhaps the epic hero Rāma had done in olden times. From the same inscription we learn that the Changāḷva capital since 1245 had been at Śrīrangapaṭṭaṇa. This does not mean Seringapatam in Mysore, but the place called Koḍagu-Śrīrangapaṭṭaṇa (see Cg 25), which is in Coorg, south of the Kāvērī near Siddapur. Malli-Dēva and his son Harihara-Dēva are mentioned in 1280 and 1297 (Bl 89, Cg 54, 55, 59). Subsequently, during the 14th century, when the Muhammadan invasions from Delhi took place, and the Hoysaḷas and other southern powers were swept away, we meet with no Changālvas. Nos. 67 of ?1360 and 58 of ?1380 are doubtful.

But in the 15th century the Changāḷvas again appear, and soon made their capital at Nanjarājapaṭṭaṇa or Nanjarāyapaṭṭaṇa, of which place they henceforward call themselves the Rājas. It still gives its name to the northern tāluq of Coorg, and is situated in Coorg, north of the Kāvērī where it turns north and becomes the common boundary of Coorg and Mysore. The following is a list of the kings in this later period. Hs 63 gives the genealogy to 1502, and Hs 24 to 1567. Mangarasa, in his *Jayanṛipa-kāvya*, written in about 1509, says that his father was descended from the minister of the Chaṅgāḷva kings, and that the latter derived their origin from Kṛishṇa, that is, were Yādavas.

Nāga	
Raṅga	
Piriya, Piryyana	
Nanja-Rāja[1]	1502-33
Nanjuṇḍa-Rāja	
Śrīkaṇṭha-Rājaiya, Śrīkaṇṭharasu	1544
Vīra-Rāja-Voḍeyar	1559-80
Piriya-Rājaiya-Dēva, Rudragaṇa	1586-1607
Nanjuṇḍa-Dēva	
Nanja-Rājaiya-Dēva	1612-19
Kṛishṇa-Rājaiya-Dēva	1617
Vīra-Rājaiya	1619-44

Nanja-Rāja was the founder of Nanjarājapaṭṭaṇa or Nanjarāyapaṭṭaṇa, the new capital, which was named after him. Śrīkaṇṭha-Rāja seems to have been an important person, and in one case (Hs 24) is given supreme titles. This was in 1567, in his son's time. But from Hs 25 it would appear that in 1544 he was indebted to Aubhalēśvara-arasu of Nandiyāla for the grant of a palanquin, and in No. 10 of that year is not mentioned at all. Piriya-Rāja rebuilt Singapaṭṭaṇa and changed its name to Piriyapaṭṭaṇa (the Periapatam of English histories), naming it after himself (Hs 15). This seems to have been a secondary capital.

All these kings were subordinate to Vijayanagar, which was represented by a Viceroy at Seringapatam in Mysore. By Piriya-Rāja's time Vijayanagar had fallen. But there still remained a viceroy at Seringapatam, named Tirumale-Rāja, who was aged and infirm, and whose authority was waning. In 1607 he is said (Hs 36) to have made a grant of the Malalavāḍi country (in Huṇsūr tāluq) to Rudragaṇa "in order that the worship of the god Annadāni-Mallikārjuna should not fail as long as the Nanjarāyapaṭṭaṇa kings of the Chaṅgāḷva family continued." But Piriyapaṭṭaṇa was taken by the Mysore army in 1644, in the reign of Kaṇṭhīrava-Narasa-Rāja, and Vīra-Rājaiya fell in its defence, after putting to death his wives and children on seeing that his situation was desperate. This was the end of the Chaṅgāḷvas, who had held the throne for 600 years or more. The Mysoreans seem not to have followed up this victory into Coorg, but contented themselves with placing garrisons in Piriyapaṭṭaṇa and Beṭṭadpur. The Koḍagas may have attempted later to retake Piriyapaṭṭaṇa or Periapatam, as they are specially named in 1722 (Sr 64) among the assailants from various quarters who were defeated by the Mysore king Chikka-Dēva-Rāja.

Koṅgāḷvas

The discovery of the Koṅgāḷva line of kings is of as much interest for the history of Coorg as that of the Chaṅgāḷvas. The origin of the Koṅgāḷvas is related in Cg 46. The great Chōḷa king, the friend of the virgin daughter of Kavēra (that is, the river Kāvērī), Rājakēsarivarmma-Permmanaḍigaḷ, that is Rājarāja, on hearing that Manija had fought in the battle of Panasoge until the enemy (evidently the Chaṅgāḷvas) were overcome and slain, resolved to reward him with a *paṭṭa*, or diadem, and give him a nāḍ. He sent orders

[1] His younger brother Mahadēva is mentioned in Hs 63 and SB 103.

accordingly to his general Pañchavan-mahārāya, who bound on him a *paṭṭa* bearing the title *Kshattriya-śikhāmani-Koṅgaḷva* and gave him Mālavve (now Mālambi in Coorg). This was in 1004.

The Koṅgāḷvas ruled over a territory including the Arkalgūḍ tāluq of Mysore and the Yēḷusāvira or Seven Thousand country in the north of Coorg. It no doubt corresponded more or less with the Koṅgal-nāḍ Eight Thousand, of which the Gaṅga prince Ereyappa is said (Hs 92) to have been the governor in about 880. The Koṅgāḷvas were Jains, and had Chōḷa prefixes to their names. Their titles, as given in Ag 99, were the following:— entitled to the *pañcha-mahā-śabda*, mahā-maṇḍalēśvara, chief lord of the city of Oreyūr (the early Chōḷa capital near Trichinopoly), sun upon the eastern mountain the Chōḷa-kula with twisted top-knot, crest-jewel of the Sūryya-vamśa (or Solar race). They thus claim to be Chōḷas.

But Pañchavan-mahārāya seems to be a recognized Pāṇḍya designation. He may perhaps be the Pañchavaṉ-Brahmādirāja to whom the Chōḷa king Rājarāja granted Tagaḍūr, said to be Dharmapuri in the Salem District.[1] But there is also a Tagaḍūr in Mysore, in the Nanjangūḍ tāluq, which is described as *hiriya-nāḍu* and *anādi-mahā-nāḍu*[2]. Of Pañchavan-mahārāya we have a farther account in an inscription at Balmuri (Sr 140), dated in 1012. He is there described as a bee at the lotus feet of Rājarāja, who invested him with the rank of mahā-daṇḍanāyaka for Beṅgi-maṇḍala (the Eastern-Chālukya territory) and Ganga-maṇḍala (the Ganga territory in Mysore). He then claims to have led an expedition throughout the western coast region, in the course of which he seized Tuluva (South Kanara), and Konkaṇa (North Kanara), held Malaya (Malabar), and put to flight Chēramma (the king of Cochin or Travancore), after which he pushed aside Teluga and Raṭṭiga (countries to the north of Mysore), and coveted even the little Belvoḷa country (in Dharwar and Belgaum Districts). He is called Rājēndra-Chōḷa in Sr 125. He appears again in 1037, conferring *paṭṭas* or badges of honour on various gāvuṇḍas or farmers (Hg 104). After Rājēndra-Chōḷa in 1022 had attacked the Poysaḷa king Nṛipa-Kāma (Mj 43), Rājēndra-Chōḷa-Koṅgāḷva also attacked him in 1026, when he claims to have gained a victory at Manni (Ag 76).

His son was Rājādhirāja-Koṅgāḷva (Cg 38), who, and his mother Pōchabbarasi, had as their *guru* Guṇasēna-paṇḍita[3], who was the disciple of Pushpasēna-siddhānta-dēva (Cg 35, 37, 38, 41). Guṇasēna had the Nāga well dug at Muḷḷūr in about 1050 (Cg 42), and died in 1064 (Cg 34). Of the same period are the following:—Cg 56, recording the death in ?1044 of Prabhāchandra-dēva, the disciple of Śubhachandra-dēva; and Cg 31, stating that Jakkiyabbe, the wife of Eḍayya, resolved to obtain *mukti* by the performance of *sannyasanam* and expired in about 1050. There is also a notice in Cg 39 that Rājādhirāja-Koṅgāḷva had set up and endowed a temple in memory of his mother Pōchabbarasi, through the agency of Rugmiṇi-Dēvi's queen's body-guard, which was at a later period restored, in 1390, when the Vijayanagar king Vira-Harihara, having read the deed making the grant, resolved to carry it on and granted Muḷḷūr-nāḍ to Gonka-Ṛaḍḍi-nāyaka, whose bravery had been noted by (the commander) Guṇḍappa-daṇḍanāyaka.

In 1058 a Rājēndra-Koṅgāḷva appears (Cg 35), presumably Rājādhirāja-Koṅgāḷva's son. He was apparently succeeded by the king whose name was Adaṭarāditya, with the titles

---

[1] Mad. No. 204 of 1909. [2] Nj 117, 115

[3] He was of the Draviḷa-gaṇa (Nos. 34, 35, 36) or Tivuḷa-gaṇa (Nos. 37)—both names meaning Tamil In Kannaḍa they take the form Draviḍa and Tiguḷa.

Rājēndra-Prithuvī-Koṅgāḷva and Tribhuvanamalla-Chōḷa Koṅgāḷva. His dates run from 1066 to 1100, and he seems to have been a powerful ruler. One of his inscriptions (Ag 99) was composed by the minister for peace and war, named Nakulāryya, who boasts of being able to write in four languages. Which these were is not stated, but Nakulāryya is a form of the name Lakula, that of a famous Śaiva teacher, the original of whom seems to have lived very early in the Christian era.[1] Cg 44 is a memorial of Uttama-Chōḷa-Seṭṭi, who, in about 1080, appears to have taken his life by cutting off his head, no doubt in accordance with some vow of self-sacrifice.

A Vīra-Chōḷa-Koṅgāḷva is the last of whom we have a record. In an inscription of ? 1176 (Cg 33) he made—in the presence of the queen mother Padmala-Dēvi, Sōmala-Dēvi and others,—a grant of the customs-dues of the Muḷḷūr-nāḍ Seventy, the country around Muḷḷūr, near Śanivārsante. Padmala-Dēvi was the queen of the Hoysaḷa king Vīra-Ballāḷa II and mother of the next king Nārasimha II. Sōmala-Dēvi was her daughter, a princess noted for her beauty and virtue. The Koṅgāḷvas seem thus to have been recognized by the Hoysaḷas, and Koṅgāḷva is mentioned along with Chaṅgāḷva in Bl 86 as coming to do homage to Ballāḷa. But they did not long survive the Chōḷa ascendancy in Coorg and the south of Mysore. In 1296 the Chaṅgāḷvas were evidently (Cg 45) in possession of Muḷḷūr. But Cg 39 shows that in 1390 a Jain priest restored a temple formerly set up there by the Koṅgāḷva king and recovered the endowments, which it is believed are continued even now. Meanwhile at that same date, the Vijayanagar king Harihara II made the grant of Muḷḷūr-nāḍ, as above mentioned, to Gonka-Ṛaḍḍi-nāyaka, through his general Guṇḍappa-daṇḍaṇāyaka. The exploits of this Guṇḍa-daṇḍanātha are extensively praised in Bl 3.

Hoysaḷas

The struggles of the Chaṅgāḷvas against the Hoysaḷas, and the establishment of the supremacy of the latter, have been described above. But the only inscriptions of the Hoysaḷas in Coorg itself, directly attributed to them, are Nos. 65 and 70, 6 and 7. The first two are of the time of Ballāḷa II, dated in 1175; the other two of the time of Nārasimha III, dated in 1255 and 1285. They are all in the north. No. 65 is at Siraha in the Bilaha hōbli (called in the inscription Biluhu-nāḍ), and records a grant for the god Mallikārjuna of Sirivūr. No. 70 is at Heggaḍahaḷḷi in the Kanime hōbli, and the subject of it is effaced. Nos. 6 and 7 are at Niḍuta on the north-eastern frontier, and are *bīragal* or *vīragal*, memorials to warriors slain in battle. The village of Kahigōḍ mentioned in them is now *bēchirākh*, or deserted, and is situated in the Arkalgūḍ tāluq of the Hassan District of Mysore, on the opposite side of the Kāvērī to Krishṇarājkaṭṭe. There are several similar memorial stones there, of the same period and relating to the same persons (Ag 37 to 40). These and the records of the preceding paragraph above show that the Hoysaḷa king and members of the royal family were at this time in the north of Coorg, in consequence perhaps of the decisive defeat of the Chaṅgāḷvas in the battle of Pālpare.

There is one inscription (Cg 40), dated in 1216, which belongs to the Hoysaḷa period, but the name of the only king mentioned in it is effaced. All that can be read is Immaḍi-A....Rāya. Who this may have been it is impossible to say. Immaḍi means 'the second'. There was an Annadāni apparently among the Chaṅgāḷvas, but no other name of a king at about that time in any line begins with A. From the inscription being at Muḷḷūr, and evidently Jain, one would be disposed to class it as Koṅgāḷva, and there was a king in that line named Adaṭarāditya. But there is no reason to suppose that the Koṅgāḷvas continued till then.

---

[1] See *JRAS* for 1907, p. 419.

The inscription records the death of a Vidyādhara Būchidēvarasa, who is described as Immaḍi-A.... Rāya's *kaṭakāchārya*, or as we might say, 'army chaplain'. He was the Jain priest to the camp or capital, but what were his functions does not appear. Kēśirāja, the author of the standard Kannaḍa grammar named *Śabdamaṇi-darpaṇa*, in like manner calls himself the Yādava-kaṭakāchārya.

KING BŌDHARŪPA

Probably belonging to the 14th century, when the Hoysaḷa power had been overthrown by Muhammadan invasions from the north, and the Changāḷvas were not in evidence in Coorg, we have two inscriptions in Tamil characters (Nos. 8 and 9), the only ones in Coorg so written. They are—the first, in the temple at Pālūr, and the second, at Bhāgamaṇḍala,[1] a sacred spot near the source of the river Kāvērī, called in the inscription the Bhagaṇḍāśrama, where the Kanake, its first tributary, unites with the Kāvērī, which emerges here from its course for some distance underground. They record grants made by a king named Bōdharūpa Bhagavar. He was a disciple of Avidyāmṛityu-bhaṭṭāraka of the Purushōttama-*parshad* (or synod), of which we know nothing more. The donor might possibly be identified with the ruler of Durga, now known as Mahārājdurga, in the south-west of the Hassan tāluq of Mysore. For in an inscription from Rudrapaṭna (Mg 87) we have a Bōdha-mahādēva on the throne of Durga in the time of Bukka-Rāya of Vijayanagar, in 1371, and this seems the most likely period of these two Coorg inscriptions. But unfortunately it is not altogether reliable, being on an alleged copper plate which was not forthcoming. The published version is from a manuscript copy furnished by the people of the village. On the other hand, grounds might be adduced for placing them in the beginning of the 11th century, the period of the Chōḷa conquest. But against this is the absence of any mention of the Chōḷas. Our information regarding the Durga principality, again, is very meagre, but its capital may have been Pālya, to the north of the hill. Compare with this the Pālayūr or Pālūr where the first grant was made.

The opening portion of both records is in Sanskrit verse. The continuation has been represented as being in the Tulu language, but this needs verification. It contains many Tamil terms.[2]

Of these two inscriptions, which have several features in common, No. 8 is a grant for Pālayūr Mahādēva (Śiva). The duty of maintaining it is laid upon the Śrīvaishṇavas, the Valañjiyar (or merchants), the arm-bearing Thousands, and the Brāhmaṇs,—all being described as of the Eighteen countries, which are not specified. A grant (TN 35, as completed[3]) made in the 20th year of the Chōḷa king Rājarāja, 1004 A.D., is similarly placed under the protection of the Śrīvaishṇavas. This designation, therefore, existed before Rāmānuja, with whom the sect of Śrīvaishṇava Brāhmaṇs is supposed to have originated, early in the 12th century. Similarly also, grants made at Āvani in 1185 (Mb 45,49b) are committed to the protection of the Valañjiyar (or merchants). The reference to the arm-bearing Thousands may be compared with 'the great army of the Right-hand of the Eighteen countries,

---

[1] This stone is cracked transversely across the middle, said to be due to the followers of Ṭīpu Sultān. For the first impressions of these two inscriptions I was indebted to Mr. Gustav Haller. But better ones were afterwards obtained through Mr. Krishna Śāstri.

[2] For the decipherment of the vernacular portion I have to thank Mr. Narasimhāchār, who says :—'The characters are a jumble of Grantha, Malayāḷam, Tamil, and a few Vaṭṭeḻuttu. There is no doubt about portions being in Tamil, but other portions are in a language which is neither Malayāḷam nor Tulu, but is related to them. I think the inscriptions are older than 1400 A.D. Some of the characters appear to go back to the 11th century'. Mr. Krishna Śāstri has also rendered good assistance in the interpretation.

[3] See MAR 1912, para. 77.

armed with great weapons', mentioned in 1072 in the time of Rājēndra-Chōḷa (Mb 49a, 119). The Right- and Left- hand factions are composed of agricultural, artisan and trading classes, divided into these two violently opposed camps. The institution is ancient, but its origin is obscure. So far as can be seen, it was a conflict of home industrial classes with outsiders from other parts. The Brāhmaṇs are then lastly named as custodians. It would seem therefore that the four orders of Hindūs,—Brāhmaṇs, Kshattriyas, Vaiśyas, and Śūdras—are intended. The penalties for neglect are somewhat peculiar.

In No. 9 we are supplied with certain astronomical data, but they are insufficient for calculation. This grant implies that it was made after the one at Pālūr, though doubtless at about the same time. Moreover the original is stated in it to have been engraved on a copper plate. Of this there is now no trace. Bōdharūpa was associated with others, not named, in making the grant. A chief named Mēlpūṇḍi Kunniyarasa was ruling the nāḍ. What nāḍ is not stated. but 'this' nāḍ is mentioned farther on as being under the rule of the king who ordered the grant. The rest of the inscription prescribes the offerings to be made, and the penalties for neglect. The arm-bearing Thousands of the Eighteen countries and the Valañjiyar are here charged to guard the temple. For whatever is omitted, reference is to be made to the treasury register and the copper plate. It was written (or engraved) by Pakaṇḍala-āyāri. The Pālūr temple is now said to be dedicated to Mahāliṅgēśvara, and that at Bhāgamaṇḍala to Bhagaṇḍēśvara, but it also has shrines to Vishṇu, Subrahmaṇya, Kinammaṇi, and Gaṇapati.

Munivarāditya Gōkula-Dēvarasa

Another local potentate appears at about this period in No. 75, which is dated only in the cyclic year and may belong to 1264. It contains some unusual items of interest. He was a maha-maṇḍalēśvara named Vīra-Munivarāditya Gōkula-dēvarasa[1], and is described as subduer of Chaüṭu, and supporter of Satyarāya (whoever they were). During his rule, there was a cattle raid by the Tengu-nāḍaka, who seized the cows of Yalaghali. The wife of his brave retainer Mēlaḷi (who was no doubt absent at the time) was so furious at this outrage that she wrestled with the marauder, overpowered and threw him down, and tied his legs with a rope. For this plucky deed, Bidaḍe, as she seems to have been named, was rewarded with a nose jewel.

The Nava Dannāyaks

On the fall of the Hoysaḷa kingdom there ensued a period of interregnum which invited attempts on the part of aspirants for power. One such was connected with the Nava Dannāyaks of Kōṭe or Beṭṭadakōṭe in the south of Mysore, where they occupied the Gōpālasvāmi hill. They seem to have been descendants from a great minister under Ballāḷa III, named Perumāḷa-dannāyaka. His son Mādhava-dannāyaka was governor of Padināl̤knāḍ[2] in the south of Mysore in 1318 (Ch 103, Gu 56), and had his residence at Terakaṇāmbi in the Gundalpet tāluq (Gu 58). He was followed by his son Kētaya-dannāyaka, ruling in 1321 (Gu 69), and by Siṅgeya-dannāyaka, ruling in 1338 (Hs 82). They call themselves lords of Svastipura, which is not identified.

The Nava Dannāyaks were nine brothers, the chief of whom was called Perumāḷ-dannāyak. Tradition says that four of them, headed by Bhīma-dannāyak, quarrelled with the

---

[1] See above, p. 15. He may be connected with the Gōpāla-dēva mentioned in No. 54.

[2] There seems no reason to connect this name, which means Fourteen Nāḍs, with Pāḍiuālknāḍ, a tāluq in Coorg, where it refers to certain Four Nāḍs (Nālknāḍ) in contradistinction to those forming Yeḍenālknāḍ. At the same time it is curious to note that the Terakaṇāmbi-nāḍ is said (Gu 11) to be also called Kuḍugu-nāḍ, which is the name of Coorg.

other five, and gaining possession of Nagarapura (Nanjangūḍ) and Ratnapur (Heḍatale), set up a separate government. After a time they returned to attack Beṭṭadakōṭe, which held out for three years before it was captured, and then only by a stratagem. Mañcha-dannāyak, who conducted the defence, on seeing the citadel taken, leaped from the hill on horseback and was killed, the spot where this occurred being still pointed out. The four victorious Dannāyaks, placing a junior member of the family in charge of the government at Beṭṭadakōṭe, set forth on expeditions of conquest, in the course of which it is said they overran the country from Davasi-beṭṭa (the southern point of Coorg) in the south, to Goa in the north, and from Satyamangalam (on the Bhavāni in Coimbatore District) in the east, to the Bisaleghāṭ (in the north-west of Coorg) on the west. There are no inscriptions in Coorg testifying to these events, which must have soon passed. But the Dannāyaks have left their name in Dannāyakankōṭṭai, 12 miles south-west of Satyamangalam. [1]

VIJAYANAGAR

The Vijayanagar empire had by this time been established, and in 1390 we are informed (Cg 39) that Harihara [II], having read the deed of the original dedication by Rājādhirāja-Koṅgāḷva, with the view of continuing it, made a grant of Muḷḷu-nāḍ to Gonka-Raḍḍi-nāyaka, whose bravery had been noticed by his general Guṇḍappa-daṇṇāyaka. Vijayanagar influence and authority are also attested by the reference made in connection with Bōdha-mahādēva above to Bukka-Rāya; by the acknowledgment of the Bēlūr chiefs below, who owed their status to Kṛishṇa-Rāya; and by the action of the Vijayanagar viceroy in regard to the Changāḷvas. Firishta says that at the end of the 16th century Coorg proper was governed by its own chiefs, called Nāyaks, who admitted the supremacy of Vijayanagar; but they seem often to have been at feud with one another. According to tradition, the country was then divided into twelve Kombus and thirty-five Nāḍs.

BĒLŪR

Of the Bēlūr chiefs there are three inscriptions—Cg 11, dated in 1693; 66 and 47, dated in ? 1755 and 1756. These show that, after the extinction of the Changāḷvas, the Bēlūr chiefs had acquired some territory for a time in the north of Coorg. The family was descended from Ere-Kṛishṇappa-Nāyaka, the bearer of the Haḍapa, or betel-bag, to the Vijayanagar king Kṛishṇa-Rāya (reigned 1509–29), who gave him the Bēlūr kingdom. It was overrun by Śivappa-Nāyaka of Bednūr before the middle of the 17th century, and by him was bestowed on the fugitive king of Vijayanagar who had fled to him for refuge. He even laid siege to Seringapatam in 1646 on the plea of restoring the Vijayanagar king to power, but was beaten off, and the Mysore army retaliated by subduing the Bēlūr country. On the conclusion of peace in 1694, six *nāḍs* of Manjarābād were restored to the old chiefs, and the rest divided between the contending parties. The genealogy of the line is given in the Hassan volume of the *Epigraphia Carnatica.*

Cg 11 records the grant of the village of Kaṭṭepura, with Hirumanahaḷḷi, to a Brāhman, in 1693, by Kṛishṇappa-Nāyaka IV. Cg 66 is the grant of an elephant and the village of Mudravaḷḷi, as an offering for Kṛishṇa, to a great *yōgi* named Kaivalya, in about 1755, by the Bēlūr king Kṛishṇa (Kṛishṇappa-Nāyaka VI). The inscription is in Sanskrit verse, and ends with the question: 'If it be asked, for what reason was this given?'—but here the record stops, and furnishes no answer. Cg 47 is of the following year, and states that the same Kṛishṇappa-Nāyaka made a grant of the village-rent to a *gauḍa* of Mālambi.

---

[1] See *Mad. Ep. Rep.* 1907, p. 80; 1910, para. 52.

Coorg Rājas

On the downfall of the Changāḷvas in 1644, the throne of Coorg was left vacant. But it did not long remain so. For a prince of the Bednūr family, in the Shimoga District of Mysore, who may have been connected in some way with the Changāḷvas, established himself at Hālēri (called Kshīra-nagara in Sanskṛit), to the north of Mercāra, in the guise of a Jangama or Lingāyit priest. Gradually levying contributions by virtue of his sacred office, and enlisting a special guard for his protection, he ended by bringing the whole country under his authority, and was the progenitor of the Coorg Rājas of the house of Hālēri (corrupted into Allory in English documents). The third from him removed the capital from Hālēri to Maḍikēri, the existing Merkāra, or Mercāra as it is now generally spelt, where he built a fort and palace in 1681. His successors continued in power till 1834, when the last was deposed by the British Government, and died in 1859.

The Coorg Rājas claim to be of the Chandra-vaṁśa or Lunar race, of the Bharadvāja-gōtra, Āśvalāyana-sūtra, Ṛikshabhānukādhyāya,[1] and the Vīra-Śaiva *mata* or religion. The titles they assume are—rājādhirāja, rāja-paramēśvara, prahuḍa-pratāpa, apratima-vīra-narapati, seated on the jewelled throne of the Koḍagu-saṁsthāna. These resemble those of the Mysore Rājas.

Their inscriptions are mostly dated according to the Kali-yuga, though the Śālivāhana-śaka is used in some. But from the time of Linga-Rājēndra I, they have this peculiarity, that not only are the particulars of the date given in the usual manner, but even the precise number of the day of the Kali-yuga. For example, No. 17 informs us that the erection of the Ōṁkārēśvara temple was commenced on the 1,796,392nd Kali day and completed on the 1,797,421st day. This method of dating seems to be a Malabar custom.[2]

No. 12 records the death of Linga-Rājēndra I in 1780, and the erection, in accordance with his wishes, of his tomb in Mahadēvapura, by his son Vīra-Rājēndra-Vaḍeyar, who also built there a temple of Basavēśvara and the *maṭha* or monastery of the Murigi sect, and endowed them with certain villages. The temple was repaired the following year, at the instance of Siddalingappa, deputy guru of Koḍagu, the repairs being completed in 1782. The subservience of the Rājas to the Lingāyit gurus will appear in the inscriptions that follow.

No. 13 is the record of a grant to the Abbi-maṭha by Vīra-Rājēndra-Vaḍeyar in 1796. In this the king describes himself as having been dedicated by the lotus hands of the *svāmi* of the Siddapura-maṭha, who was an adherent of those (high priests) enthroned in the upper cave at Śivaganga (in the north-west of the Bangalore District of Mysore). The inscription refers to grants originally made to the Abbi-maṭha in 1728 by his great-grandfather Doḍḍa-Vīrappa-Vaḍeyar, first of two villages, and afterwards of a third, when Doḍḍa-Virūpāksha-svāmi visited Maḍikēri, on which occasion the king held the *guru's* feet and made petition (that he might offer the grant). These gifts Vīra-Rājēndra now renewed and confirmed, inscribing the details on a copper plate, which was placed at the feet of Nirañjana-dēva of the Abbi-maṭha, representing the Murigi-svāmi. (The chief monastery of the Murigi-svāmi is near Chitaldroog in Mysore). In granting this charter the king directs that at the time of Śiva-pūjā blessings may be continually invoked (for him) with the hymn of benediction (saying).—

> Recollection of former births, dominion of the world, the glory of good fortune, surpassing beauty,
> Faith in thee, knowledge, long life, (objects of) desire—(of these) be thou giver to me, Śankara, from age to age.

---

[1] In the latest inscriptions Ṛik-śākhā is substituted for this.

[2] It has also been found in one case, from the North Arcot District, of the Chōḷa king Parāntaka I, in 943 (*Rep. Arch. S. of India*, 1905-6. p. 171).

The witnesses are thus described:—Sun and moon, wind and fire, sky, earth and water, heart (or conscience) and Yama, day and night, morning and evening; these know the deeds of a righteous man.

No. 14 is a grant of land made at the same time by the same king for the Mahadēvapura-maṭha. When the *paṭṭada-svāmi*, or crown high-priest, of the Siddapura-maṭha paid a visit to the Mahadēvapura-maṭha, the king performed obeisance to him with the eight members (*sāshṭ-āṅga*—hands, breast, forehead, knees and feet, touching the ground), and holding his feet, made the gift as an offering to Śiva. The copper plate on which it was inscribed was placed at the feet of Śāntavīra-svāmi, deputy of the Koḍali-mahanta-svāmi, deputy of the Mahā-Murigi-svāmi. The directions as to invocation of blessings at the time of Śiva-pūjā, and the witnesses are as in the preceding inscription.

No. 17 is dated in 1820, and contains an account of the erection of the Ōṁkārēśvara temple at Mercāra and its endowment by Linga-Rājēndra-Vaḍeyar II. Considering that by the performance of good deeds in this world must be obtained perfect fruition in the present world and the next, he resolved to set up a Śiva-linga, as an act ensuring the acquisition of the highest merit. Accordingly, he commenced building this beautiful new temple, a lotus ornament to the earth, at the date specified, on the 1,796,392nd Kali day. And in 2 years, 9 months and 25 days the building was completed, and he set up the Śiva-linga named Ōṁkārēśvara in it on the 1,797,421st Kali day, through the power bestowed by the great mercy of the holy Chandraśēkhara (Śiva). Then follows a specification of the allowances granted for up-keep, and the services to be performed, adding that the accounts and papers of the temple were to be audited and examined annually.

No. 25, dated in 1824, is of quite a different character from any of the above, and may perhaps be described as sporting. It relates that when Vīra-Rājēndra-Vaḍeyar II, with various laudatory epithets, his fame pervading all the points of the compass, was ruling with justice, purity and uprightness[1], at all times devoted to meditation on Mahādēva;—elephants multiplied so greatly in his country that they were destroying the fruits and crops raised by men for their own sustenance, killing travellers, and doing damage to houses; so much so that the subjects represented that they were unable to bear these calamities. Considering in his mind that it is the duty of a king to put down the evil and uphold the good, he prayed to Gaurīdhava (Śiva) to give him power to remove these troubles. Having received a token of supreme favour from Sāmba-Śankara (Śiva), he had a chariot made, painted like a lion (according to Hindū belief the natural enemy of the elephant), and by means of this entered, beginning on the auspicious 1,798,128th Kali day, into the middle of the forests where the herds of rutting elephants were ranging, and during 2 years, 1 month and 25 days (March 1822 to April 1824), to the 1,798,913th Kali day, by the power of his arm having destroyed them in various ways, made a pause, while at the same time others had by his orders been captured alive with chains by trained soldiers. He thus made good the pronunciation of *gaja* (elephant) in the popular form *aja* (goat).

An account is then given in detail of the numbers killed and captured, the places where they were bagged, and the dates on which the hunts took place. The forests visited were those in the east and south of the country—in Nanjarāyapaṭṭaṇa tāluq, Uluguli-Mūḍigēri-nāḍ and Horūr-Nūrokkal-nāḍ (both in Mercāra tāluq), Koḍagu-Śrīrangapaṭṭaṇa, and Kiggaṭnāḍ tāluq. The actual number of days occupied in the hunt was 38, during which

[1] Unfortunately very unlike his real character.

the Rāja killed with his own hand 233, and his troops captured alive 181. A total of 414 elephants was thus accounted for.

Great was the astonishment at the success of the operations, which is expressed in verse as follows:—Though herds of elephants, towering like mountains, hid the sun as when the sky is overcast with storm-clouds, and roamed about trumpeting in the forests,—with seven-tongued weapons (fire-arms) like thunderbolts he slew them in a moment, while his men captured alive huge and lofty rutting elephants as if they were mice. What a marvel indeed was this!

Such are the inscriptions of the Coorg Rājas, and they give a very inadequate account of their history. It may be well therefore to supplement the information by a table of the Rājas and a summary of the main points connected with their reigns, as well as a notice of the circumstances under which the line came to an end [1]. The following is the pedigree:—

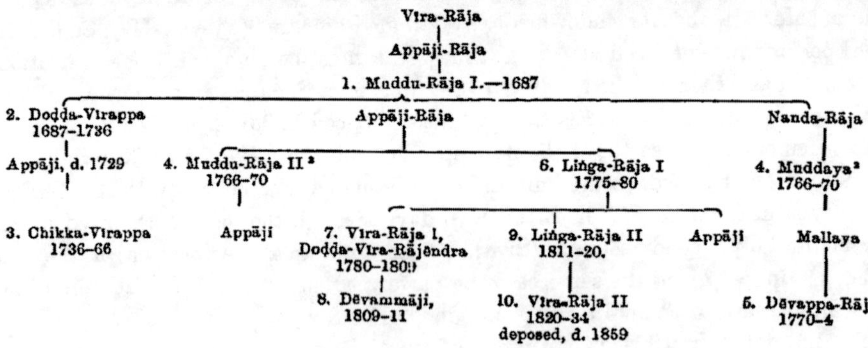

Muddu-Rāja I, as already stated above, made Mercāra the capital in 1681. In 1690, when Mysore and Bednūr were contending for the Bēlūr and Manjarābād territory, Doḍḍa-Vīrappa took possession of the Yēḷusāvira country. He also gained the district of Amara-Sulya by aiding the Chirakkal-Rāja against Bednūr. His brothers Appāji-Rāja and Nanda-Rāja settled at Hālēri and Horamale respectively. He died in 1736, at the age of 78. His only son had died in 1729, after being imprisoned for twelve years. But Chikka-Vīrappa, the son of the latter, who had been imprisoned with him, succeeded to the throne. During his reign Haidar Ali rose to power in Mysore, who, on his conquest of Bednūr in 1763, laid claim to Yēḷusāvira, but in consideration of a payment of three lakhs of pagodas consented to grant Uchingi to Coorg. Chikka-Vīrappa died in 1766 without leaving any heir. The succession therefore passed to the Hālēri and Horamale branches.

Muddu-Rāja II and Muddaya, representing the two houses, ruled together at the same time. The promised cession of Uchingi having been delayed, eventually they succeeded in obtaining Panje and Bellāre instead. These joint rulers both died in the same year, 1770. A dispute for the throne now arose between Muddu-Rāja's son Appāji, supported by his uncle Linga-Rāja, and Muddaya's grandson Dēvappa, supported by his father Mallaya. Dēvappa was preferred and became Rāja, on which Linga-Rāja went off to seek the assistance of Haidar Ali, taking with him his son Vīra-Rāja and his nephew Appāji. As soon as a respite in the war which Haidar was waging with the Mahrattas allowed, he furnished Linga-Rāja with a force which enabled him to march upon Coorg. Dēvappa-Rāja

[1] A fuller account will be found in Vol. III of my *Mysore and Coorg*, published in 1878 (Government Press, Bangalore).

[2] Ruled together, at the same time.

fled to the Chirakkal-Rāja, but meeting with a cold reception, escaped to Harihar, where he was taken prisoner and sent to Seringapatam. There he was put to death, with all his family, the Horamale branch being thus brought to an end. Haidar now offered Coorg to Linga-Rāja on condition of paying tribute, but deprived him of Amara-Sulya, Panje, Bellāre, and Yēḷusāvira, giving him instead permission to occupy a part of Wainād. On Linga-Rāja's death in 1780, Haidar assumed entire possession of Coorg under the pretext of being guardian to his sons until they should come of age. Meanwhile they were made to reside at Gorūr, on the Kāvērī, in the Hassan District of Mysore. A former Brāhman treasurer of the Coorg Rāja was appointed governor, and a Musalmān garrison held the fort at Mercāra.

These measures drove the Coorgs into rebellion, and in 1782 they rose and expelled the Musalmāns. Haidar was at this time engaged in war with the British in the Carnatic, and his death soon after prevented immediate retribution. But his son Ṭīpu Sultān was fully determined on the reconquest of Coorg. He removed the family of the Coorg Rājas to Piriyapatṇa or Periapatam, and when he had retaken Nagar, and reduced Mangalore in 1784, marched through Coorg to Seringapatam. After denouncing the Coorgs as guilty of polyandry, and for their rebellions, he said he would forgive them this once, but if they rebelled again he vowed that he would honour every man with Islām and banish them from their country. Scarcely had he left when they again took up arms in 1785 and repossessed themselves of their native hills. A force sent to put them down was driven back, on which Ṭīpu himself marched to Coorg with an army. Having allured most of the Coorgs to meet him at Tale-Kāvērī, under pretence of peaceable intentions and conciliatory measures, he suddenly seized them, and hunting out their families, drove them, altogether about 70,000, like a herd of cattle to Seringapatam, where all the males were forcibly circumcised. Coorg was partitioned among Musalmān landlords, to whom the slaves of the country were made over. The only condition laid on the new owners was that they were to search out and slay all such Coorgs as might have escaped his vengeance, as he was resolved on their extermination. The country was held in four forts, at Mercāra (Jāfarābād), Fraserpet (Kushālnagar), Bhāgamaṇḍala, and Beppunāḍ.

But in December 1788 Vīra-Rāja or Vīra-Rājēndra-Woḍeyar, with his wife and his two brothers Linga-Rāja and Appāji, managed to escape from Piriyapatṇa, after a confinement of six years. The Coorgs rallied round him, and before long he had possessed himself of the whole country, the large force sent against him by Ṭīpu being diverted to the western coast owing to a revolt of the Malayāḷam Rājas. The British now entered into a treaty with Vīra-Rājēndra in view to the impending struggle with Ṭīpu. He assisted the Bombay army on its march to Seringapatam with supplies procured by wholesale plunder of the neighbouring countries; and at the spot where he first met the British Commander, General Abercromby, he founded Vīrarājēndrapet (generally called Vīrājpet for short), now the second place in Coorg.

On the night in February 1792 when Lord Cornwallis drove Ṭīpu back into Seringapatam and the British occupied the island, 5,000 Coorgs who had been carried away by Ṭīpu escaped in the confusion and regained their native country, making with their wives and children a body of some 12,000. In the final war with Ṭīpu in 1799, Vīra-Rājēndra again rendered assistance with supplies and transport, and laid waste the enemy's country around Coorg. He was rewarded with some of the trophies of the victory, and was granted Panje and Bellāre in South Kanara.

His great anxiety now arose from his having no son to succeed him. He had married a second time in 1796, but only daughters were born to him. His mind was affected, and he became subject to paroxysms of sanguinary rage in which he ordered executions and massacres for which he was filled with remorse when he recovered. A plot to assassinate him failed. With the death of his wife in 1807 all hopes of an heir being extinguished, he wrote to the Governor-General requesting that the succession to the throne might be settled on his four daughters or their male issue in order of seniority. Before this matter could be decided, he felt that his end was approaching, and maddened with concern for the safety of his daughters if he should die, he sent executioners to put his two brothers to death, but coming to himself again, despatched messengers to countermand the orders. They were too late in the case of Appāji, the younger one, but were in time to save Linga-Rāja. He also had a history of the Coorg Rājas, called the *Rājēndranāme*[1], compiled in Kannaḍa or Kanarese, which was translated for him into English by Lieutenant Abercromby at Mangalore in 1808. At length, in June 1809, he sent for his beloved daughter Dēvammāji, gave his seal into her hands, and shortly after expired.

Dēvammāji, though under age, was now acknowledged as Rāni of Coorg, and the Sōde Rāja, who was married to the late Rāja's daughter by his first wife, continued to act as Dewan. But Linga-Rāja induced the Coorgs to accept him as Regent instead of the Sōde Rāja, who retired to his own country. Linga-Rāja next persuaded the Rāni to sign an abdication of the throne in his favour, and in 1811 permanently assumed the government. He also strove to get possession of the large sums invested at Bombay and Madras in the name of Dēvammāji by her father. But these the Governor-General pronounced to be state funds, only the interest of which might be paid to Linga-Rāja as guardian of Dēvammāji and Regent of Coorg. Linga-Rāja strengthened all the fortifications, and carried out a regular survey of the land; but reduced the people to a state of abject slavery by a rigid system of terror, of which no hint was allowed to be heard outside the country[2]. He died in 1820, at the age of 45, and his wife, full of fear for her future, committed suicide and was buried with him.

His son, Vīra-Rāja II, who was about 20 years old, succeeded. His first act was to put to death all who had displeased or thwarted him in his father's lifetime. He was grossly sensual and most sanguinary in his rule, bloody executions continually taking place. At length, in 1832, his sister and her husband escaped to Mysore and put themselves under the protection of the British Resident. Their restoration was refused, and inquiries were made into the proceedings of the Rāja, who was warned of the consequences if he did not reform. But he paid no heed. Dēvammāji, the daughter of Vīra-Rājēndra, was murdered, as well as all the surviving members of the families of his predecessors. As his disaffection openly increased, and he wrote insulting letters to the Governor of Madras and the Governor-General, it was decided in 1834 to depose him. This resolution was met by a most abusive proclamation against the British. A force advanced into Coorg in four columns from different sides, and encountered but little serious opposition at most of the stockades. The British flag was hoisted at Mercāra on the 6th of April. The Rāja, who had retired to Nālknāḍ with his women and treasures, had not the courage to face the invaders.

---

[1] Not altogether to be relied on. It relates to the period from 1633 to 1807.

[2] Interesting light is thrown on the system of administration by the translation of the *Hukumnāma*, or Regulations for Public Servants, issued in the name of this king, which has recently been published (Mercara, 1911), with an Introduction, by Mr. A. J. Curgenven, I.C.S.—Some graphic accounts of his visit to Coorg in 1811 and 1812 are given by Colonel James Welsh in his *Reminiscences from a Journal of Forty Years Active Service in the East Indies.*

On the 11th, Colonel Fraser, the Political Agent with the force, issued a proclamation that "the rule and dominion of Rāja Vīra-Rājēndra-Woḍeyar over the country of Coorg had now definitely and for ever ceased." The Coorgs breathed freely when they found that he was not to remain in their country, and unanimously voted to be placed under the British Government. The annexation was accordingly proclaimed on the 7th of May 1834. The ex-Rāja was deported to Vellore, and was subsequently allowed to live at Benares. In addition to the pension granted to him, he demanded the payment to him of the capital, originally the inheritance of Dēvammāji, of which the interest had continued to be paid to the Coorg Rājas. In 1852 he obtained permission from the Governor-General, Lord Dalhousie, to visit England with his favourite daughter Gauramma, then ten years old, in order to give her a European education. Arrived there, he expressed a wish to have her brought up in the Christian faith. Queen Victoria took an interest in the Indian princess, and at her baptism, on the 30th of June 1852, stood sponsor through the Archbishop of Canterbury, and gave her the name Victoria Gauramma. Feeling himself now strong in the royal favour, the ex-Rāja commenced a Chancery suit against the East India Company for the recovery of the sums formerly invested for Dēvammāji. The suit dragged on a weary course till in 1858 the Government of India was transferred to the Crown, and his suit thus failed. The Coorg princess was carefully brought up[1] and eventually married a British officer, but she died in 1864, leaving one child, a girl. Her husband afterwards mysteriously disappeared and is supposed to have fallen a victim to foul play. Vīra-Rāja himself died in London on the 24th of September 1859. His body was at first temporarily placed in the catacombs at Kensal Green cemetery, and next year sent to India for interment, two of his wives going with it to Benares.

British Period

Of three inscriptions falling in this period, only one (Cg 29) need be noticed. It is dated in 1857 and records the restoration of the temple of Mahādēva on the Kunda hill in Beṭṭiyattu-nāḍ. The work was commenced three years before, on the 1,810,060th Kali day, by agreement between the Takka-mukhyastaru of Beṭṭiyattu-nāḍ and Ammati-nāḍ. These Takkas are recognized elders among the Coorgs in each village and nāḍ, and are the censors of morals and regulators of social affairs. The institution is hereditary in certain families. The inscription gives a list of the principal people who assisted in the work, and mentions what parts of the temple they provided. One was actually a Muhammadan by name, the Jāgīrdār of the Kunda village, and he had the Nandīśvara or sacred bull in front of the temple made. A blessing is invoked on all who took part in the erection.

Architecture

The ruined Jain temples at Muḷḷūr may have been worthy of notice. But the principal architectural monuments now standing are the tombs of the Rājas at Mahadēvapura, near Mercāra, built in 1809 and 1821. They are square buildings, much in the Muhammadan style, on well raised basements, with a handsome dome in the centre, and minaret-like turrets at the four corners surmounted by *basavas* or bulls. On the top of the dome is a gilded ball, with a vane. All the windows have well carved syenite frames, with solid brass bars. The palace at Mercāra, first erected in 1681, is also of interest, though alterations have been made to fit it for its present uses. Good wood-carving may sometimes be seen in the domestic architecture.

[1] By Sir John and Lady Login. He had been Residency Surgeon at Lucknow when the King of Oudh was ruling, and they were after that guardians of Duleep Singh, the young Sikh Mahārāja.

CLASSIFIED LIST OF THE INSCRIPTIONS ARRANGED IN CHRONOLOGICAL ORDER

Date A.D.	Name of Ruler	Tāluk No.	Date A.D.	Name of Ruler	Tāluk No.
		Kadambas			
1095	Duddharasa	57	..	....	..
		Gangas			
466	Avinīta	1	c. 910	Ereyapa	74
888	Satyavākya II	2	944	....	28
c. 890	do.	3	978	Satyavākya IV	4
c. 900	Ereyarasa	60	1000	....	5
		Chōḷas			
c. 1004	Rājarāja	46	..	....	..
		Changāḷvas			
c. 1095	Changāḷva	61	? 1297	Harihara-Dēva	59
1106	Annadāni	51	? 1345	....	63
1218	....	32	? c. 1350	...	64
c. 1220	Changāḷva	27	? 1360	....	67
1278	....	32	? 1380	....	58
c. 1280	Malli-Dēva, Harihara-Dēva.	54	1544	Śrīkaṇṭharasa	26
c. 1280	do. do.	55	1544	....	10
c. 1290	....	52	1597	Rudragaṇa	24
1296	Harihara-Dēva	45	..	....	..
		Kongāḷvas			
c. 1030	....	41	1064	....	34
? 1044	....	56	c. 1070	Prithuvī-Kongāḷva	36
c. 1050	Kongāḷva's son	30	1070	Rājēndra-Prithuvī-Kongāḷva.	49
c. 1050	....	31	1070	do. do.	50
c. 1050	Kongāḷva	48	1077	Rājēndra-Chōḷa-Dēva	43
c. 1050	Rājādhirāja-Kongāḷva	37	c. 1080	....	44
c. 1650	do. do.	38	c. 1100	....	62
c. 1050	....	42	? 1115	Vīra-Chōḷa-Kongāḷva	33
? 1055	Kongāḷva-Dēva	53	..	....	..
1058	Rājēndra-Kongāḷva	35	..	....	..
		Hoysaḷas			
1175	Ballāḷa-Dēva II	65	1255	Nārasiṁha III	6
1175	do.	70	1285	do.	7
1216	....	40	..	....	..
		Munivarāditya			
? 126	Gokula-Devarasa	75	..	....	..
		Durga			
c. 1371	Bōdharūpa Bhagavar	8	c. 1371	Bōdharūpa Bhagavar	9

Date A.D.	Name of Ruler	Tāluk No.	Date A.D.	Name of Ruler	Tāluk No.
		Vijayanagar			
1390	Harihara (II)	39	..	....	..
		Bēlūr			
1693	Kṛishnappa-Nāyaka IV ..	11	? 1756	Kṛishnappa-Nāyaka VI ..	47
c. 1755	do. VI ..	66	..	....	..
		Coorg Rajas			
? c. 1700	....	71	1820	Linga-Rājēndra .. .	17
1731	....	68	1824	Vīra-Rājēndra II	25
1731	....	69	1828	....	63
1782	Vīra-Rājēndra I	12	c. 1830	....	64
1796	do.	13	1831	Vīra-Rājēndra II	18
1796	do.	14	1831	do.	19
1808	....	15	1831	....	20
1815	....	16	1831	Vīra-Rājēndra II	21
		British Period			
1841	....	22	1857	....	29
1842	....	23	..	....	..

TEXT IN ROMAN CHARACTERS

1

On copper plates found in the Treasury at Mercara[1].

(*Ib*) [2]svasti jitām bhagavatā gata-ghana-gaganābhēna Padmanābhēna śrīmad-Jāhnavīya[ku] lāmalā-vyōmāvabhāsana-bhāśkaraḥ sva-khaḍgayka-prahāra-khaṇḍita-mahā-silā-stambha-labdha-bala-parākramō dāraṇōri-gaṇa-vidāraṇōpalabdha-braṇa-vibhūshaṇa-vibhūshita Kaṇvā yana-sa-gōtrasya śrīmān-Koṅgaṇi-mahādhirāja ‖ tat-putra pitur-anvāgata-guṇa-yuktō vidyā-vineya-vihita-vṛittaḥ samyāk-prajāpalanā-mātrādhigata-rājyāt-prayōjana vidvat-kavi-kāñcha na-nikāshōpala-bhūtō nīti-sāstrasya vaktri-payōktri-kusalasya Dattaka-sūtra-vrittiḥ-praṇētāṁ śrīmān-Mādhava-mahādhirāja ‖ tat-putra pitṛi-paitāmahā-guṇa-yuktō vanēka-chāturddanta-yuddha-vāpti-chatur-udadhi-salila-svādita-yasa śrīmad-Harivarmma-mahādhirāja ‖ tat-putra ‖ dvija-guru-dēvatāḥ-pūjana-parō Nārāyaṇa-charaṇānuddhata śrīmad-Vishṇugōpa-ma-(*IIa*) hādhirāja ‖ tasya putra ‖ Tṛiyambhaka-charaṇāṁbhōruha-rājāḥ-pavittṛi-kṛitōttamāṅga sva-bhuja-baḷa-parākrama-kṛiyā-kṛita-rājya Kali-yuga-baḷa-paṁkāvasanna-vṛishōddharaṇa-nitya-sannaddha[3] śrīmān-Mādhava-mahādhirāja ‖ tasya putra ‖ śrīmad-Kadaṃba-kula-gagana-gabhasti-mālina Krishṇavarmma-mahādhirājasya pṛiyā-bhāginēyō vidyā[4]-vinēyatisaya-pari pūritāntarātma[5] niravagraha-prathāna-sauryya vidva-suprathama-gaṇya śrīmān-Koṅgaṇi-mahādhirāja Avinīta-nāmadhēya dattasya Dēsiga-gaṇaṃ Koṇḍakundānvaya Guṇachandra-bhaṭāra sishyasya Abhaṇandi-bhaṭāra[6] tasya sishyasya Sīḷabhadra-bhaṭāra-sishyasya Jaya ṇandi-bhaṭāra-sishyasya Guṇaṇandi[7]-bhaṭāra-sishyasya Chandaṇandi-bhaṭārargge ashṭā-asīti-uttarasya trayō-satasya[8] saṁvatsarasya Māgha-māsaṁ Śōmavāraṁ Svāti-nakshatra suddha pañchami Akāḷavarsha-Pṛithuvī-Vallabha-mantri Taḷavana-nagara-Śrīvijaya-Jinālayakke Pūnāḍu-chhā-sahasra Eḍenāḍu-saptari-madhyē Badaṇeguppe-nāma Avinīta-mahādhirājēna dattēna paḍiye āṟ oḷaṃ-ūr-ū (*IIb*) roḷ pannir-kkaṇḍugaṅ geydu ambali-maṇṇuṁ Taḷavana-puradoḷ taḷa-vittiyamaṇ Pogarigeḷeyoḷ pannir-kkaṇḍugaṁ Pirikeṟeyolaṁ rāja-mānaṁ-anumōdana pannir-kkaṇḍugaṁ manōharaṁ dattaṁ Badaṇeguppe-grāmasya sīmāntaraṁ pūrbbasyāṁ-disi keṁjige-moṟaḍiē Gajaseleye Karivaḻḻiya-Koṭṭagara-Badaṇeguppeya-trisan dhiya satti-koṟaḍu āgnēyadin ante bandu Kāgaṇi-taṭākam puna dakshiṇasyāṁ-disi bahuśnuhiye balkaṇi-vṛikshame puna paśchima-mukhade sanda bahumūlika-pantiye puna Badaṇeguppeya-Koṭṭagara-Muḻtagiya-tṛisandhiya koḷe Chaṇḍigāle puna nairatyade sandu kathaka-vṛikshame puna paśchimasyāṁ-disi peḻd-uḻdil-vṛikshame sānteṟetiya vaṭa-vṛikshame puna tore-vaḻḻame uttarā-mukhade sanda bahumūlika-pantiye jambupaḍiya-taṭākame puna vāyavyade gaḻe-chiṁcha-vṛikshame puna Badaṇeguppeya-Muḻtagiya-Koḷeyanūra-Dāsanūra-tṛisandhiya-nerggiḻa-guṁbe niḍuveḷuṅge puna Gajaseleya-grāma uttara-disi kāyga-moṟaḍie iḻidu keṁba

---

1 Originally deciphered by me and published in 1872, *Ind. Ant.* i, 363; see also xii, 12. The facsimile now published is from an impression by Dr. Fleet. The original impression by Dr. Burgess is given in the *Indian Antiquary*, vol. i.

2 A symbol here supposed to represent Ōm.

3 The *nna* is inserted below the line.

4 *Vidyā* is inserted below the line, with a small cross above, to show where it should come.

5 By mistake *tna* has been engraved for *tma*.

6 This name should most probably be Abhayaṇandi.

7 The second *ṇa* is inserted below the line.

8 The first *sa* is inserted below the line between two vertical strokes.

9 The *ya* is inserted below the line.

i.

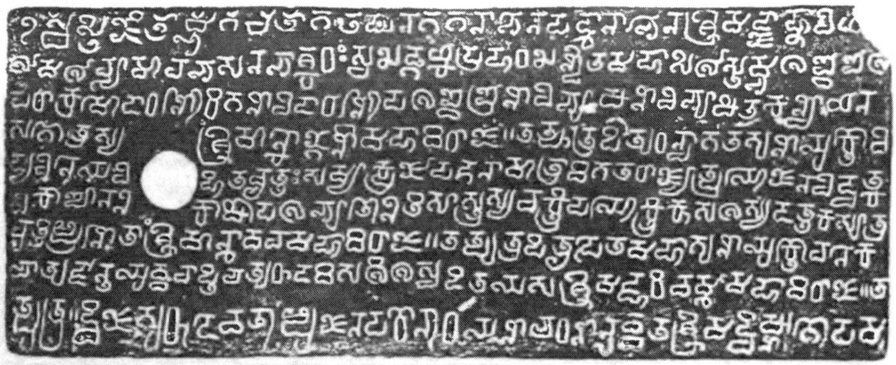

ii a.

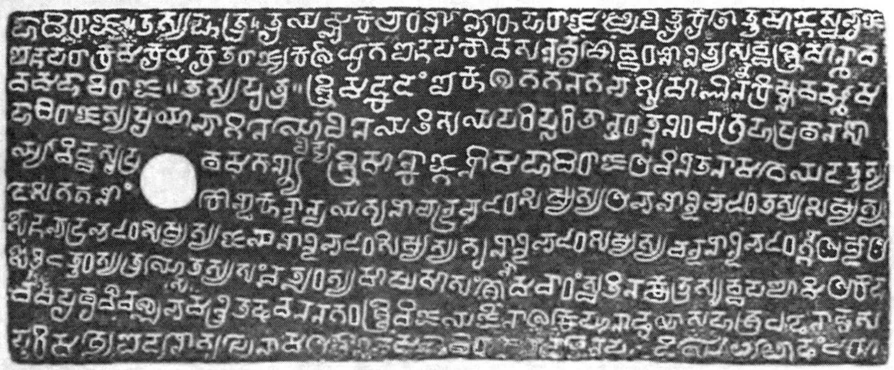

ii b.

L. RICE. SCALE NINE-TENTHS W. GRIGGS & SONS, LTD., PHOTO-LITH.

FROM INK-IMPRESSIONS BY DR. FLEET.

No. 2.—Biliur stone Inscription of Satyavakya; A.D. 888.

iii.

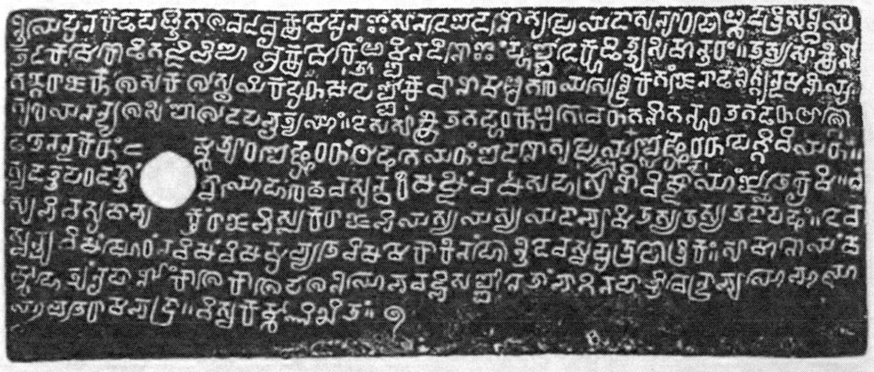

Ring and Seal.

reye puna pūrbba-mukhade sanda bahumūlika-pa (*IIIa*) ntiye puna kaḍapaḻtigāla vaṭa-vṛikshame puna isānade Badaṇeguppeya-Dāsanūra-Poḻmada-trisandhiya taṭākame koḍigaṭṭi chiñcha-vṛikshame keṁtaṟambina[1] diṇeim pūrbbade kūḍittu sīmāntaraṁ || tasya sākshiṇā Gaṅga-rāja-kula-sakalāsthayika-purusha Perbbakkavāṇa Maṟugareya Sendrika Gaṁjenāḍa Nirggunda Maṇiyugureya Nandyāla Siṁbāl Ādapa bhṛityayāṁ dēsa-sākshi Tagaḍūra Kuḻugō varu Gaṇiganūra Tagaḍaru Ālgoḍate Nandakaruṁ Ummatūra Beḷḷuraruṁ Āḷageyaruṁ Badaṇeguppeya Jhaṁsanda[2] Beḷḷuraru Perggiviyaruṁ || svadatta paradattāṁg vā yō harētha vasundharī shashṭiṁ varsha sahasrāṇi vishṭāyāṁ jāyate[3] kṛimi || vasubhi vasudhā bhuktaṁ rājabhis Saka-rājabhi[4] yasya yasya yadā bhūmi tasya tasya tadā paḷaṁ || dēvasvan tu vishaṁ ghōraṁ na vishaṁ visham uchyatē vishaṁ ēkākinaṁ hōnti dēvasva putra pautrikaṁ || sāmān-[y]ōyaṁ dharmma hētuṁ[5] nṛipāṇām kālē kālē pālanīyō bhavadbhi sarbbān ētāṁ bhāgina[6] pārttivēndrā bhūyō bhūyō yāchatē Rāmabhadrā[7] || Visvakarmma likhitaṁ ௐ

2

On a stone at Biḷiūr (in Kiggaṭ-nāḍ).

[8] bhadram astu Jina-śāsanāya Saka-nṛip-atītā-kāla-saṁvatsaraṁgaḷ eṇṭunūṟ-ombattaneya varsham pravarttisuttire svasti Satyavākya-Koṁguṇivarmma-dharmma-mahārājādhirāja Kovaḷāla-puravarēśvara Nandagiri-nātha śrīmat-Permmanaḍiya rājyābhishēkaṁ geyda padi neṇṭaneya[9] varshad andu Pālguṇa-māsada śrī-pañchame yandu Śivaṇandi-siddhāntada-bhaṭārara śishyar Ssarvbaṇandi[10]-dēvargge [11]Peṇṇe-gaḍaṅgada Satyavākya-Jinālayakke Peddoṟegareya Biḷiūr-ppannir-ppaḷḷiyumaṁ sarvba-pāda-parihāra Permmanaḍi koṭṭō tom bhattaṟu-sāsirvbarum ay-sāmantaruṁ Beddoṟegareya eḷpadimbaruṁ eṇṭ-okkaluṁ idakke sākshi Male-sāsirvbarum aymurvbaruṁm[12] ay-dāmarigaruṁ idakke kāpu idan aḻidoṁ Bāraṇāsiyumaṁ sāsirvbar-ppārvbarumaṁ sāsiraṁ kavileyuman aḻidoṁ pañcha-mahāpātakan akkuṁ Sedōjana likhitta[13] Beḷiūra[14] eṇbattu-gadyāṇa ponnū eṇṭu-nūṟu-battamum teruvoṁ.

3

On a stone at Kotūr (same nāḍ) in the Lakkuṇḍa forest.

svasti Satyavākya-Koṁguṇivarmma-dharmma-mahārājādhirājaṁ Kuvaḷāla-puravarēśvaraṁ Nandagiri-nāthaṁ śrīmat-Permmanaḍigaḷ Jeḍala Eṟeyaṅga-gāvuṇḍana magaṁge Permmaḍi-

---

1 The *ta* is inserted below the line between two vertical strokes.
2 What looks like this name is inserted below the line here in a different cursive hand.
3 The *ya* is inserted below the line.
4 Generally *Sagarādibhiḥ*.
5 Properly *sētum*: the collocation *dharmma hētum* recalls the Buddhist formula.
6 Generally *bhāvina*.
7 Generally *Rāmachandraḥ*.
8 See note 2, p. 30.
9 The first *ne* is inserted below the line.
10 For the subscript *va* the earlier form of *ba* is used; also in l. 8, 9.
11 The sign for subscript *ṇa* is the same as for *na*, as usual at this period.
12 Read *aynūrvvarum*. The subscript *va* in this and the next line has the modern form of *ba*.
13 Read *likhitam*.
14 This name begins with the old form of *ba* here, but with the new form in l. 8.

vaṭṭaṁ gaṭṭi biṭṭa stiti-kramam āvud endoḍe siddhāyada ponnoḷ pattu gadyāṇa ponnuṁ biḻtiya bhattadoḷ nūṟu-bhattamumaṁ ellā-kālakkaṁ sāsanam āge biṭṭar Būvayyan akkaraṁ maṁgaḷaṁ Eṟeyaṁgaṁge kalnāḍu mahāśrī.

4

On a stone at Peggūr (same nāḍ).

svasti Saka-nṛipa-kāḷ-ātīta-saṁvatsara-sataṅga 899 ttaneya Īsvara-sa[ṁ]vatsaraṁ pra varttise[1] ꣸ svasti Satyāvākya[2]-Koṅgiṇivarmma-dharmma-mahārājādhirājā Kōḷāḷa-puravar ēśvara Nandagiri-nātha śrīmat Rāchamalla-Parmmanaḍigaḷ tad-varsh-[ā]bhyantara Pālguṇa-sukla-pakshada Nandīsvaraṁ talpa-devasam āge svasti samasta-vairi-gaja-ghaṭ-āṭōpa-kuṁbhikuṁbha-staḷa-spuṭit-ānargghya-muktāphaḷa-grahaṇa-bhīkara-kar-āse-nivāsita-dakshiṇa-dōrddaṇḍa-maṇḍita-prachaṇḍaṁ aṇṇana[3]-baṇṭa baḍavara-naṇṭaṁ śrīmat Rakkasa Beddoṟegareyan āḷuttire bhadram astu Jina-śāsanāya śrī-Beḷgoḷa-nivāsigaḷ-appa śrī-Bīrasēna siddhānta-dēvara vara-śishyar śrī-Goṇasēna-paṇḍita-bhaṭṭārakara vara-śishyar[4] śrīmat Anantavīryyayyaṁgaḷ Pe[r]ggadūruṁ posa-vādagamuman abhyantara-siddhiyāge paḍedar adarkke sākshi tombhattaṟu-sāsirbbarum ay-sāmantaruṁ Beddoṟegare-yēḻpadiṁbarum eṇṭ-okkalum idaṁ kāvar nnâlvar Mmaleparum aynūrbbarum ay-dāmarigaruṁ Śrīpurusha[5]-mahārājaradattiyan āvon orbban aḻidoṁ Bāṇarāsiyuṁ sāsirbba-Brāhmaṇaruṁ sāsira-kavileyu man aḻida pañcha-mahāpātakan akkuṁ idan ār-orbbar kādar avarge piridu punyaṁ[6] Chandaṇandiyayyana likhitaṁ|| Perggadūra basadiya śāsanaṁ.

5

On a stone at Mercara Central School, brought in from the country ; now in the Commissioner's office.

svasti śrī Śaka-varisha 921 neya Sārvvari-saṁvatsarada Pālguṇa-māsada puṇṇame Uttare-Bhādrapada Arkkavārad-andu Gaṇagūra Biha-gāmuṇḍana magaṁ Hañcha[da]rma-seṭṭi Kuṇin dor-oḷege gēdu kālaṁ tiḻdiū Kālūraṁ māḍi Muḷḷūr-nnāḍa Bōkanahaḷḷiyu Hakādi vāḍiya Gorahaḷḷi . . yu . . . ḷeyu-nāḍa Kūḍalūrumaṁ tanna bhuja-baladinda paḍedu modal kāluśiyaṃ mindu Rāmēśvaram archi . . battu kabbiḷ-angaḷeū dha[rmma]kke biṭṭa maṇṇu khaṇḍuga ī dharmmavau aḷidam kavile . . . .

6

On a vīrakal at Niḍuta (in Yēlusāvirashīme).

svasti śrī-jayābhyudaya-Śaka-varusha 1177 ne Rākshasa-sam 1 Vaiśākha śudha 11 śi śrīmat-pratāpa-chakravarti Hoysaṇa bhuja-bala śrī-Vīra-Narasimha-Rāyana . . . kāladalli Kahigōḍina Bīra-gavuḍana maga Sōmaiyanu boguḷuttā Bumbiya-nāyakanu tāu dūta Bīmaiya Sōmaṇṇan oḍane yatti hōgi kādidalli biddanu ā Sōmaiyanu dēva-lōkakke salla-bēkendu ātan oḍane-huṭṭida Māri-gavuḍanu ā Sōme-gavuḍana maga Māyiganu paripāya māḍisida bīragallu mangala-mahā śrī śrī śrī.

---

1 The subscript *t* in this and the next word is formed in a peculiar manner. The engraver seems to have had some original ideas. See the stop in line 2, and *nd* in Nandagiri.

2 Read *Satyavākya*.

3 The double *ṇṇa* is here expressed by *ṇna*.

4 These two phrases might be read *dēvar avara śishyar* and *bhaṭṭārakar avara śishyar*.

5 The original impressions showed *Śrīpurada*.

6 Read *puṇyaṁ*.

No. 3.—Kotur stone inscription of Satyavakya.

H. KRISHNA SASTRI. GOVT. PHOTOZINCO OFFICE, POONA.

SCALE ONE-SIXTH.

No. 4.—The Peggur stone Inscription of Satyavakya; A.D. 978.

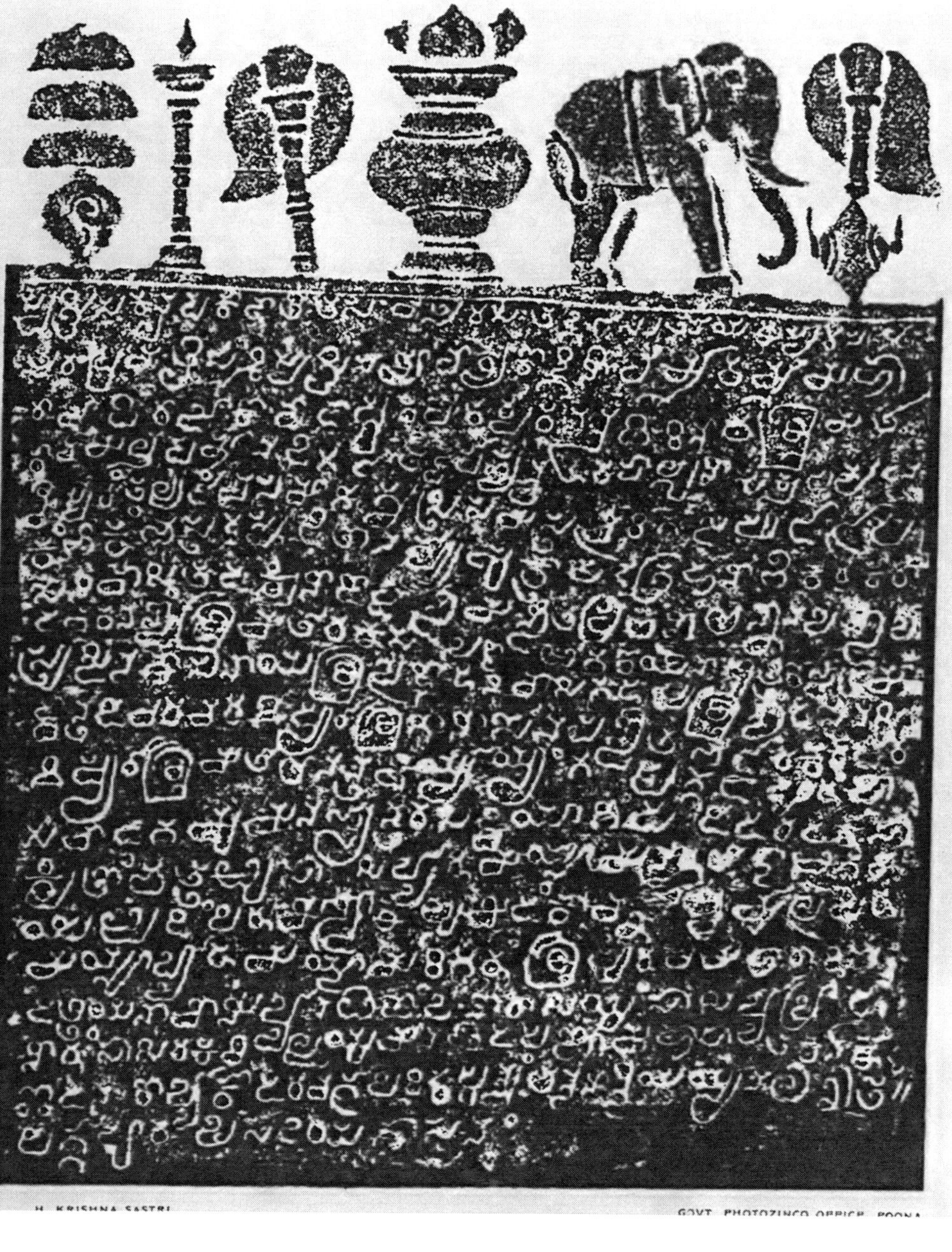

No. 8—The Palur stone inscription.

H. KRISHNA SASTRI. GOVT. PHOTOZINCO OFFICE, POONA.

SCALE ONE-FIFTH

No. 9—The Bhagamandala stone inscription.

H. KRISHNA SASTRI. GOVT. PHOTOZINCO OFFICE, POONA.

SCALE ONE-FIFTH.

7

On another vīrakal at the same place.

svasti śrī-vijayābhyudaya Śaka-varusha 1208 Pārthiva-sam | rada Vaiśākha śudha 12 śrīmat pratāpa-chakravarti Hoysaṇa bhuja-bala śrī-Vīra-Narasimha-Dēvarasara rājyābhyu daya-kāladallu Kahigōḍina Māra-Tammanu tanna kochaṇa-pratittu-matsara-virōdhangaḷa kūḍi kāḷagadallu kādi biddanu ā Māra-Tammanu dēva-lōkakke saḷa-bēkeudu ātana tamma Maleya-nāyaka ā Māra-Tammana makkaḷu Sōmanna . . . . . . vīragallu mangala mahā śrī śrī śrī.

8

On a stone in the Mahālingēśvara temple at Pālūr (in Beṅganāḍ Kuyaṅgerināḍ, Pāḍinālknāḍ tāluq).

svasti śrī | Vināyakam viśēshajñaṁ guruṁ dēvīm Sarasvatīn
namaskṛitya [ya]thā śaktyā karishyē śāsanam śubham |
svasti śrī | śrīma[t]-Purushōttama-parshad-Avidyāmṛityu-bhaṭṭāraka śishya
Bōdharūpa-Bhagavar Pālayū[r] Mahādēvarkku cheyda śilā-śāsanam |

padinenḍēśi Śrīvaishṇavar muntāna padi[ne]ṉ-ḍēśi Vaḷaṇchiyar padineṉ-ḍēśi ppaḍa-piḍichcha-Pallāyiravar padineṭṭu- nāṭṭu-Brāhmaṇar ivagaḷil kanḍār kanḍ irakshikka kaḍavar-eṉṟu cheyda śilā-śāsanam-āvadu śāntinōḍu pūvisthāna nnōkkiy amachchān amachchapaḍi chelu ttānāgil tan-tandayai koṉṟun-tāyai kaḷatram vachchun tām piṟanda nāḍu vāḷum araśaittān koṉṟavan nāṭṭul[1] valattu keṭṭiyā iḍattu piḍichchānai mūkk-aṟutt-avan penḍilai kaḷatram vachchān paḍakkaḍava danḍam paḍakkaḍavan nitya chchelav[u]m mikka saṁkētaṁgaḷum śrī-bhanḍāra-pottagam āṭṭ-orukkāl eḍuttu vāśippittu [a] dil paṭṭapaḍi chellāda chilavu cheluttakkaḍavar padineṉ-ḍēśi-Vaḷañchiyar nālu muttāmay-āḷum-muṉūṟka-muntayi.

9

On a stone at the Bhagaṇḍēśvara temple in Bhāgamaṇḍala (in Tavunāḍ-Sampajināḍ, Pāḍinālknāḍ tāluq).[2]

svasti śrī [|] namaskṛittya gurum bhaktyā | Kanyārūḍha-Bṛihaspatau[|]
Vṛiśchik-ākhyē mahā-māsē Bṛihaspatty-uttarā-dinē ||
karishyē śāsana[ṁ] sarvvam | gurōr ānanda-rūpiṇaḥ[|]
śāsanāṁ Bōdharūpō-' haṁ śrī-Bhagaṇḍāśramē 'pi hi [||]

Mēlpunḍi-Kunniyarasan-nāḍu[3]-vāḷānikka śrīmat Pu[r]shōttama-pa[r]shat[4] Bōdharūpa-Bhaga var-arasu muntāy-chchaivitta cheppēṭṭil akappaṭṭa nichcha-chchilav-aḍayav-oru-nāḷ tappich chānukku Kunniyarasan-muntāyāṉ-peṇṇ-akappaḍa mēl-in-nāḍu-vāḷakkaḍav-arasan-āṇa āṇa ttappu pannirandu kāṇam pon kāsanmi oru-nāḷukku iraṭṭippaḍi dēvarkku appaḍi āchchi-vaṭṭam adil ēṟil panniru-kaḷañchu ponn-eḷu māṟṟu araśukku nandāviḷakku padinēḷu | nāḷ-amu du mudalāy poduvāḷar-iḍakkaḍav-ariy-iruvattaṟu nāḷi | oḷukk-avikk-iru-nāḷi pushpattukku

---

[1] Read *nāṭṭil*.

[2] The stone is cracked across transversely, between the 16th and 22nd lines, — said to have been done by the followers of Ṭīpu Sultān.

[3] Malayāḷam *ṭa* is used throughout in place of Tamil *ḍa*.

[4] Read *parshad*.

nā-nāḻi agamañchu-māla muppatirandu Vṛiśchika-viḷakk ādi śāntinōḍu pūvisthānamnōkkiy amachchānam uchchapaḍi cheluttānākil tāṇ pıṟanta nāḍu-vāḻum arasanai kula-karu dum-āṇa avan nāṭṭil valattu kaṭṭiy-iḍattu piḍichchānai mūkk-aṟuttu [a]van-peṇḍilai-ttān kaḷatra-vachch[ān] paḍa-kkaḍava daṇḍam ivv-ā ināṇa-miṟā nai kaṇḍum kēṭṭum-upēkshittu pōm arasukku tan-nāṭṭil prakṛitiyāṇa āṇatappi nāḍu viḍuvittatt-aiyyattukku viḍakkaḍavar prakṛiti paḍaka muntāya paṇiy-añchu Mahābhāratam oṉṟu i-chchilavil-oṉṟu tappil nāḷukkiraṇḍ-arai-kkāṇam padineṇ-ḍēśi paḍa-piḍichcha-Pallāyiravar| Vaḷañchiyar| rakshikka Va kaṇḍālaiya| sannyāsikaḷumm-arasum muntāyaidil mikkadu bhaṇḍāra-ppottakattilum cheppēṭ ṭilum u . . Pakaṇḍala āyāri eḻuttu.

10

On a stone at Añjanagiri.

śrī-Śāṁtināthāya namaḥ || nirvvighnam astu || śubham astu ||

śrīmat-parama-gaṁbhīra-syād-vād-āmōgha-lāṁchchhanaṁ|
jīyāt trailōkya-nāthasya śāsanaṁ Jina-śāsanaṁ||

svasti śrī-Mūla-saṁgha Dēśī-gaṇa Pustaka-gachchha Kuṁdakuṁdānvayada Yiṁguḷēśvara-vaḷiya śrīmad-Beḷuguḷa-puravar-ādhīśvara Gummaṭa-Jinēśvara-pāda-padma-matta-madhukarāyamānar-āda tat-kāla-dharmma-pravarttakar-āda Dharmmāchāryyara birudāvali yeṁt eṁdoḍe|| paṁḍita-puṇḍarīka-kulamaṁ paribōdhisiy urvvī-kormma-uddaṁḍa-kuvādi-hṛittamaman-ōḍisi kūḍe Digaṁbara-prabhā-maṁḍana- vṛittamaṁ taḷedu Bhavya-rathāṁgamanōvut-āvagaṁ Paṁḍita-dēva-sūryyan esedaṁ naya-vāg-ruchiyiṁ niraṁtaraṁ|| svasti śrīmad-rāya-rājaguru-maṁḍal-āchāryya mahā-vāda-vādīśvara rāyavādi-pitāmaha sakala-vidvajjana-chakravarttigaḷuṁ Ballāḷa-Rāya-jīva-rakshapālakādy-anēka-birudāvalī-virājamānarum-appa śrīmach-Chārukīrtti-Paṁḍita-dēvarugaḷa praśishyar-āda tach-chhishya śrīmad-Abhinava-Chārukīrtti-Paṁḍita-dēvarugaḷa priya-śishyar-āda tasy-āgraja-śishya śrīmach-Chārukīrtti-Paṁḍita-dēvarugaḷa sa-tīrtthyar-āda śrīmach-Chhāṁtikīrti-dēvaru[ga]ḷu Śaka-varsha || 1466 saṁda varttamāna Krōdhi-saṁvatsarada Kārtika-śudha 15 lū barasida śilā-śāsanada kramav-eṁt-eṁdoḍe tamma guru śrīmad-Abhinava-Chārukīrtti-Paṁḍita-dēvarugaḷu | Kali-kāla-dharmma-tīrttha-pravarttana-nimittavāgi Suvarnnāvati-nadiyiṁda svayaṁ-pratyaksharāgi Śāṁti-tīrtthēśvaranu Anantanātha-svāmiyu Śaka-varusha 1453 neya Vikṛitu-saṁvatsarada Chaitradalu bije-māḍalāgi Aṁjanagiriya-agra-nivāsiyāg-irdda Śāṁtinātha-svāmiya basadige bijemāḍisi giriy-agradalli dārumayada-basadiya māḍisi Khara-saṁvatsarada Chaitra-māsadalli svānujar-āda Koṇasanagarada Śāṁtōpādhyāyara kayyiṁda pratishṭeya māḍisi śilā-mayavāda basadiya māḍis-eṁdu buddhi gatisalāgi alliṁda muṁde Krōdhi-saṁvatsarada Kārttika-śu 15 nelege kalu-gelasa hāladāregaḷa naḍasida vivara Naṁjarāyapaṭṭaṇakke saluva Beṁmatti Būtanhaḷi-Malaganakereya samasta-halariṁ kalu-gelasakke saṁda hoṁnnu ga 200 Hanasogeya Ādi-Śrī-Avvagaḷu Aṁmana-Hosahaḷḷiya Bhujabali-Śrī-Avvagaḷiṁda garbba-gṛihavagaivalli kalu-gelasakke sandadu ga 30 hoṁnnu taṁma guru śrīmach-Chārukīrtti-Paṁḍita-dēvarugaḷige tāv ittaṁḍakke mūṟu hāladāre madhya-bāgilali voṁdu-hottina naivēdyakke śela saṁdadu ga 50 āhāra-dānakke śela sandadu ga [50] | Śubhakrutu-saṁvatsarada Pālguna śu 15 lū Aṁjanagiriya Śāntīśvarage bidire sītāḷa-maḷigeya samasta-halaru Kaṁnaḍiga-halaru Nānādēsiya-halaru māḍida dharmma| [n]āu kaṭṭida kālu-naḍe vondakke ga 0·1 vanu āhāra-dānakke koḍuvcu yeṁdu barasida ī dharmma-śāsana yī-dharmmakke tappidavaru gō Brāhmara koṁda dōshakke hōvaru[||] (*left side*) śaka varushaṁ 1465 neya Śubhakṛitu-saṁvatsarada

No. 10.—The Anjanagiri Jaina stone inscription of A.D. 1544.

H. KRISHNA SASTRI.

SCALE ONE SIXTH.

GOVT. PHOTOZINCO OFFICE, POONA.

Chaitra śuddha 13 Budhavāra Vṛishabha-laghnadalli muṛu taṁḍa dehāragaḷu kula-pratishṭe yāyittu || dānaśālege haḷḷi vayala gaddeya krayada maulya ga 70 kolāyaru hosa gadde gaiduda kke koṭṭadu ga 50 ubhayam vechcha ga 120 kke ādāya śrīmach-Chārukīrtti-Paṁḍita-dēvaru gaḷa śishyaru Hanasogeya Ādi-Śrī-Avvagaḷu Bhujabali-Śrī-Avvagaḷiṁ ga 24 Basavapa [ṭṇa]da Anaṁtamati-Avvagaḷu Nēmi-Śrī-Avvagaḷiṁ saṁdadu ga 24 Muddi-saṭṭiya Vijey[a]-Śrī-Avvagaḷiṁ saṁdadu ga 10 Maluganahaḷiya Ādyakkagaḷiṁ saṁ ga 12 Hāruva-saṭṭiya Vijeya-ṇa-śaṭṭiriṁ ga 30 Kaṁṇanūra Dēvaraṁma-śaṭṭiyariṁ ga 12 [A]suṁ[ḍi]ya A[ra] sa . . . . . (*rest buried underground*): (*right side*) [ll. 79 to 107 contain the three usual imprecatory verses beginning with *svadattām paradattām*, *dānapālanayōr* and *svadattād-dviguṇam*]. ī māḍida dharmmaū āchaṁdrārkka-sthāyiyāgi naḍeyali yeṁdu barasida dharmma-śāsanakke maṁgala-mahā śrī śrī.

11

On a copper plate at Kaṭṭepura.

śubham astu. ||

namas tuṅga-śiraś-chumbi-chandra-chāmara-chāravē |
trailōkya-nagar-ārambha-mūla-stambhāya Śambhavē ||
vandē līlā-varāhasya daṁshtra-daṇḍa sa pātu naḥ |
udhrutā mēdinī yēna kalaṅkam iva yatra sā ||

svasti śrī-vijayābhyudaya-Śālivāhana-śaka-varushagaḷu 1615 neya Śrīmukha-nāma-saṃvatsa rada Pushya śu 12 lu Kāsyapa-gōtrada Āpastamba-sūtrada Bēlūra Kṛishṇappa-Nāyakara pautra rāda Vēnkaṭādri-Nāyakara putrarāda Kṛishṇappa-Nāyakaru Vasisṭha-gōtrada Āś[va]lāyana-sūtrada Rik-śākhādhyāyanarāda Subramaṇya-dēvagaḷa pautrarāda Puṭṭarasaiyana putrarāda Yōgapaiyage barisi koṭṭa grāma-dāna-śāsana-kramav ent endare pūrvadalli śrīmad-rājādhirāja rājā-paramēśvara śrī-vīra-pratāpa śrī-vīra Kṛishṇa-Rāya-Dēva-mahārāyaravaru namma vṛid dha-pitāmaharāda sindhu-Gōvinda himakara-gandha dhavalānka-Bhīma Maṇināgapura-varā dhīśvara balīyada saptānga-haraṇarāda Yara-Kṛishṇappa-Nāyakaraiyanavarige pālista Bēlūra śīmege saluva Arakalgōḍā valitada Tungi-nāḍa Nīrugunda-staḷadalli Koṇiganahaḷḷige pūrva Hēmāvatī-nadige dakshinada jamīnige paśchima Niluvāgilige vuttaravāda Kaṭṭepurada grāma Yippugaḷalege pūrvavāda Hirumanahaḷḷi sahā Kāśyapa-gōtrada Āpastamba-sūtrada Kṛishṇappa-Nāyakara pautrarāda Vēnkaṭādri-Nāyakara putrarāda Kṛishṇappa-Nāyakaru Vasishṭa-gōtra Āśvalāyana-sūtrada Ṛik-śākhādhyāyanarāda Subrahmanya-dēvagala pautrarāda Puṭṭarasaiyana putrarāda Yōgapaiyage Kaṭṭepurada-grāma Hirumanahaḷḷi saha yī tathā tithi Makara-sankramana-puṇya-kāladalli sa-hiraṇyōdaka-dāna-dhārā-pūrvakavāgi koṭṭēvāgi yī grāmakke saluva akshin-āgāmi-nidhi-nikshēpa-jala-pāshāna-siddha-sādhyangaḷ-emba ashṭa-bhōga-svāmyavannu āgu-māḍikoṇḍu nimma santānā-parampar-āchandr-ārka-sthāyigaḷ-āgi dānādi-vinimaya-vikrayagaḷige yōgyavāgi sukhadalli anubhavisikoṇdu yihadu yendu Kāśyapa-gōtrada Āpastamba-sūtrada Kṛishṇappa-Nāyakara pautrarāda Vēṅkaṭādri-Nāyakara putra rāda Kṛishṇappa-Nāyakaru Vasishṭa-gōtrada Āśvalāyana-sūtrada Rik-śākhādhyāyanarāda Subrahmaṇya-dēvagaḷa pautrarāda Puṭṭarasaiyana putrarāda Yogapaiyage barisi koṭṭa śāsana yidakke dharma-sākshigaḷu

āditya-chandrāv anilō nalaś cha dyaur bhūmir āpō hṛidayam manaś cha |
ahaś cha rātriś cha vubhē cha sandhyē dharmasya jānāti narasya vṛittaṃ ||

dāna-pālanayōr madhyē dānāt śrēyō'nupālanam |
dānāt-svargam avāpnōti pālanād achyutam padam ||
svadattā dviguṇam puṇyam paradattānupālanam |
paradattāpahārēṇa svadattam nishphalam bhavēt ||
svadattā putrikā dhātrī pitṛi-dattā sahōdarī |
anya-dattā sva-mātā cha datta bhūmim parityajēt ||
yēkaiva bhaginī lōkē sarvēshām ēva bhūbhujām |
na bhōjyā na karagrāhyā vipradattā vasundharā ||

śrī-Kṛishṇa

12

On a copper plate at Mahādevapura (Mercāra).

Linga-Rājēndra-Vadeyaru

Vi

Koḍagina charamūrtigaḷāda Śidhalingappadavaru Śārvari-samvatsarada Kārtīka-śudha 13 yu Mandavāradallu jīrṇōddāra māḍisiddu.

śrīmad rājādhirāja rāja-paramēśvara prahuḍa-paratāpa apratima-vīra-narapati Koḍagina samsthānada śrī-ratna-simhāsanārūḍharāgi prithvī- sāmrājyam gaiyutt-idda Bhāradvāja-gōtrada Āśvalāyana-sūtrada Rukshabhānukādhyāya Vīra-Śaiva-matastar-āda Appājēndra-Vaḍeyaravara putrarāda Linga-Rājēndra-Vadeyaru—

namas tunga-śiraś-chumbi-chandra-chāmara-chāravē |
trailōkya-nagar-ārambha-mūla-stambhāya Śambhavē ||

svasti śrī-vijayābhudaya Kali-sanda 4881 ne varatamānakke salluva Vikāri-samvatsarada Māgha-bahuḷa 10 yu Budhavāra divi gaḷige 7½ ge Śivādhīnav-āddu—

yī Śivādhīnav-āguva tat-kāladallu yī Mahārājara garbhābdhi-sudhākarāyamānarāda Vīra-Rājēndra-Vaḍeyaru sannidhānadallu yiddu sat-karmavannu virachisi appane-prakāra Mahādēvapuradallu kriya-samādhiyannu māḍisi dēvasthānavannu kaṭṭisi ā-samādhi-mēle Basavēśvara-dēvara-pratishṭeyannu māḍisi Murige-sampradāyada-maṭhavannu kaṭṭisi sadā-kāladaḷḷu gaṇārādhane yī-dēvatārādhane vuddiśya yī-Mahādēvapura-bhūmi Chikka-Harade Jambūru Bēlūru Basavanahaḷḷi grāmakke saha linga-mudre-śilā-pratishṭeyannu māḍisi Nala-samvatsarada Chaitra-śudha 1 vu Bhārgavāradallu vappisi dāna-śāsanavannu baradu-koṭṭu-yidheyāgi jīrṇōddāra-āddu Śārvari-samvatsarada Kārtīka-śudha 13 divasa prārambha Śubhakṛitu-samvatsarada Vaiśākha-śudha 10 Guruvārakke ākairu āgi-yidhe.

13

On a copper plate at the Abbi maṭha in Yaḍava-nāḍ.

Murigi-svāmiyavara pādaka Mallikārjuna-svāmiya Pākōdu-Mahanta-svāmiyavara chara mūrttigaḷāda Śāntavīra-svāmiyavara charamūrttigaḷāda Abbi-maṭhada Niranjana-dēvara pādakke.

namas tunga-śiras-chumbi-chandra-chāmara-chāravē |
trailōkya-nagar-ārambha-mūla-stambhāya Śambhavē ||

svasti śrī-vijayābhyudaya-Śālivāhana-śaka-varusha 1718 ne vartamānakke salluva Nala-samvatsarada Chaitra śu 1 Bhārgavāradallu Śivagange-mēlana-gavi-simhāsanārūḍhara-sāmpradāyastarāda Śidhapurada maṭhada svāmiyavara kara-kamala-sanjātarāda Vīra-Śaiva-matastar-āda śrīmad rājādhirāja rāja-paramēśvara prahuḍa-pratāpa vipratima-vīra-narapati

Koḍagina samsthānada śrī-ratna-simhāsanārūḍharāgi prithvī-sāmrājyam gaivutt-iralu Bharadvāja-gōtrada Āśvalāyana-sūtra Rukshabhānukādhyāgaḷāda Appājēndra-Vaḍeyaravara pautrarāda Linga-Rājēndra-Vaḍeyaravara putrarāda Vīra-Rājēndra-Vaḍeyaravaru baradu vappista jīrṇōddārada dāna-śāsanada kramav-entendare—prāku Śālivāhana-śaka-varusha 1650 ne Kīlaka-samvatsarada Kārttika-śuddha 2 Budhavāradallu hire-ajjayanavarāda Doḍḍa-Vīrappa-Vaḍeyaravaru Yaḍava-nāḍu Abbi-maṭhakke prāku naḍaḍu-baruttidda grāma Hosaḷḷi-grāma vandu Jigaṭṭaḷḷi-grāma vandu vubhaya-grāma yeraḍu yidallade Doḍḍa-Virūpāksha-svāmiyavaru Maḍikērige chittaisalāgi pāda-viḍidu binnaha-māḍikoṇḍu āchan drārkavāgi dharma-barabēk-endu nūtanavāgi Abbi-maṭhakke biṭṭu koṭṭa grāma Bāchaḷḷi-grāma-vandakke kandāya ga 16 hadināru-varaha saha Hosaḷḷi-grāma 1 Jigaṭṭaḷḷi-grāma 1 Bāchaḷḷi-grāma 1 antu grāma 3 ra chatuś-śīme-yellekaṭṭinalli yiruva nidhi-nikshēpa-jala-taru-pāshāṇa-akshīna-āgāmi-siddha-sādhyangaḷ-emba ashṭa-bhōga-tēja-svāmya muntāda ā sakala-bhūmiyannu Śivārpitavāgi gaṇārādhaneyannu naḍiśikoṇḍu āchandrārkvavāgi dharmavannu naḍista Śivapūjā-kāladallu āśīrvādada ślōka—

jāti-smaratvam prithvī-patitvam savubhāgya-lāvaṇṇyam atīva-rūpam |
tvad-bhakti vidyā paramāyur ishṭam tvam daś cha mē Śankara janma-janmanī ||

yamba āśīrvādavannu māḍuttā-yirabēk-embadāgi baradu vapista jīrṇōddhārada bhū-sādhanakke sākshigaḷu—

āditya chandrō anilō nalaś cha dyaur bhūvir āpō hṛidayam Yamas' cha |
ahō rātriś cha ubhayaś cha sandhyā dharmasya jānāti naṛasya vṛittaḥ ||
svadattā dviguṇam puṇyam paradattānupālanam |
paradattāpahārēṇa svadattām niśphalam bhavēt ||

yamba bhū-sādhanakke appaṇe-prakāra Bhārgavāra baradāta khāsa-rahasyada Śambhaiya.

śrī Vi.

14

On a copper plate at Mahādēvapura (Mercāra).

śrīman mahā-Murigā-svāmigaḷavara charamūrttigaḷāda Koḍali-Mahanta-svāmigaḷavara charamūrttigaḷāda Śāntavīra-svāmiyavara pādakke—

namas tunga-śiraś-chumbi-chandra-chāmara-chāravē |
trailōkya-nagar-ārambha-mūla-stambhāya Śambhavē ||

svasti śrī-vijayābhyudaya-Śālivāhana-śaka-varsha 1718 ne vartamānakke salluva Nala-samvatsarada Chaitra-śuddha 1 Bhārgavāradallu Śivagange-mēlana-gavi-simhāsanārūḍhara-sāmpradāyastarāda Vīra-Śaiva-matastarāda Siddāpurada maṭhada paṭṭada-svāmiyavara kara-kamala-sanjātarāda śrīmad rājādhiraja rāja-paramēśvara prahuḍa-pratāpa apratima-vīra-narapati Koḍagina samsthānada śrī-ratna-simhāsanārūḍharāgi prithvī-sāmrājyam gaiyyutt-iralu Bhāradvāja-gōtrada Āś [va] lāyana-sūtrada Rukshabhānukādhyāyagaḷāda Appājēndra-Vaḍeyaravara pavutrarāda Linga-Rājēndra-Vaḍeyaravara garbhābdhi-sudhākarāyamānarāda Vīra-Rājēndra-Vaḍeyaravaru Śivārpanakke samarpisida dāna-śāsanada kramav-entendare—Mahādēvapurada maṭha yidakke svāmiyavaru chittaisalāgi sāshṭānga-praṇāpisi pāda-viḍidu āchandrārkavāgi dharma-barabēk-endu baradu vappisida vuttārada-bhūmi-vivara—Śivār panada-bagye maṭhakke yī bhūmi bijavari bhaṭṭi 17kke beliyuva bhaṭṭi 700 maṭhakke mēlu-vechchada-bagye linga-mudre-śilā-pratishṭeyannu māḍisi biṭṭu koṭṭa grāmagaḷinda baruva kandāyada vivara Chikka-Harade Jambūru grāmakke bija bhaṭṭi 43 kke kandāya 39 varaha prākina vuttāra yī grāmada pura-varga dēva-mānya bhūta-vuttāra saha bija bhaṭṭi 6½ ge 6½ varaha hōgalāgi śuddha-ninta-bhūmi bijavari bhaṭṭi 36½ varaha Yaḍāva-nāḍu valittada

Thenka-nāḍu-mandege śērida Bēlūru Basavanahaḷḷi vaḷagaṇa Guḍugūru saha grāma 2 kke bijavari bhaṭṭi 50 kke kandāya 50 varahakke prākina vuttāra yī grāmada pura-varga dēvamānya bhūta-vuttāra gavuḍ-umbali nāyi-mannu saha khaṇḍi ga 17½ ge kandāya 17½ hōgalāgi śudha nintaddu bija bhaṭṭi 32½ ge kandāya 32½ varaha antu grāma 4 kke prākina vuttāra hōgalāgi śuddha-nintadu yī maṭhakke baruva kandāya 69 varaha bhatta bhaṭṭi 700 beḷeyu chavu-grāmadavara munḍiṭṭu linga-mudre-śilā-pratishṭeyannu mādisi koṭṭu yī tithiyallū pitṛādi samasta-pitṛigaḷigu akshaya-Śiva-lōka-prāpti-yāgabēku-yamba apēksheyinda bhū-sādhanavannu baradu vappistēvāgi yī grāmakke chavu-kaṭṭu-linga-mudre-śilā-pratishṭevaḷagāda nidhi-nikshēpa-jala-taru-pāshāna-akshīna-āgāmi-siddha-sādhyangaḷ-emba ashṭa-bhōga-tēja-sāmya muntāda ā sakala-bhūmiyannu Śivārpitavāgi gaṇārādhaneyannu maḍisikonḍu Śiva-pūjā-kāladallu āśīrvādada ślōka—

jāti-smaratvam pṛithvī-patitvam savubhāgya-lāvaṇṇyam atīva-rūpam |
tvad-bhakti vidyē paramāyur ishṭam tvam daś cha mē Śankara janma-janmanī ||
yamba āśīrvādavanu māḍutta-yirabēk-embadāgi baradu vappista bhū-sādhanakke sākshigaḷu—
āditya chandrō anilō nalaś cha dyaur bhūmir āpō hṛidayam Yamaś cha |
ahaś cha rātriś chā vubhayaś chā sandhyā dharmasya jānāti narasya vṛittaḥ ||
svadattā dviguṇam puṇyam paradattānupālanam |
paradattāpahārēṇa svaduttam nishphalam bhavēt ||
yamba bhū-sādhanakke sva-hastā vappitā—

śrī Vi.

15

On the throne.

Kali sandda 4909.

16

On a stone at Danagal.

Virājapurada maṭha.

Iva-samvatsarada Jēshṭha-śudha 5 rallu Chīlaḷa Shāka-svāmigaḷa virakta maṭṭa.

17

On copper plates in the Ōmkārēśvara temple at Mercāra.

svasti śrī-vijayābhyudaya-Śālivāhana-śaka-varsha 1739 ney Īśvara-samvatsarada Jēshṭha-bahula-bidigeyu Bhānuvārakke Kali-dina 1796392 ne yī-śubha-divasadalli Chandra-vamśa-kshīra-pārāvāra-pārijātāyamānarāda Bhāradvāja-gōtra-sanjātarāda Āśvalāyana-sūtra Rik-śākhigaḷāda Vīra-Śaiva-mata-dhurīṇa-pravīṇarāda śrīmat-Koḍagu-samsthāna-samsthita-samādya Kshīranagara-madhya-paribhrājamāna-maṇi-gaṇa-khachita-chāru-simhāsanārūḍharāda apratima - pratāpa - prakāśa - prahasita - mārtāṇḍa - maṇḍalarāda akhaṇḍākhaṇḍa[1]-vaibhava-samētarāda sakala-digantarāla-vidyōttama-samāna-kīrti-prakhyātarāda samasta-praśasta-rājadharm-āvadhāraṇa-Yudhishṭhirarāda mahārāja-Appāji-Rājēndraravara pautrarāda Linga-Rājēndra-Vaḍeyaravara putrarāda śrī-Linga-Rājēndra-Vaḍeyaravaru yī-lōkadalli sukruta-kriyegaḷannu virachisidare iha-para-yeraḍaralliyū śāśvita-phala-bharitarāgi-yirabēku tat-kāraṇadinda mahattāda-puṇya-phala-pradāyakavāgi-yiruvanthā Śivalinga-pratishṭāpanaū kartavyav-endu chittadalli niśchaiśi tad-divasa-śubha-muhūrtadalli asadruśa śrī-kuśala-

---

[1] See No. 25.

maṇṭapādi-yukta rājakamalākar-ākhyā padmakarābhirāma nūtan-Ōṁkārēśvara-dēvasthāna vannu prārambhisi tad-ārabhya Vikrama-saṃvatsarada Chaitra-śuddha-dvādasiyu-Bhānuvā rada-varige varusha 2 tingaḷu 9 dina 25 Kali-dina 1797421 ne yētadruśa su-divasadalli aty-āścharyakavādanthāddannu sāmagriyavāgi nirmiśi śrīkaravāgi-yiruvantha Ōṁkārēśvara-nāmaka-Śivalingavannu pratishṭāpisi santushṭa-chittarāddu hyāgandare śrīmach-Chandra-śēkharana parama-kṛipānugraha-sāmarthyadinda sakala-manōratha-pradavāgi-yiruvantha yētad-dēvatā-yatna Śivalinga-pratishṭāpana-u nirvighnadinda virachitav-āyitu yāru bhakti-yinda śrī-Mahēśvarana bhajisuttārō avarige sarvatra-anikara-sādhyavāgi-yiruvantha śubha-phala-u svayam-ēva sādhyav-āguttade yendu sarva-jana parijnānārthavāgi barasi-yiruvantha śāsana || śubham astu ||

antu varusha 1 kke Ōṁkārēśvara-Gaṇādhīśvara-Kumārēśvara-śrī-Nandīśvara-dēvarige saha āchandrārkavāgi śāśvitadinda naḍadu-baratakka-bagye nitya-kaṭle amṛita-padi nandā-dīpa viśēsha-kaṭle pancha-parva sambaḷagāra-janakke saha appaṇe koḍisi yiruva Kaṇṭhīrāyi 1221 vandu-sāvira-yinnūra-yippatt-ondu-varahakke h a ṇ a d i n d a jiniśi-jauḷi-muntādarinda uttāravannu dharma-sangrahada-bagye aramane-divān-kachēri-hastāntradinda prati-samvat saradallu koḍisi-koṭṭu sēvārthavāgi v i n i y ō g a k k - e n d u nēmisi-yiruvanthavarinda kāla-trayadallu śāstra-prakāra dēvatā-sēveyannu sāngavāgi māḍisutta dinam-prati vichārisikoṇḍu varusham-prati yī-dēvasthānada lekka-pakka-muntāddannu jaḍti-tegadukoḷḷutta-baruvadāgi yamba tastīku-nirūpakke appaṇe-prakāra Kali-varsha 4922 ne Vikrama-samvatsarada nija-Jēshṭha tārīku 22 ne Bhānuvāra ||

śrī-Linga-Rājēndra-Vaḍeyaravaru ||

18

On a stone at Kibbeṭṭa.

Kara-samvatsarada Kārtīka-ba 1 rallu Channaina guru-u Rājaiyyanavara t a m m a n a kumāra Channa Mallikārjuna-dēvarige dūpa-dīpa-ārādhanege Vi || Vaḍeyara namaskāra-māḍi koṭṭa vivara udeya-kāladalli stāpane-māḍiddu.

19

On a stone at Iggoḍlu.

. . . . de ka bauḷa 1 neyallu Vīra-Vaḍeyaru Hālēri Mamadai-arasinavara k u v a r a vīriyadalli māḍida bhakti-tāmbra [Hālēri]-bhūmiya Aigaḷa-maṭhakke.

20

On a stone at Danugal.

śrīmatu Khara-nāma-samvatsarada Āsvīja-śuddha 10 rallu Yeḍatore-m a ṭ ṭ a d a Sidda-linga-svāmiyarige.

21

On a stone at Mayamuḍi.

śrī-Gangādhara-dēvaru.

Vīra-Rājēndra-Vaḍeyaravaru.

22

On a stone at Irpi.

Śālivāhana-śaka-varsha 1763 ne Śārvari-samvatsaradallu Kiggaṭṭu-hattu-nāḍu raihitaru tamma-bhaktiyinda Lakshmaṇatīrthada-bali yiruva Irpina Rāmēśvara-dēvara dēvastanavannu jīrnōddāra māḍisi yiddāre.

23

On a stone at Mahādēvapura (Mercāra).

śrī-Murigā-svāmigaḷavara charamūrttigaḷāda Śāntavīra - s v ā m i y a v a r a kara-kamala-sanjanitarāda Sōmaśēkhara-Śivayōgīśvararu Kali sanda 4643 ne Śōbhanakṛitu-samvatsarada Kārttīka-śuddha-bidigeyu Guruvāra Rōhini-nakshatra prātaḥkāla ganṭe 7 ra vaḷage yīgaddige-mēle kaḷaśa-sthāpane-māḍisiddu.

24

On a stone at the old village site of Gaṇagūr in Beṭṭiyaṭṭ-nāḍ.

. . . . . . svasti śrī-vijayābhyudaya-Śālivāhana-śaka-varusha 1519 n e y a Hēvilamba-samvatsarada Aśvayūja-śu 5 Bhaumavāra . . . . . gōtrada Āśvalāyana-sūtrada Ruk-śākhe [Nanjarāya] paṭṭaṇada Śrīkanṭha-Rājayana putrarāda Rudragaṇangaḷu . . . . . . ravarige Gaṇagūru maha . . . . ngaḷu tamma tande-tāyi . . . . pitrugaḷige Kailāsa-padavi āgali yendu koṭṭa bhāmi-dāna koṭṭa-gramakke āvan . . . . aḷipidare tande-tayi . . . . . . Nanjarāyapaṭṭaṇada . . . . śrī

25

On a stone slab in the wall of the Commissioner's Office, Mercāra

VI

Maharaja Veer Rajender Wadeer [1]

svasti śrī-jayābhyudaya-Sālivāhana-śaka-varsha 1743 ne Ishu-saṃvatsarada Pālguna-śuddha 11 yu Bhānuvārakke Kali-dina 1798128 ne yī-śubha-divasadalli Indu-vamśa-kshīra-pārāvāra-pārijātāyamānarāda Bhāradvāja-gōtra-sañjatarāda Āśvalāyana-sūtra-Rik-śākhigaḷāda Vīra-Śaiva-mata-dhurīṇa-pravīṇarāda śrīmat-K o ḍ a g u-samsthāna-samsthitānavadhya-Kshīranagara-madhya p a r i b h r ā j a m ā n a-maṇi-gaṇa-khachita-chāru-simhāsanārūḍharāda apratima-pratāpa-prakāśa-p r a h a s i t a-mārttaṇḍa-maṇḍalarāda akhaṇḍalākhaṇḍa-vaibhava-samētarāda sakala-dig-antarāḷa vidyōttamāna-kīrti-prakyātarāda samasta-praśasta-rājadharm-āvadharana-Yudhishṭhirarāda mahārāja-Linga-R ā j ē n d r a-V a ḍ e y a r a pautrarāda Linga-Rājēndra-Vaḍeyaravara putrarāda śrī-Vīra-Rājēndra-V a ḍ e y a r a v a r u sad-dharma-suśīla-sucharyadinda prithvī-sāmrājyam geyutta anugāladallu Mahādēva-dhyāna-pararāgi irut-iruva tad-anantara sva-dēśadallu varaṇagaḷu mitimīri mānavaru t a m m a u d a r a-pōshaṇ-ārthavāgi rachisi-iruvanthā phala-pairugaḷannu karaḍu-māḍiddarindalu pāntha-j a n a r a n n u himse-gaiddarindalu bhavan-ōpadrava-goḷisiddarinda saha i n t a p p a-bhādhegalinda nistarisalārev-endu prajegaḷu binnaisalāgi dushṭa-nigrāha-śishṭa-paripālane yesaguvanthāddu rājadharmav-endu chittadallu avadharisi y i d a n n u pariharisatakka-sāmarthyavannu karuṇisabēk-enta

[1] In English capital letters.

Gaurīdhavanige prārthisalāgi tat-Sāmba-Śankarana parama-kripānugraha-sahāyav-āda-kāraṇa tad-dinad-ārabhya Tārana-samvatsarada Chaitra-ba 12 yu Chandravāra-paryanta varusha 2 tingalu 1 dina 25 kke Kali-dina 1798913 ētādṛiśa-divasada-valage a r a ṇ y a-madhyadalli aitaruva-matta-gajagaḷa samūhakke tad-vāhanālankāra-yuktadim chittaisi kaṇṭhīravanavol paḍi-paṭṭi gajagaḷ-emba uchcharaṇege nāṇnuḍi-kāṇipante aja-sadṛiśam gaidu sva-sāmarthyada bhuja-bala-parākramadinda vidha-vidhadallu virāma-gaida-kunjaragaḷu appaṇe-prakāra paṭu-bhaṭaru sa-jīvadinda kaisere-hiḍida dantigalu saha gaṇane-yashṭ-endare Chitrabhānu-samvatsarada Āshāḍha-ba 10 lu Nanjarāyapaṭṭaṇa-tālōkinalli layavāda āne 6 kaisere-hiḍida-āne 9 Śrāvaṇa-ba 3 llu sadari-tālōkinalli layavāda-āne 42 kaisere-hiḍida-āne 22 adhika-Āśvayuja-śuddha 5 llu sadari-tālōkinalli Uluguli-Mūḍigēri-nāḍinalli saha layavāda-āne 47 kaisere-hiḍida-āne 15 ī śuddha 11 lu Nanjarāyapaṭṭaṇada-tālōkinalli Horūru-Nūrokkalu-nāḍinalli Uluguli-Mūdigēri-nādinalli saha layavāda-āne 34 kaisere-hiḍida-āne 6 nija-Āśvayuja-śuddha 11 lu Nanjarāyapaṭṭaṇada-tālōkinalli layavāda-āno 20 kaisere-hiḍida-āne 6 Svabhānu-samvatsarada nija-Chaitra śuddha 5 lu Koḍagu-Śrīrangapaṭṭaṇadalli layavāda-āne 4 kaisere-hiḍida-āne 18 Vaiśākha-śuddha 3 llu Beṭṭiyatta-nāḍinalli Channanakōṭeyallu saha layavāda-āne 21 kaisere-hiḍida-āne 41 Tāraṇa-samvatsarada Chaitra-ba 12 llu Kiggaṭṭu-nādinallu layavāda-āne 10 kaisere-hiḍida-āne 40 yitara-trimśad-dinadallu layavāda-āne 49 kaisere-hiḍida-āne 24 antu ashṭa-trimśad-divasakke sva-hastadinda layavāda-āne 233 paṭu-bhaṭaru appaṇe-prakāra prāṇa-yuktavāgi pāṇi-grahaṇav-esagida-āne 181 ubhayam gaja 414 ī-teradallu sakala-manōratha-prada-āgalāgi vismaya-paṭṭaddu hyāge andare vipinagaḷallu adri-samānvitav-āda kari-samūhavu dinakaranannu mēgha-jāla-mutthva teṛadante bhōrguḍi sutā gamisal-āgi siḍilin-ōpādi-yiruvanthā saptārchitāstra-āyudhagaḷinda tat-kshaṇadallu nigrahisidanthāddu sthūlōnnatav-āgiruvantha mada-gajagaḷannu mūshikan-ante bhāvisi manujaru prāṇa-samētavāgi parigrahisi-iruvantha atyāścharya.

26

On a stone at Chērala-Sirimangala (Horūr-Mūḍigeri-nāḍ), lying in Bhaktanakōṭe in the Minakolli forest.

śrīmatu Śālivāhana-śaka-varusha 1466 neya Krōdhi-saṁvatsarada Chaitra-śu 1 lū śrīman mahā-maṇḍalēśvara Chaṁgāḷva-Śrīkaṁṭharasugaḷu Liṁgaṁṇ-oḍēru-dēvarige Bagutanakōṭege salluva bhūmiyanu sarvamānyavāgi koṭṭaru yī koḍageyan aḷupidavaru raurava-narakadalli yiruvaru.

27

On a vīrakal at Herūr (same nāḍ), lying in paisāri land, Survey No. 56/1.

. . . . haraha be . . . . leya Māchiga . . rānega
svasti śrīmatu . . Munivarādityam nahō . . uḷiya Hērūra etti kaṭṭisidake . . . .
dha magam Herūra kō . . . karambha ga handala . . . mudēvaḷa . . . . . ma
negardda . . . nahaṇa arasa . . . eṇḍala mannaṇe sā . . . . munna nela .
. . . . vandu huṭṭidam niba . . . . . . isuva . . ḷda Herūra Ālapa yidam
Chaṅgāḷuva alankarisida . . . Munivarāditya Malala . . karaśi va . . . . .
. . baḍaḷadu paṭṭaṇa-svāmiya sē . . ya koṇḍu hosa mu . . kāvaka . . .
. . . . ga oppiga meraba . . . . kaṭi .
. . . .

28

On a vīrakal at Andagōve-Kallūr (same nāḍ) in Basavēśvara-dēva's jōḍi land, Survey No. 89.

svasti Śaka 866 Krōdhi-saṃvatsara . . . . ma tale gaḍisi satta ātana santati . . . . . koṭṭa . . . . . . hāra . . . . . . para koṇḍa saḷi . . . ṟam . . . Gaṅge . . . . . kavileyan aḻida Brahmatti Būchagan abbā tana ma . . parōksha-vinayava ma . . . ṟisida baredam Bavanayya.

29

On a pillar of the Ayyappa temple on the Kunda hill (Beṭṭiyatt-nāḍ).

śrī . . . . īśvara-prasannanāgi . . Beṭṭiyattu-nāḍu Kundada-beṭṭada mēle nelasiruva Mahādēvara śilāmayavāda purāṇa-guḍiyannu nava-nettavāgi Śivālayadallu jīrṇōdhāra-māḍuvadakke yī-nāḍu Takka-mokastarū ādiyāgi sarvē-janaru mattu Ammati-nāḍu Kakkēri-grāmada Takka-mokastarū saha anumati-paṭṭu Śālivāhana-śakābda-varusha 1776 kke Kali-varusha 4955 ne Ānanda-nāma-samvatsarada Tulā-māsa 18 ne Kārtika-śuddha 15 Guruvārakke Kali-sanda-dina 1810060 dina sanda-śubha-mūrtadali prārambhisida yī-mahāsthaḷa jīrnōdhāradallu Maneppaṇḍra . . . . Īśvarārpitav-endu maulya-koṭṭu śēva-māḍida janara vivara . . . Kaṇḍeya-rāvuta . . . tadalūra . . . māḍisida . . sāya māḍidavaru śāṇabhāgaru Brāhmaṇa-Veṅkapaiya śubhēdāru Koḍandēra-Mudaiya pāru pātyagāru Maneppaṇḍra-Puchaiya bāgilu-nilake sāya māḍiśida Koḍandēra-Mēdaiya dēvara pāṇivaṭa terekala meṭukela saha sāya māḍidu Saṇvaṇḍra-Bōḷaiya Maṇiṇḍe-Timmaiya-gavuḍa Chinnē-gauḍana Channappa Nandīśvarana prasannakke sāya mādidu Kunda-grāmada jahāgīradār Hayātta-Kāna-sābi yī-mēre sarvē-janaru kūḍi jīrṇōddhāra-māḍida yī-Śivālayada kelasaū Paingaḷa-nāma-saṃvatsarada Vaiśākha-śuddha 15 Śukravāra śubha-muhūrtadalu yī-Śivānugrahadinda pūraisidhe yī-sēve-mādidavarige . . . . yihadali saukhya paradali mukti.

30

On a stone at Nallūr (Hattugaṭṭu-nāḍ) in a hittal west of Tītaramāḍu Mādayya's house.

. . . . . Koḍangāḷa . . . e maga . . . . . . diḷe āḷdaḍe mendu yati-varargg-ellam sādaradi Bīḻiya-seṭṭiyā-pādadoḷ eṟagi tāḻidad ī-sura-kīrtti bhadram astu Jina-śasanāya śrīman Maduvanga-nāḍa dora Kiviriy-Ayyangaḷ Chāngaḷada basadiyoḷ panneraḍam nōntu muḍipidan avara makkaḷ Bākiyu Bukiya niṟisidar.

31

On a stone on the tank bund at the same village, Survey No. 117, near Tītaramāḍu's house.

bhadram bhūyāj Jinēndrāṇām śāsanāyāgha-nāśinē |
ku-tīrtha-dhvānta-sanghāta-prabhinna-ghana-bhānavē ||

svasti śrī.

pa . . dhanaṃ paratra-hita-kāraṇakam paramōpakārakam |
kuḍe ta . . tāḻdi . . yatiga . . matiga . . bhayā . . dantama. . |
taḍeyade muktiyaṃ paḍeven endu vichārisi bandhu-varggava . . |
biḍisi samādhiyam paḍedud elliyum achchari Jakkiyabbeya ||

Kastūri-bhaṭṭārargge avara śrāvaki Chandiyabbe-gāvuṇḍi . . . yara mantraki Jakkiyabbe sanyasanam geydu muḍipidaḷ || ākeya gaṇḍa parama-śrāvaka Eaḍyya mangalam.

No. 34.—Mullur Epitaph of Gunasena, A.D. 1064.

A.

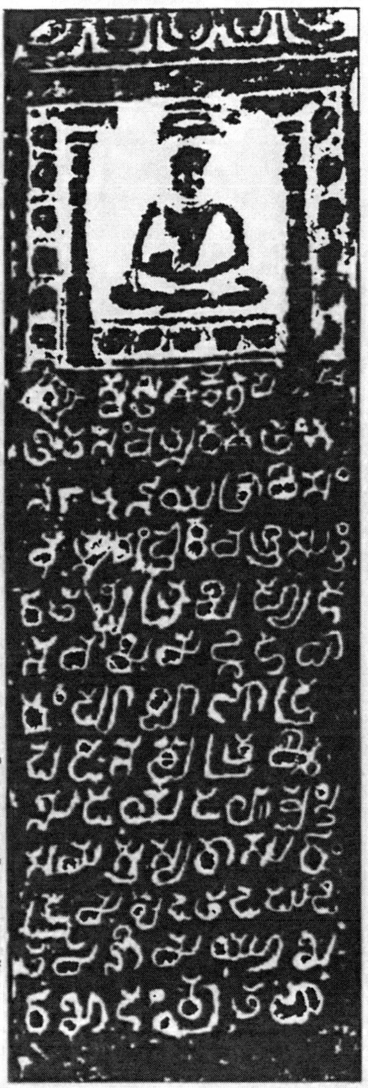

B.

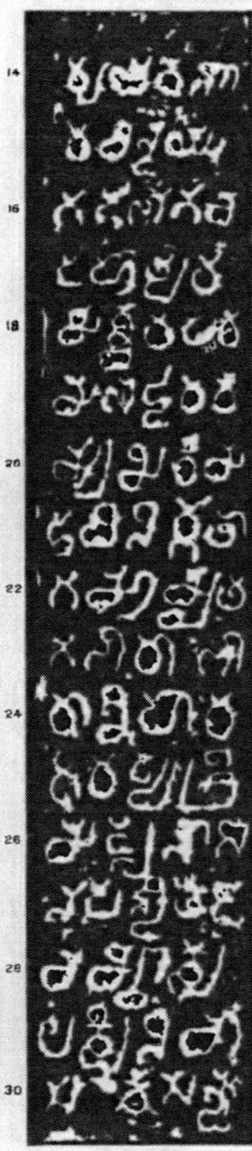

C.

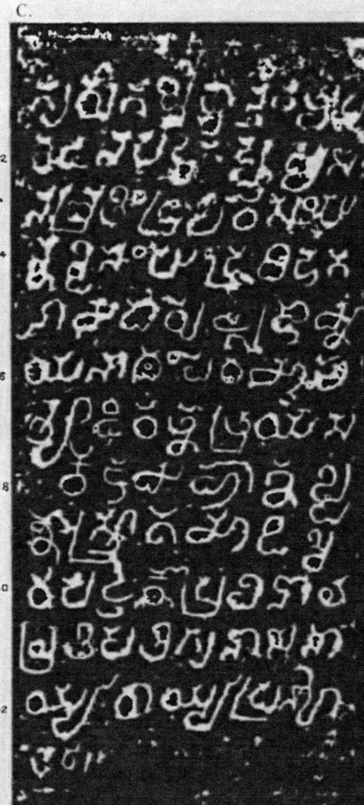

H. KRISHNA SASTRI.

SCALE ONE-FIFTH.

GOVT. PHOTOZINCO OFFICE, POONA

32

On a stone at Niḍuta (Niḍuta hōbli) in Bīre-dēvara vana.

svasti śrī . . . dbhayat-Syakalra-vorusha 120[1] [Bahu |dhānya-saṁvatsarada Vai śākha-ba . . . . haḷiya gu ga . . . dava . . . Malapanahaḷḷiya Mallikārjjuna-dēvara-pra . . . [Gaḍi]-nāḍu Aṇi[le]nā . . . [Mu]ḷḷu-nāḍu ekōṭi . . . . tā mun[ta]ṭṭu ā-Mallikārjju[na-dēvara] . . . hora-bhūmiya ja- . . ṇam . . . . yaṇṇa Lakaṁṇa [Jaka]-Rāma[ya] . . . . . . Hiriya-Vīraṁṇa Chika-Vīraṁṇa . . . . . . tiya taṇḍakkavu (||) ā-nāḍa-muṁ[de] . . . . [ṭṭa] gadde bedalu Banasamudrada . . . . ko 10 dēvara keṟeya keḷage kāra [gadde] . . . [hu]vina gadde ko 10 Baniganahaḷḷiya[lu Tiru]male-gaüḍa kattisida ā-keṟeya keḷa[ge ko 3 . . [yo]lage sa 2 dēvara hiṁdaṇa-pareya ga[dde] . . . . yaṁṇage sa 2 ko 1 [ā]-hatreya teṁkaṇada [ho] . . ṁge [ko] 1 ali paḍuva haḷḷa gadde sa 1 Koṟakaḍahu Hariyamṇage sa 1 Koṟakaḍahu Vīraṇṇa . . . [maṇṇa] dēvana gadde sa 1 [Māka] lakeṟeya . . . . . sa 6 Hiḍijīyakeṟeya . . . . . . lu ūra muṁdaṇa ko . . [te]ṁdaḍe . . m 100 ūra hindaṇa ke . rike 600 aṁntu bedalu . . 700 gadde sa 22 nū Malli-gauḍa . . Hariyaṇṇa Vīraṇṇaṁgeyū samavāgi amrutapaḍige biṭṭa dharmmam āru aḷipida[ḍe] Gaṁgeya taḍiyali ka[vi]leya koṁda pā . . . . taṁ vā paradattaṁ vā yō harēta vasundha . . . r-vvarisha sahasrāṇāṁ vishṭāyāṁ jāyatē . . . . sāsana . . . . .

33

On a stone at Nandigunda (same hōbli) in Government kharāb land, Survey No. 147.

svasti śrīman-mahāmaṇḍaḷēsvaraṁ Vīra-Chōḷa-Koṁgāḷuva-Dēvar prithivī-rājyaṁ gaiyutt ire tāyi-Padumala-Dēvi Sōmala-Dēvi Tōḷūra-Duddarasa Balleya-daṇḍanāyaka Haḍiyiṟa-Kirikaṇa yiṁtt-inibaruṁ muṁtāg-irddu Manumata-saṁvachharada Kuṁbha-māsa Ādivāra dasami yaṁdu Muḷḷu-nāḍ-eppattakaṁ Aṇṇattammana makkaḷa makkaḷig ett eydo saluvudu suṁkada beḍuṁgoḷu nall-ettu parihāra heggaḍe-gadyāna Ganahūralu oṁdu haḷḷige haṇav aidu kāṇike gadyāna Ganahūral oṁdu haḷḷige haṇav aidu ara teṟe haṁdala-haṇa parihāra Gaṁga-siddhāya hoṟagāgi āya daya[1] biṭṭi besa haḍu vagērige parihāravaṁ biṭṭa [||] Vīra-Chōḷa-Koṁgāḷvu-Dēva koṭṭudaṁ tappa nuḍida Gaṁgeya taḍiya kavileyam Brām maṇanaṁ koṁda brahmātiyaṁ koṁḍa || eppattaroḷage maneg ai-guḷa bhatta saluvudu Gaṁg-ōjaṁge Būchaṇaṁge ||

34

On a stone at Muḷḷūr (same hōbli), west of the Pārśvanātha basti in the Basti temple.

(*1st side*) svasti-Śaka-nripa-kāl-ātīta-saṁvatsara-śataṁgaḷ 986 neya Krōdhi-saṁvatsaraṁ parivarttisuttire [2]tach-Chaitra-bahuḷa navami Maṅgaḷavāraṁ Pūrvva-Bhādrapade-naksha tram Mīn-odayadal || svasti samasta-surāsurēṁdra-makuṭa-taṭa-ghaṭita-maṇi-mayūkha-rēkh-āḷaṁkṛita-chā (*2nd side*) ru-charaṇāravinda-yugaḷa-bhagavad-Arhat-paramēśvara-parama-bhaṭṭāraka-mukha-kamaḷa-vinirggat-āgam-āmṛita-gaṁbhīr-āṁbhōrāśi-pāragar appa śrīmad Guṇasēna-Paṇḍita-dēvar Mōksha-Lakshmī-nivāsakka[ṁ] sanda[r] [||]

---

[1] Read *dāya*.

[2] Read *pravarttisuttire*.

(*3rd side*) gurugaḷ siddhānta-tatva-prakaṭana-paṭugaḷ Pushpasēna-vratīṁdrar | vvara-saṁghan Nandi-saṁghaṁ Draviḷa-gaṇa ma[hĀ]ruṅguḷ āmnāya-nāthaṁ[|]param-ārhanty-ādiratna-traya-sakaḷa-mahā-śabda-śāstr-āgamādi sthira-shaṭ-tarkka-pravīṇar vratipati-Guṇasēn-āryyar āryya-praṇōtar||

35

On a second stone at the same place.

(*1st side*) Dharmma-seṭṭi baredam svasti Śaka-varsha 980 tteneya Viḷaṁbi-saṁ vatsarada uttarāyaṇa-saṁkrāṁti-yaṁdu śrī-Rājēṁdra-Koṁgāḷvaṁ taṁm ayyaṁ māḍisida basadige koṭṭa Hāruvanahaḷḷi Arakanahaḷḷi (*2nd side* Niḍutada-gōḍal khaṇḍugaṁ 3 ke Sakuniyu oḷageṟeyuṁ khaṇḍuga [3] Hēnnellūra bhūmi khaṇḍugaṁ 10 oṁdu gāṇad eṇṇe (*3rd side*) Kāṅgoṇḍahaḷḷi haṁgala [b]āni khaṇḍugaṁ 10 Huṇisedāṟu khaṇḍugam 10 Gaṇapati gōḍalu khaṇḍugaṁ 3 Asagavoḷe khaṇḍugaṁ 4 (*4th side*) śrī-Rājādhirāja-Koṁgāḷvan abbe Pōchabbarasiyar ttamma gurugaḷu Draviḷa-gaṇada Naṁdi-saṁghad Aruṁgaḷ-ānvayada Guṇasēna-paṇḍita-dēvargge māḍisi dhārā-pūrvvakaṁ koṭṭaru || svadattaṁ paradattaṁ vā yō harēti vasundharā[ṁ] shashṭēr vvarsha-sahasrāṇ[i] vishṭāyāṁ jāyatē krimiḥ ||

36

On a third stone at the same place.

. . . . ya nidhi Satyā . . . . la Dēvi bhūtaḷa . . . . vinirgata . . . . lōkya-vikhyāte . . . yaṇa mōkshade . . . . . varṇṇa . . . . ydāmulam . . panida . . māḷi . . . . . . n urvvīpāḷa bhūta . . barasida kāruṇiy odava . . . na vachana kāya vaddiga . . . tuḷḷina . . . yamb ant ire sa . . . . . . ta divija lōka || kham . . . . . . Prithuvī-Koṁgāḷvan arasi . . .

37

On the north wall of the same Pārśvanātha basti.

svasti śrī-Rājādhirāja-Koṁgāḷvan abbe Pōchabbarasiyar Draviḷa-gaṇada Nandi-sanghad Arungaḷ-ānvayada Guṇasēna-paṇḍita-dēvara guḍḍi māḍisida basadi mangaḷa mahā.

38

On the basement of the same basti.

. svasti śrī-Rājēndra-Chōḷa-Koṁgāḷvana putra śrī-Rā[jādhirāja]-Koṁgāḷva . . . . vāsa-sthānamaṃ tamma gurugaḷ Tivuḷa-gaṇad Arungaḷ-ānvayada Nandi-sanghada Guṇasēna-paṇḍita-dēvargge dhārā-pūrvvakaṃ koṭṭam mangala mahā śrī śrī.

39

On a stone near the Chandranātha basti in the same basti.

svasti śrī Śaka-varsha 1313 neya Pra[mō]dōta-saṁvatsarada Vaiśākha-su 3 Bhāna vāradallu śrī-Mūla-saṁgha Dēsi-gaṇa Pustaka-gachchada . . . Koṇḍakuṁd-ānvayar

No. 35.—Mullur Pillar inscription of Rajendra-Kongalva and Rajadhiraja-Kongalva's Mother, A.D. 1058

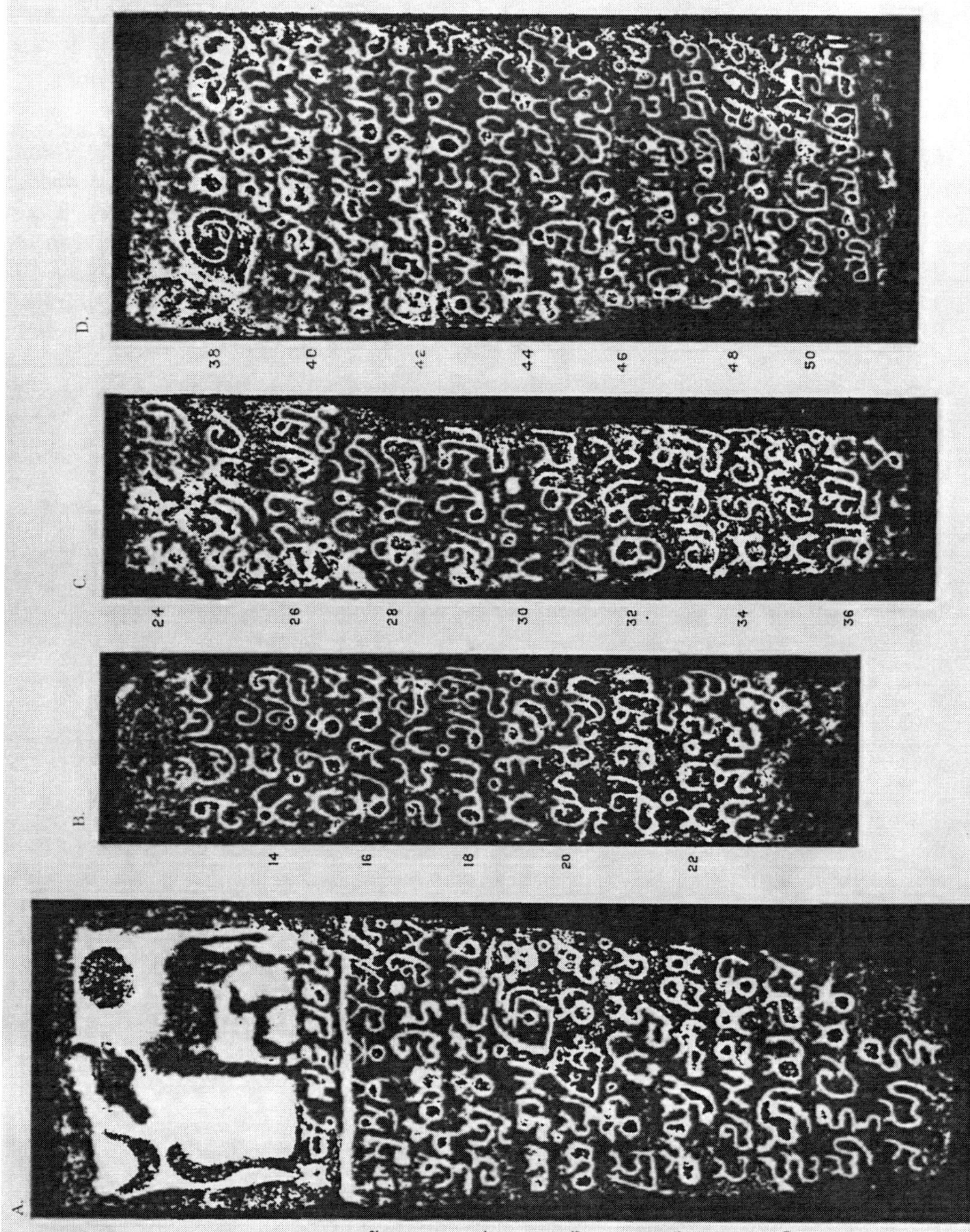

H. KRISHNA SASTRI. SCALE ONE-SEVENTH. GOVT. PHOTOZINCO OFFICE, POONA.

Āryya-Śubhēndu kaṁda Vija[ya]kīrtti-dēvara priya-śīshyar-appa Bāhubali-dēvaru ī-stānamaṁ paḍad uddharsidaru śrī-Rājā[dhirājānu] Komgālva-Rugmiṇi-Dēviya dēviya dēhārada Vijaya-dēvara dvārā nele niṁd aṁdu sva janani . . ta putra ā-Pōchab barasige puṇyārtthavāgi pratishṭheyam māḍsi aṅga-raṅga-bhōga biṭṭa ūru Aṇilavāḍiya Nulabihaḷḷiyaṁ Nāḍudaṟaśinahaḷḷi Muḷḷūra Hāruvahaḷḷie sīme mūḍa Hariva-haḷḷa teṁka Badanaguttiga . . baḍagaṇ agaḷa naṭṭa kallu paḍuva beṭṭa-baḍagaṇa agala Kāragōḍa haḷḷiya sīme mūḍa Nelliyahāḷi naṭṭa kallu teṁka beṭṭada kone harigala baḍaga kere ēri īśānya naṭṭa kallu Muḷḷūra gadde gaḷegala vōni kha 1 . . ḍigeṟeya keḷage kha 2 āgaḷ ottu ko 10 . kina gōḍalu . . ko 10 gāla kha 1 Koḍagōḍalu [kha] 2 Abba-gadde ko 10 Lōke-gadde ko 10 . . . . . nāgasampage-gadde kha 1 bō[ḷa]-gadde kha 1 ko-ālada-kōḍi kha 1 ko 10 asagavakki kha 1 kō . . siku kha 1 Niḍitada gōḍalu kha 3 Myaṇasadalli kha 1 ko [10] Honnedēviya saraṇa gōḍalu kha 1 Heṇṇanūra bhūmi kha 2 oṁdu gāṇad eṇṇe biṭṭadu āchandrārkkaṁ sarvvā-janānandar dīkshateya paṭṭa ōdi pravarttiseyāge Vīra-Hariharōrvvīśa palavara kādi rāya-maṟe-vokkaṟa-kāva śaraṇāgata-vajra-paṁjara saṁkha-chakra-gajadāra[1]-bhṛitya Goṁkā-Raḍḍi-nāyakage Guṇḍappa-daṇḍanāykaru kurittu Muḷḷu-nāḍaṁ kuḍuvantar-ādar svabhāvārtthavāgi Siddha-gauḍa prajagaḷa karekoṁḍu Aṁṇā-dēviya Kumāranahaḷḷiya Bhīmāpuram eṁdu pesar-iṭṭu chatus-sīmeya kallu naṭṭu dhārā-pūrvvakavāgi koṭṭarū || Kāragōḍam A[ṁṇā]ṁgapurav eṁdu pesaran iṭṭu dhārā-pūrvvakavāgi Pārśvanāthaṁg ittarū || [Ki]ratyadugakke dānaśāle gōmāle Jayamāḷapuriyalli gadde kha 3 || Gaṇapati gōḍalu kha 3 Huṇisedāṟu kha 1 eḷutt Ārjuna śāsanam || śrī ī dharmava aḷipidavaru paśu sisu heṇṇu guru ivara kōti [ko]ṁda pāpadali hōharu handiya tiṁbaru.

40

On a stone near the maṇṭapa in front of the Chandranātha basti.

svasti śrī Śaka-varsha 1138 ne Dhātu-saṁvatsarada Jeshṭa śu 15 Man . . . vāradallu Immaḍi-A . . . . ya-Rāya kaṭakāchāryyar appa Vidyādhara-Bāchidēv-arasaru muḍipi .

41

On the footprint stone in front of the Śāntīśvara basti, in the same basti.

Guṇasēna-paṇḍitasya gurōḥ Pushpasēna-siddhānta-dēvasya śrī pādaṁ.

42

On a stone in the north-west angle of the enclosure of the same basti.

svasti śrī-Guṇasēna-paṇḍita-dēvar agaḷisida Nāga-vāvi nakarada dharma.

(Figure of a cobra)

43

On a vīrakal on the tank bund of the same village.

śrī Śaka-varsha 999 neya Piṅgaḷa-saṁvatsara . . . . śrī-Rājēndra-Chōḷa-Koṅgāḷvam rājyam geyyutt i . . . . ātana paṭṭad-arasi Padmala-Dēvi sattu . . . . ṇipa kāvaradindam tānum tanna peṇḍa. . . . . .

[1] No doubt a mistake for *gadādhara*.

44

On a stone at the same place.

Uttama-Chōḷa-Seṭṭi sa . . . bāleya . . . . . khaḻgadindam . . . . . . tale gaḍisi sattam

45

At the same village, on a vīrakal in Vīrarāja-gauḍa's threshing-floor.

(*First section*) Ōm namaḥ || svasti samasta-praśasti-[sa]hitaṁ maṇḍalīka-Nārāyaṇanuṁ Maleya-beṁkoṇḍa-gaṁḍanuṁ śa ra]ṇāgatavajra-paṁjjararum appa śrī-Harihara-Dēva-Chōḷa-Dēvara rājyad aṁdu [Du]rmmukhi-saṁvatsarada Chai (*Second section*) tra-śuddha paṁchamī Sōmavārad aṁdu Muḻḻūra kōṭege Beḷuhu-nāḍu Godduṁbāḍi Muḷivarādityanāḍa Mallikārjjuna Nidita Meṇasa modalāgi nāḍ-ella nerad ettibaṁdu mutti kōṭeya hattisida alli Boppa-gauḍiya Malleya Muḻḻūra kōṭeya kādu aṭi hoy (*Third section*) du vaṁkai dhāradoḷage biddanu biddalligey ātange vīra-sēseyāgi Māsāvi-mukhyavāgi ūra mūnūṟ āḷu nerad-irddu Muḻḻūra gaddeyoḷage Mākoveya maṁnoḷage gadde 3 Hiḍijegallali gadde 5 yiṁt eṁṭu ga[d]de Boppa-gauḍiya Mālaiya Mādaiyanavaru hosamāni-keṟe sa (*round the stone*) hita ga 9 kke Māsāvi ūru neradu avarige sarvvā-bādhā-parihāravāgi māṟidaru ī-mariyāde ḻēsōdeṁ baṁdadu || ī-kalla Kōgoḷaliya Bāchāchāriya maga Bairōji māḍi[da] kal[l]u śrī Kopaṇa-tīrthada sēnabōva Sātaiya ī-śāsanada akharava bareda maṁgaḷa mahā śrī śrī śrī.

46

On a stone at Mālambi (same hōbli), near the old village-site.

svasti Sūryyānvaya-surataru-staṁbhāyamāna Chōḷa-kuḷa-gaghana-gabhastimāḷi sakaḷa-jana - durita - haraṇa - nipuṇa - Kavēra - kanyakā-sakhīyamāna Chōḷa-mahā-mahīpati śrī-ManiRājakēsarivarmma-Permmanaḍigaḷ jaṁge Panasogeya kāḷegadal oṭṭi keydaṁ neṟid ikku barēn endu ātanan[1] aḍahidar ssattar endu piriduṁ kāruṇyadinda[2] paṭṭava kaṭṭi nāḍa kuḍug endu Pañchavan - mārāyargg aṭṭal ātaṁ Kshatriya - sikhāmaṇi- Kongāḷvan endu paṭṭavaṁ kaṭṭi Mālavviyan ittar idarkke gāvuṇḍa-Rāchammana vaṁśamē sākshi Kaṇṇavaṁgalada Āditya-gāvuṇḍanuṁ . gaḷaniya Nanniya Mēruvuṁ Keḷane. . . . . . cha-gāvuṇḍanum Nallūr Eṟeyaṁga-gāvuṇḍa . . . ḻḻūr-nnāḍe Kel-nāḍe poṟag endu nuḍiyal kā. . . . . . (*the rest is effaced*).

47

On another stone at the same place.

Dhātu-saṁvatsarada Āsvīja-śudha 5 lū śrīmatu-Veṁ[ka]ṭādri-Nāyakara Krushṇappa-Nāyakarru Mālambi-Rāche-gauḍage pālisi koṁḍadu [ka]ndāya ga 12 haṁneraḍu varahaṁnu pālisi koṁḍadu idhēve.

48

On a stone at Mesaṇa (same hōbli), in the trench of the fort ruins.

svasti śrī-Koṁgāḷva rājyam ge-e Komārayan Sundara . . . . . ede tuṟu koḷe kaṭṭistaralli . . . n ā-hāra turuhāran oṭṭi . . . . sāmantara . . . da Koṁgā . . Gōkipayana . . Māra vūrā . . . ppaṭṭi koṭṭa . . daṇida sēniyara . . . . . .

(Images of Sundaran and Komāran, with the names attached.)

---

[1] The first *na* is inserted below the line, with a cross above to show where it should come.

[2] *ru* is below the line, at the end.

No. 45.—A Virakal from Mullur.

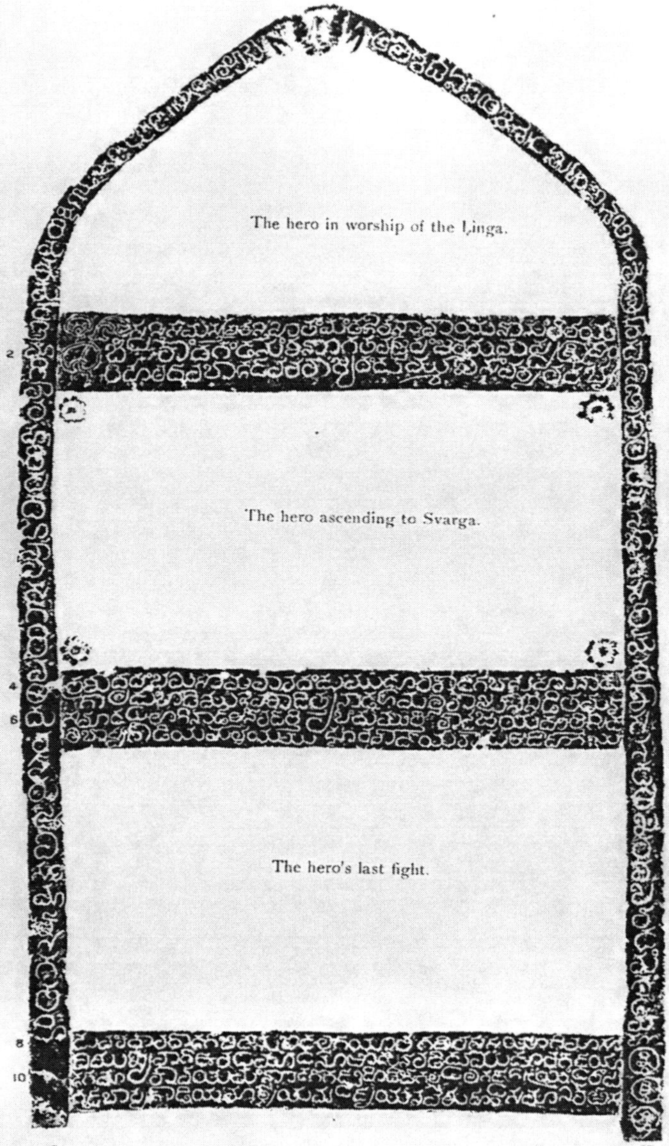

H. KRISHNA SASTRI. GOVT. PHOTOZINCO OFFICE, POONA.

SCALE ONE-SIXTH

No. 46.—The Malambi stone of the time of Rajakesarivarma-Permanadigal.

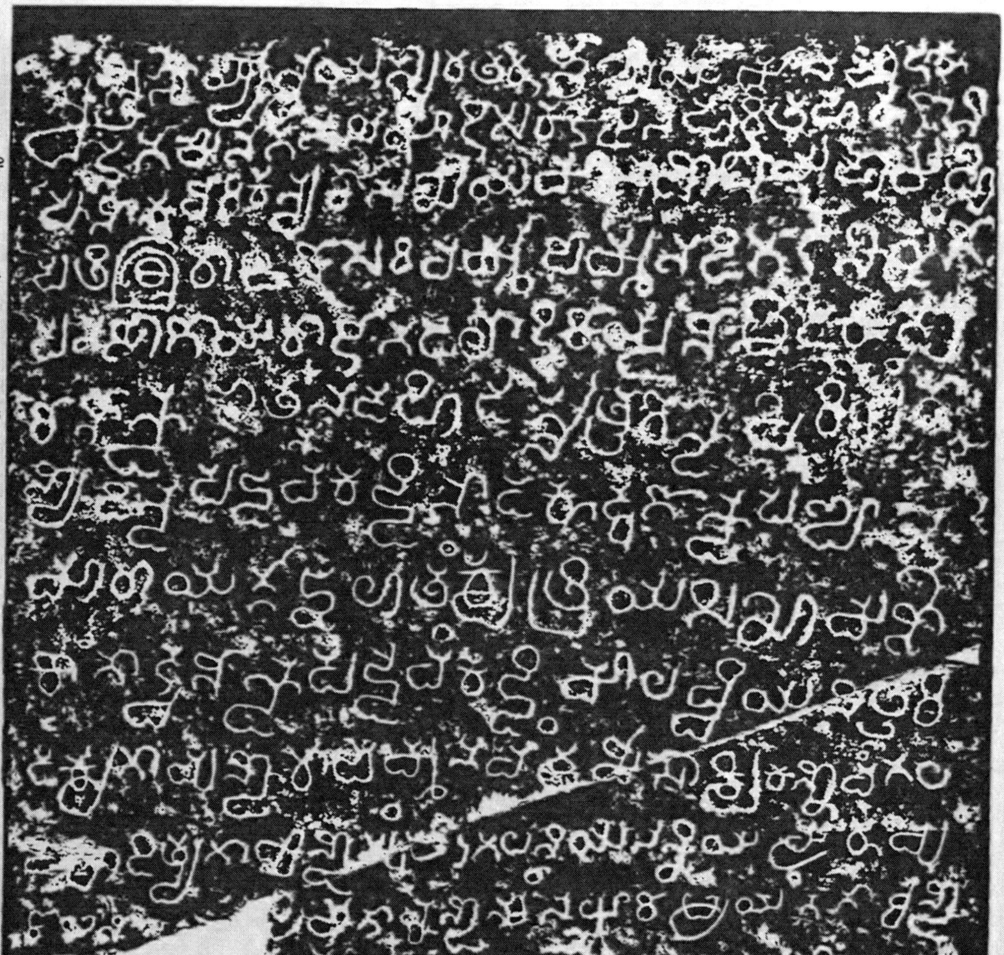

H. KRISHNA SASTRI.

GOVT. PHOTOZINCO OFFICE, POONA.

SCALE ONE-FOURTH

49

On a stone at Hosahalli (same hōbli), near Paṇiyālada-kaṭṭe.

(One line and a half at the top, beginning *svasti*, is illegible except for a letter here and there. It is perhaps a subsequent addition.)

svasti Śaka-varsha 993 neya Sādhāraṇa-saṁvatsarada Chaitra-māsada amāvāse yaṁdu śrīmad-Rājēndra-Pṛituvi-Koṁgāḷvaṁ Suḷḷigōḍina Gauratiya-keṟeya keḷagaṇa makke mūḍaṇa haḍuvaṇa gōḍa bāḷagāgi ayvattu-khaṇḍuga biḍa bhūmiyaṁ Hoshavaḷḷi-Vīra-Siddhēśvara-dēvarggaṁ archchanā-bhōgakkaṁ dhārā-pūrvvakaṁ biṭṭaṁ Rājavallabha-seṭṭi keṟege koṭṭa gadyāṇaṁ 40 āḍavalam gadyāṇaṁ 1½ tappidaṁ kavileyan aḷidaṁ svadattaṁ paradataṁ vā yō harēta vasundharāṁ shashṭir vva[rsha sahasrāṇi vishṭhāyāṁ jāyatē krimiḥ].

50

On a stone at the same village, in the paddy field near Timmayyana-kere.

svasti Śaka-varsha 993 ne . . Sādhāraṇa-saṁvatsarada Chaitra-māsada amāvāsi yandu śrī-Rājēndra-Pṛithuva-Koṁgāḷva rājyam geyutt-ire Hoshavaḷḷi Vira-Siddhēśvara-mahā dēvargge Posavaḷḷiya Nīra-gāvuṇḍana keyyal ponnaṟe koṭṭu maṇṇaṟe koṇḍu pattu-khaṇḍuveya āḍavalam koṭṭam tappidaṃ kavileyan aḷidam.

51

At Doḍḍa-Maḷate (same hōbli), on the sluice of Honnammana-kere.

śrīmatu Pārtthiva-saṁvatsarada Phālguṇa-śu 10 Guruvāra Annadāni-arasinavaru yītūba kaṭṭisidaru kaṭidavaru Venkaṭaiya Malaiyya Bomarasaina baraha Basalinga-dēvaru Nanna-gauḍana kāladali āyitu.

52

On a stone at Ganagūr (same hōbli), near the village entrance.

. . . . rada Vaiśākha-su 10 Mangaḷavārad-andu tenka-Gunda-nāḍ-eppattakkaṁ kāruṇyam geydu . . . . . rtoḍe gaṇḍ illadirddaḍe heṇṇinge heṇṇu-makkaḷinge saluvudu ī dharmmava tappa-naḍadam pāpa Naraka bidda Gangeya taḍiyalu kavileyam Brāhmaṇanu vam konda Brammātiyam koṇḍa śrīman-mahā-pradhāna Paḍivala-Bānam-marājana putra Heggade-Nākana barada mangala mahā śrī . . damaṭṭa-vesa . . . . Vajjaragāḷa Bayala-nāḍa Bammōja geyda śāsana.

53

On another stone at the same place.

. . . . pṛithivī-rājyam gaiyutt-ire tā iva . . . . daṇḍanāya kan int anibaru mukhya . . . ku-nāḍ-eppattakkaṃ āya dāya Voḍeyappa Honnapaya haṇa kāṇike . . sa biṭṭam . . . . . . sarvvāya . . . . . Manumatha-saṁvatsarada Jēshṭa . . . Śukra vārad andu āya dāya saha . . . . va kāruṇyam gaiydd . . . . Koṁgāḷva-Dēva ||

54

On a stone at Gōṇi Marūr (same hōbli), near a Kenchuvāḷa tree.

. . . . . . mattiya ga . . . . . keṟeya kelage gadde gaṇṇu . . . . . Dēvi-geṟeya keḷage gade gaṇṇu āṟa . . ko 1½ Māvina-makkivoḷage ko 10 antu ga 4 beddalu vūru-mūḍaṇa-vōṇiyim baḍagaṇa-kaḍe eraḍ āra beddale . . kōpa voṇṇangi tale meṭṭi sale kondu Gōpāla-Dēvana daṇḍina kāṇike mane vāṇa solage biṭi yinn ishṭu sarvvamānyavāgi sva-ruchiyinda koṭṭaru yint appudakke ā-Malli-Dēva-Harihara-Dēvarasar-oppa—śrī Chenna-Sadāśiva.

55

On another stone at the same place.

(*The first part is gone*). . . . Dēvarasaru pṛithvī-rājyaṃ geyutt-irddali Yaḍavu-nāḍa Gaṭṭa bāḍiya gaḍiya kāḷegada bavaradali Chikkeya-Nāyaka bidd-andu Chikkeya-Nāyakana makka lige ā Malli-Dēvarasaru Harihara-Dēvarasaru Tenka-nāḍa samasta. . . . . .

56

On a stone at Doḍḍa Kaṇagālu (same hōbli), in the Gauḍa's field.

śrī-Mūla-sangha Dēśiya-gaṇa Pustaka-gachchha Koṇḍakund-ānvaya Ingulēśvarada-baḷiya . . . . Śubhachandra-dēvara priyāgra-śishyarum-appa Prabhāchandra-dēvara nisidhi Tāraṇa-saṁvatsara Chaitra-śudha-panchamī Śukravārad-andu muktar ādaru.

57

On a stone at Yaḍūr (Yaḍava-nāḍ), in the Suggidēva temple.

svasti Sakha-varsha 1017 neya Yuva-saṁvatsarada Srāvaṇa-māsada sudi-bidige Ādivārad-aṁdu śrīmanu-mahā-maṇḍaḷēsvara Tripurādhīsvara Balīndra-kuḷa-kamaḷa-mārttaṇḍa Chaturmukha-gaṇḍa saraṇāgata-vajra-paṁjara vairi-gaja-kēsari baliyara-Bhīma saṁgrāma-Rāma Malepara-naṁdana-vanaṁ saṁstutya-vandi-janaṁ para-maṇḍaḷa-sūṟekāṟa ayyan-aṁkakāṟa Śiva-pāda-sēkharaṁ śatya-ratnākaraṁ ripu-hṛideya-karkkasaṁ aras-aṁka-rakkasan anēka-nāmāvaḷī-mukhyan-appa Duddharasaṁ Hiṭṭeyarasaṁga[ṁ] Juṁjala-Dēvigaṁ puṭṭi atuḷa-baḷa-parākraman-āgi nava-yauvan-ārūḍhanuṁ vijaya-Lakshmī-kāntanum-āgi Maleyaṁ pratipāḷisi ripugaḷam bedaṟi beṁkoṇḍu kōṭegaḷaṁ nirddhāṭisi vīrāvatāranuṁ Kaliyug[āṁ] (*on the back*) tekaṁ Saṁhatha-nāḍumaṁ Pākuvāḍiyuṁ modal āgi pratipāḷisiy āḻdu padinaydu-kudureyu ayvattu-leṁkaruṁ innūṟ-ayvattu-ekkaṭigaruṁ nāluvatt-aydu kuḷaputtigeg-āyad-āḷum anēka-praje-parivāra-baṁdhu-varggamuṁ taḷa-varggamuṁ kula-strī-Chikala-Dēviyuṁ besakeyye su . . jalideyiṁ Rāja . . keṟeyaṁ kaṭṭisi . . . . yaman ettisi diva . . . ru Brāhmaṇargge chatramaṁ nilisi toṟe-gaḻdeya māḍisi anēka-dhammama beḷagi Śiva-lōka-prāptan āgal sahōdaraṁ Jūjarasaṁ snēhadiṁ parōksha-vineyaṁ geydu vīra-sāsanamaṁ bareyisidaṁ Moḷateya Duddhamalla sandhi-vigrahi sēnabōva - Rājimayyana magaṁ Bamma-dēvan ī intu Duddharasaṁ māḍisida toṟe-gaḻdeyaṁ māṟikoṇḍavaṁ Bāṇarāsiyalu hasuvuṁ hāruvanaṁ koṁda maṁgaḷa mahā śrī śrī||

58

At Kalakandūr (same nāḍ), on the pedestal of Brahma-dēva.

Raudri-saṁvatsarada Jēshṭa-suda-panchamī Ādivārad-andu Handra . . dūra Pāri . . ru bije māḍisida śrī-Māṇika-dēvaru maṁgaḷa mahā śrī śrī.

59

On a stone at Chauḍlu (same nāḍ), on the path near the Suggi temple.

svasti śrīmanu-mahā-manḍalēśvara . . . . Nārāyaṇa . . . . Harihara-Dēva . . . . āḷutt-ire Hēviḷaṁbi-saṁvatsarada Māgha-māsa pūrva-paksha panchamī Aśvinī-nakshatra Guruvārad-andu Harihara. . . . Kundūringe pūrvvadali heṇṇinge saluva svāste mariyādiya koṭṭa kramav ent endaḍe heṇṇinge heṇṇu-makkaḷinge tottina makkaḷinge saluvudu Chavaḍa . . . . māneyoḷu Māra-janakā . . Molateya . . . . . . Pārisa. . . . . . Kundūra ṭhāvamāneyoḷu Māchi . . kāriyana gaha| Mācha-jīyana kaṇan aigaṇaleya Kāmanapaḻḻi gundada Ājaṇa Beṇacha Heggaḍehaḷḷiya Māḍaṇa Abiyūra Mali-gauḍa yī gauḍugalu mukhyavāgi yint ī-nāḍu-nakharake chandrādityar-uḷḷannabara koṭṭa śāsana-mari yādiya bareda sēnabōva Jinayya kalla hoyda Malōja. . .

No. 57.—Vira-Sasana from Yadur, A.D. 1095.

A. B.

H. KRISHNA SASTRI

GOVT. PHOTOZINCO OFFICE, POONA.

SCALE ONE-FIFTH.

60

On a stone at Hārōhaḷḷi (same nāḍ), in the Gauḍa's paddy field.

Teyalayya Jūbu kālam kaḷchi . . . . . rvvadim Baraṟiya Eṟeyaru . . . sange biṭṭ agrahāra| mattaṃ Chaṭṭayyam Dhāraka-balaha Koṅgaṇivarmmaṃ kālam kaḷchi koṭṭaṃ . . biṭṭa Ponna maṇṇange vaṭṭadiṃ . . . .

61

On a vīrakal at Garagandūr (Gaḍi-nāḍ), in the path to Śāntavīramma's house.

. . . . svasti śrīmanu mahā-maṇḍalēśvara Tribhuvanamalla Vīra . . . . matu Changāḷva . . . mahā-ma . . ditya dēvage . . . . .

62

On a stone at Hārangi (same nāḍ), on the north-east, in the bamboo forest of the Chikka maṭha.

svasti samasta-praśasti-sahita śrīmat Shaṇmēdō-Kōkam Kaliyuga-Brahma ēṟida.

63

On a stone at Tākeri (same nāḍ) in Balagai-Īrana's paddy field.

Sarvadhāri-saṃvatsara Chaitra ba 5 Ā lu Gauḷi-Nanjarappaya-aṇanavarū Hānagala Linge-gauḍarige bā . . ṭṭa gauḍike.

64

On a stone at Kājūru (Bilaha hōbli), lying north of the Basavana guḍi.

śrīmatu Biḷu-gauḍa Aṇaba-gauḍa Bayirukanigu Yirāma Nāgajyaya Kempaṇa nālvarige koṭṭa grāma.

65

On a stone at Siraha (same hōbli), in front of the Rāmēśvara temple.

śrī Jaya-saṁvatsarada Phālguṇa-suddha pavurnami Brihavāradali Hoysaṇa bhujabala śrī-Vīra-Ballāḷa-Dēvarasaru prithvī-rājyaṃ geyutt-iddalli Biluhu-nāḍa paḍa . . Śiriyūra Kasapa . .-gavuḍagaḷa Bīrayana maga Māyaṇṇange Śirivurada Mallikārjuna-dēvara ashṭa-bhōga-tējas-svāmya nidhi-nikshēpa-jala-pāshāṇa-āgāmi-mukhyavāgi Māyaṇṇange kāluga berasāgi dhāreya yeṟadu koṭa sāsana yidanu āru aḷihidaḍe Gangeya taḍiyali kavileya konda dōshadali hōharu mangaḷa mahā śrī śrī śrī— . Maṟe-vokkara-kāvaru śrī.

66

On a stone at Mūdarahaḷḷi (same hōbli), under the tamarind tree at the village entrance.

śubham astu

śrīmat-parama-haṁsānām parivrājaka-sattamaṃ|
Kaivalyākhya mahā-yōgim sadā jnānaika-tatparaṃ|
Bēlūru-Krishṇa-bhūpas tu āhūya ya . .-kuñjaraṃ|
Mūdravaḷḷī cha grāmas tu dattaṃ Krishṇārppaṇaṃ śubhaṁ||

kimarthaṁ dattam ity uktē (*stops here*).

67

On a stone at Hulakōḍu (Koḍli hōbli), at the Kannēśvara temple, east of the village.

Vikāri-saṁvatsarada Phālguṇa-śudha 5 Vaḍavāra-di Trinamēra-Dēvaṇṇanavaru Ghaṭada-keḷage hōgi . . li Hulukōḍa-Chikkaṇṇaya Bomma-gauḍana bīragallu Kalina-Bōja gaḍadu . . . . Dēmmayyam Chikkaṇṇaya . . . ge . . .

68

On a stone at Heggaḍahaḷḷi (Kaṇime hōbli), near the Basava temple.

śrī svasti śrī-vijayābhyudaya-Śālivāhana-śakada varusha 1652 neya Sādhāraṇa-saṁvatsarada Māgha-ba 2 Bhārgavāradallu Kuḍumada Mañjunātha-svāmiyavara sannidhiyallu naḍava dēvatā-śēve-bagye Hāvēri-Vīrap-oḍēru sarvamānya-saṅkētavāgi biṭṭa Heggaḍahaḷḷi Sirangāḷa . . ubhaya-gaḍige saluva upagrāma 29 nu śilā sthāpita māḍisi biṭṭu koṭṭadu śrī.

69

On another stone at the same place.

śrī-Kuḍumada Mañjunātha-svāmiyavara sankēta śrī (*ḍamaruga* and *triśūla*).

70

On a third stone at the same place.

svasti samasta-bhuvanāśrayaṁ śrī-pṛithvī-vallabhaṃ mahārājādhirāja paramēśvaraṁ parama-bhaṭṭāraka Yādava-kulāmbara-dyumaṇi samyaktva-chūḍāmaṇi Malerāja-rāja Mala paroḷu gaṇḍa gaṇḍa-bhēruṇḍa kadana-prachaṇḍan asahāya-śūra ēkānga-vīra Śanivāra-siddhi giridurgga-malla Magara-Rāya . . ranaya . . . . . gaṇḍa śrī-Vīra-Hoyisaṇa . . . .

71

On a stone at Sirangāla (same hōbli), in the field of the Basava temple.

svasti śrī Sirivangalada Mācha-gāvuṇḍaṁ Siriyama-tandi vīra[gallu] Mācha-goṇḍana maga Kāva-goṇḍa kalla niṟisidaṃ Mariyōja besada mangalaṃ.

72

On a stone at Bāḷāji (in Beṭṭiyattu-nāḍ, Kiggaṭnāḍ tāluq).

Illegible, owing to the letters being nicked all over.

73

On the wall of a temple at Bāḷele (in Hatgaṭ-nāḍ, same tāluq).

Paḍubara jōgi silā golā
Paḍuva rāya silā
Paḍubara jōgi namaḥ||

74

On a stone called Kirakaṇabailu-gālikallu, near Hardūr (in Mercāra tāluq).

svasti śrī Eṟeyapana . . dāhanu raṇāntya vaḷ eṇṇuvaḷu sattu paḍeda kalnāḍuṁ idan aḻivaṁge kavileyuṁ Bāṇarasiyuṁ aḻida pātakaṁ ondu bāḻu parihāraṁ maṁgaḷa mahā śrī.

75

On a stone in Mudduvīraṇa Puṭṭamma's coffee garden in Uluguli (in the same tāluq).

svasti śrīmanu mahā-maṇḍalēsvara Chaüṭu-vibhāḍa chhaladanka-Rāma Satyarāya-saṁvaraṇa tira-vajra-Rudira maṟe-vokkasa-kāva śrīmad-Vīra-Munivarāditya Gōkula-dēvarasaru | Raktākshi-saṁvatsarada Kanyā-māsad andu Tengu-nāḍakam Yaḷaghaḷeya tuṟu iḍidelli māsala-baṇṭa Mēlāḷiya marulakāra-yōśiyāḷu Bidaḍe garuḍu vaśa tallibiṭṭu dāṇige kāḷege sandudu mukk-oḍave.

TRANSLATIONS

1

Date 466 A.D.

Be it well. Success through the adorable Padmanābha, resembling (in colour) the cloudless sky.

A sun illumining the clear firmament of the Jāhnavī (or Ganga) kula, possessed of strength and valour from the great pillar of stone dividing with a single stroke of his sword, adorned with the ornament of a wound received in cutting down the hosts of his cruel enemies, of the Kaṇvāyana gōtra, was śrīmān Koṅgaṇi-mahādhirāja.

His son, inheriting the qualities of his father, possessing a character for learning and modesty, having obtained the honours of the kingdom only for the sake of the good government of his subjects, a touchstone for (testing) gold the learned and poets, skilled among those who expound and practise the science of politics, author of a commentary on the *Dattaka-sūtra*[1], was śrīmān Mādhava-mahādhirāja.

His son, uniting the qualities of his father and grandfather, having entered into war with many elephants (so that) his fame had tasted the waters of the four oceans, was śrīmad Harivarmma-mahādhirāja.

His son, devoted to the worship of the twice-born, gurus, and gods, not leaving the feet of Nārāyaṇa, was śrīmad Vishṇugōpa-mahādhirāja.

His son, whose head was purified by the pollen from the lotuses the feet of Triyambhaka, having by personal strength and valour purchased his kingdom, daily eager to extricate the ox of merit from the thick mire of the Kali-yuga in which it had sunk, was śrīmān Mādhava-mahādhirāja.

His son, the beloved sister's son of Kṛishṇavarmma-mahādhirāja,—who was the sun in the firmament of the Kadamba-kula,—his mind illumined with the increase of learning and modesty, of indomitable bravery, reckoned the first among the learned, was śrīmān Koṅgaṇi-mahādhirāja, named Avinīta.

Of whose gift to Chandaṇandi-bhaṭāra, the disciple of Guṇaṇandi-bhaṭāra, who was the disciple of Jayaṇandi-bhaṭāra, who was the disciple of Śīlabhadra-bhaṭāra, who was the disciple of Abha[ya]ṇandi-bhaṭāra, who was the disciple of Guṇachandra-bhaṭāra, of the Dēsiga-gaṇa and Koṇḍakundānvaya, in the year eighty-eight beyond three hundred, the month Māgha, Monday, the Svati-nakshatra, the fifth day of the bright fortnight,—the minster (*mantri*) of Akālavarsha-Pṛithuvī-Vallabha—having obtained (it) by grant from Avinīta-mahādhirāja—presented the charming (village) named Badaṇeguppe, (situated) within the Eḍenāḍu Seventy of the Pūnāḍu Six Thousand, to the Śrīvijaya Jina temple of Taḷavana-nagara, together with twelve *kaṇḍuga* in each of the six dependent hamlets, the *ambali-maṇṇu*, the *tala-vitti* in Taḷavana-pura, twelve *kaṇḍuga* in Pogarigeḷe, and twelve *kaṇḍuga* according to the accepted royal measure in Pirikeṟe.

---

[1] Dattaka was an early poet, of perhaps the 1st century, who, induced by the dancing girls of Pāṭalīputra, wrote a work on one section of the *Kāma-sūtra* (See *JRAS.* 1911, p. 183). In Kannaḍa his name appears as Jattaka. Thus the Hoysaḷa prince Eṟeyanga is styled in an inscription (Ak 102a) *abalā-Jattakan*, or a Jattaka to the weaker sex.

Boundaries of the village of Badaṇeguppe[1] : east, the red rock, Gajasele, the *śakti* post at the tri-junction of Karivaḷḷi, Koṭṭagara and Badaṇeguppe, and so coming to the Kāgaṇi pond on the south-east ; again south, the milk hedge, the *balkuṇi* tree ; again facing west, the row of medical plants, then the pond at the tri-junction of Badaṇeguppe, Koṭṭagara and Muḻtagi, Chaṇḍigāla ; thence to the clearing-nut tree at the south-west ; again west, the *peḻd-uḻdil* tree, the banyan tree called Śāntaṟa, thence the bed of the stream ; facing north, the row of medical plants, the pond of the rose-apple, thence to the sacred tamarind tree at the north-west ; again the *neggila* clump at the tri-junction of Badaṇeguppe, Muḻtagi, Koḷeyanūr, and Dāsanūr, the long ? sacrificial circle, thence the hill which protects the north of the village of Gajasele, descending to the big rock ; again facing east, the row of medical plants, then the *kaḍapaḻtigāla* banyan tree ; again north-east, the pond at the tri-junction of Badaṇeguppe, Dāsanūr and Poḻma, the tamarind tree at the paddy fields by the sluice, and so to the level red mound which joins the eastern boundary.

Witnesses thereto :—Pērbbakkavāṇa, the man who is a friend in all things to the Ganga royal family ; Maṟugareya Sendrika, Ganjenāḍ Nirggunda Maṇiyugureya, Nandyāla Simbālādapa, servants.

Country witnesses :—Tagaḍūr Kuḷugōvar, Gaṇiganūr Tagaḍar, Ālgoḍate Nandakar, Ummatūr Beḷḷurar and Aḷageyar, Badaṇeguppe Jhaṃsanda-Beḷḷurar and Perggiviyar.

Whoso takes away land presented by himself or by another is born a worm in ordure for sixty thousand years. The earth has been enjoyed by many kings and Saka kings[2] ; whosesoever at any time is the land, his at that time is the fruit. The property of the gods is a dreadful poison ; call not poison poison, poison kills a single person, but a gift to the gods (if seized) destroys sons and grandsons. Merit is a common bridge for kings, this do ye support from age to age, O kings,—thus does Rāmabhadra beseech the kings who come after him.

Visvakarmma's writing.

2

Date 888 *A.D.*

Prosperity to the Jina-śāsana.

Of the years expired since the time of the Saka king, the eight hundred and ninth year being current,—

Be it well. Satyavākya-Konguṇivarmma-dharmma-mahārājādhirāja, boon lord of Kovaḷāla-pura, lord of Nandagiri, in the eighteenth year of śrīmat-Permmanaḍi's anointing to the kingdom, on the auspicious fifth day of the month Phālguṇa, to Śivaṇandi-siddhānta-bhaṭāra's disciple Sarvvaṇandi-dēva, for the Satyavākya Jina temple of the Penne kaḍanga, Permmanaḍi gave the twelve hamlets of Biḷiūr in Peddoṟegare, free of entry from all feet.[3]

They of the Ninety-six Thousand, the five tributary chiefs, the seventy of Beddoṟegare, and the eight householders are witnesses to this.

---

[1] Badaṇeguppe still exists under the same name, and is in the north of the Chāmrājnagar tāluq of Mysore. Of the other villages mentioned in the boundaries and witnesses,—Dāsanūr is in Nanjangūd tāluq, Poḻma. now called Homma (see Ch 63) and Ummatūr are in Chāmrājnagar tāluq, Tagaḍūr is in Nanjagūḍ tāluq, Ganiganūr in Yelandūr, and Nandyāla is named in Yl 27.

[2] Generally the phrase is 'Sagara and others.'

[3] Or, perhaps. 'free of all imposts.'

They of the Male Thousand, the Five Hundred, and the five ? garland-makers are guardians of this.

Whoso destroys this destroys Bāraṇāsi, a thousand Brāhmans and a thousand tawny cows, and is guilty of the five great sins.

Sedōja's writing.

Biḷiūr will bring eighty gadyāṇas of gold and eight hundred (measures) of paddy.

3

Date about 890 *A.D.*

Be it well. Satyavākya-Koṅguṇivarmma-dharmma-mahārājādhirāja, boon lord of Kuvaḷāla-pura, lord of Nandagiri, śrīmat-Permmanaḍi:—when on Jeḍala Eṟeyaṅga-gāvuṇḍa's son he bound the *Permmāḍi-vattaṁ*, the order for the estate granted was as follows:—the fixed land-rent forty gadyāṇas of gold, and of seed paddy one hundred (measures) of paddy; thus for all time was a decree granted.

Būvayya's letters.

Prosperity. Kalnāḍ for Ereyaṁga. Great good fortune.

4

Date 978 *A.D.*

Be it well. Of the hundreds of years expired since the time of the Saka king, the 899th, the year Īsvara being current:—

Be it well. Satyavākya-Koṅgiṇivarmma-dharmma-mahārājādhirāja, boon lord of Kōḷāḷa-pura, lord of Nandagiri, śrīmat-Rāchamalla-Permmanaḍi, within that year, on the Nandīśvara *talpa* day of the bright fortnight of Phālguṇa,—

Be it well. When the valiant one adorned with a powerful right arm—the abode of his sword—vigorous in seizing the priceless pearls scattered from the frontal globes of the troops of proud elephants of all his enemies, his elder brother's warrior, a friend of the poor, śrīmat-Rakkasa was ruling Beḍḍoṟegare;—

Prosperity to the Jina-śāsana. A resident of śrī-Beḷgoḷa, śrīmat-Anantavīryyayya, the beloved disciple of śrī-Goṇasēna-paṇḍita-bhaṭṭāraka, who was the beloved disciple of śrī-Bīrasēna-siddhānta-dēva, acquired Peggadūr and the new trench, secure against obstruction.

Witnesses to it:—They of the Ninety-six Thousand, the five tributary chiefs, the Peddoṟegare seventy, and the eight householders.

Guardians of this:—The four Malepar (or hill chiefs), the Five Hundred, and the five ? garland-makers.

Whoso destroys Śrīpurusha[1]-mahārāja's gift destroys Bāṇarāsi, a thousand Brāhmans and a thousand tawny cows, and is guilty of the five great sins. Whoso protects this acquires great merit.

Chandaṇandiyayya's writing. Grant of the Perggadūr basadi.

---

[1] So apparently in the latest impression; but in those given in my first edition and in *Ind. Ant.* vi, 102, it was clearly *Śrīpurada*. It is doubtful if Śrīpurusha would have been read unless for this name being now familiar. It looks more like Śrīṛ-parama-mahārāja.

5

Date 1000 *A.D.*

Be it well. Fortune.

In the Śaka year 921, the year Śārvvari, the full moon day of the month Phālguna, Uttara-Bhādrapada, Sunday,—Gaṇagūr Biha-gāmuṇḍa's son Hañcha[da]rma-seṭṭi, having served with Kuṇindora and finished his time,—made (or established) Kālūr, and by the power of his arm having acquired Bōkanahaḷḷi in Muḷḷūr-nāḍ, Gorahaḷḷi of Hakādivāḍi, and Kūḍalūr of . . . . -nāḍ ;—first bathing away the guilt, and worshipping Rāmēśvara,—together with ? nine fowler's (front) yards, gave for *dharma* a *khaṇḍuga* of land.

Whoso destroys this *dharma* incurs the guilt of destroying tawny cows.

6

Date 1255 *A.D.*

Be it well. In the victorious increasing Śaka year 1177, the year Rākshasa (the month) Vaiśākha, the 11th day of the bright fortnight ; in the time (of the auspicious reign) of śrīmat-pratāpa-chakravarti Hoysaṇa bhujabala śrī-Vīra-Nārasimha-Rāya :—Sōmaiya, the son of Bīra-gavuḍa of Kahigōḍu, shouting—, Bumbiya-nāyaka himself, taking with him his servants Bīmaiya and Sōmaṇṇa, fighting with him, he fell. In order that Sōmaiya may attain to the world of gods, Māri-gavuḍa who was born with him, and Māyiga, the son of that Sōme-gavuḍa, have prepared and raised this *bīragal*. Great prosperity. Fortune.

7

Date 1285 *A.D.*

Be it well. In the victorious increasing Śaka year 1208, the year Pārthiva, (the month) Vaiśākha, the 12th day of the bright fortnight ; in the time of the increasing reign of śrīmat-pratāpa-chakravarti Hoysaṇa bhujabala śrī-Vīra-Nārasimha-Dēvarasa :—Māra-Tamma of Kaihigōḍu, joining fight with his boasting bitter enemies, fell in the fight.

In order that Māra-Tamma may attain to the world of gods, his younger brother Maleya-nāyaka, and his sons Sōmaṇṇa . . . . this *vīragal*.

Great prosperity. Fortune.

8

Date about 1371 *A.D.*

Be it well. Fortune.—Doing obeisance to Vināyaka the all-learned guru, and to the goddess Sarasvatī,-- so far as I am able an auspicious śāsana will I make [1].

Be it well. Fortune.--The disciple of Avidyāmṛityu-bhaṭṭāraka of the auspicious Purushōttama-parshad, Bōdharūpa-Bhagavar, had this stone śāsana made for (the god) Mahādēva of Pālayūr. That whoso among the Śrīvaishṇavas of the Eighteen countries, the Vaḷañjiyar (merchants) of the Eighteen countries, the arm-bearing Thousands of the Eighteen countries, or the Brāhmaṇas of the Eighteen nāḍus, seeing it, will dutifully maintain it, is this stone śāsana set up.

Whoso does not pay as laid down by the *amachchān* after examination of the temple and the requirements of the worship, incurs the penalty of the man who murders his own father, or takes to wife his own mother, or murders the king of the very nāḍu in which he

---

[1] The translations of the vernacular portions of this inscription and the next are in parts tentative.

was born, or cuts off the nose of him who having bound on the right side seizes on the left, or marries a woman within the prohibited degrees of relationship.

The Valañjiyar of the Eighteen countries and others . . . will have the daily expenses and other provisions noted in the treasury accounts of the temple read out once a year, and see that each item mentioned therein which has been omitted to be carried out is properly conducted as directed.

9

Date about 1371 *A.D.*

Be it well. Fortune.—Doing obeisance to the guru by devotion,—Bṛihaspati (Jupiter) being in conjunction with Kanyā (Virgo), in the great month named Vṛiśchika (Scorpio), on the day following Bṛihaspati's (that is on Friday),—a universal sāsana, a sāsana for the guru, who is a form of joy, will I, Bōdharūpa, make even at the holy Bhagaṇḍāśrama also.

When Mēlpuṇḍi-Kunniyarasa was ruling the nāḍu,—Bōdharūpa-Bhagavar-arasu of the auspicious Purushōttama-parshad, with others, had a copper plate engraved. Whoever stops for a day the daily expenses laid down in the plate, whether male or female, including Kunniyarasa (himself), violates the order of the king ruling this nāḍu. The penalty for such violation for one day is 12 *kāṇam* and twice the offerings for the god; and when continued for a whole week, 12 *kaḻañju* of gold of 7 touches to the king.

There will be 17 perpetual lamps. The quantity of rice to be supplied by the *poduvāḷ* for daily offerings, etc., is 26 *nāḻi*. For the high oblation there will be 2 *nāḻi*, and for flowers 4 *nāḻi*. There will also be supplied daily 32 garlands of flowers and 6 lamps in the month of Vṛiśchika.

Whoso does not pay as laid down by the *amachchān* after examination of the temple and the requirements of the worship, shall be looked upon as a traitor conspiring to murder the king of the very nāḍu in which he was born, and incurs the penalty of the man who cuts off the nose of him who having bound on the right side seizes on the left, and of one who takes to wife a woman within the prohibited degrees of relationship. Should the king be indifferent towards a man who does not pay the above fine, even after seeing and hearing him, the people of his nāḍu will curse him. . . . .

The people have to perform five items of service, of which the Mahābhārata is one. If even a single item of the expenses is stopped, the penalty shall be $2\frac{1}{2}$ *kāṇam* for every day.

May the arm-bearing Thousands of the Eighteen countries and the Valañjiyar protect the Vagaṇḍa temple. May the ascetics and the king ? prosper.

Whatever is omitted here may be found in the treasury register and the copper plate.

Pakaṇḍala-āyāri's writing.

10

Date 1544 *A.D.*

Obeisance to śrī-Sāntinātha. Be it free from obstruction. Be it fortunate.

May it prevail, the auspicious supreme profound syād-vāda, a fruit-bearing token, the doctrine of the lord of the three worlds, the Jina doctrine.

Be it well. Of the śrī-Mūla-sangha, Dēśi-gaṇa, Pustaka-gachcha, Kuṇḍakund-ānvaya, and Ingulēśvara circle, a bee intoxicated from the lotus feet of Gummaṭa-Jinēśvara, the lord of the auspicious Beḷuguḷa-pura, promoter of the religious merit of the time, (was) Dharmāchārya, whose titles were as follows :—nourishing the groups of lotuses the learned, he at the same time drove away the darkness from the minds of evil-speakers proud as the tortoise that bears up the earth, upholding the character of a Digambara shining ornament, he ever protected the ruddy goose the Bhavyas (or Jains),—thus was the sun Pandita-dēva ever distinguished with the rays his gentle speech.

Be it well. The auspicious Āchārya of the circle of the royal rājagurus, the great lord of powerful orators, a Brahmā of royal speakers, emperor of all the learned, preserver of the life of Ballāla-Rāya,—distinguished with these and many other titles, was śrīmach-Chāru kīrtti-Paṇḍita-dēva; the disciple of whose disciple's disciple was śrīmad-Abhinava-Chāru kīrtti-Paṇḍita-dēva; whose beloved disciple, his elder brother's disciple, śrīmach-Chāru kīrtti–Paṇḍita-dēva's fellow-student, śrīmach-Chhāntikīrtti-dēva[1], in the Śaka year 1466 expired, the year Krōdhi being current, on the 15th of the bright fortnight of Kārtika, caused to be written a stone inscription as follows :—

His guru śrīmad-Abhinava-Chārukīrtti-Paṇḍita-dēva,—when, for the promotion of religious merit in the Kali age, Śanti-tīrthēśvara and Anantanātha-svāmi themselves came and manifested themselves from the Suvarṇāvatī river in the Śaka year 1453, the year Vikṛitu, in Chaitra,—having paid a visit to the basadi of Śāntinātha-svāmi who dwells on the summit of Anjanagiri, and made on the crest of the hill a basadi of wood—in the year Khara, in the month Chaitra, he caused it to be consecrated by the hand of his own younger brother Konasanaguḍḍa Śāntōpādhyāya, and left instructions for the erection of a stone basadi.

After that, in the following year Krōdhi, the 15th of the bright fortnight of Kārtika, the stone work done to the foundation and the *hāladhāres* were as follows :—to all the *halaru* of Bemmatti Būtanhaḷḷi and Maganakeṟe belonging to Nanjarāyapaṭṭaṇa, paid for stone work ga 200 honnu; to Ādi-Śrī-Avvagaḷ of Hanasoge[2] for having the stone work of the inner shrine done by Bhujabali-Śrī-Avvagaḷ of Ammana-Hosahaḷḷi, paid ga 30 honnu; to his guru śrīmach-Chārukīrtti-Paṇḍita-dēva for two sets of three *hāladhāre*, and for a curtain for the centre door at the one time of the offering, paid ga 50; and for a curtain at the distribution of food ga ? 50.

In the year Śubhakṛitu, the 15th of the bright fortnight of Phālguna, all the *halaru*, the Kannaḍiga *halaru* and Nānādēśi *halaru* of Bidire and Sītāḷamaḷige for (the god) Śāntīś vara of Anjanagiri made a *dharma* and had it written in their dharma śāsana, saying the 81 paṇa due for the footpath that we have built, we will give for distribution of food. Whoso fail in this dharma are guilty of murdering cows and Brāhmans.

In the Śaka year 1465, the year Śubhakṛitu, the 13th of the bright fortnight of Chaitra, Wednesday, the Vṛishabha-lagna, the family consecration was performed of the three sets of *dēhāragaḷu*[3]. For a dānaśāle the price of the Haḷḷivayalu paddy field, 70 ga, and the sum given to the *kōlāyaru* for work at the new paddy field, 50 ga, both together an outlay of 120 ga, was received from śrimach-Chārukīrtti-Paṇḍita-deva's disciples Ādi-Śrī-Avvagaḷ of Hanasoge and Bhujabali-Śrī-Avvagaḷ, 24 ga; Basavapaṭṇa Anantamati-Avagal paid through Nēmi-Śrī-Avvagaḷ 24 ga; Muddi-seṭṭi's Vijayi paid through Śrī-Avvagaḷ 10 ga; through Muluganahaḷḷi Ādyakka was paid 12 ga; from Haruva-seṭṭi and Vijeyaṇa-seṭṭi, 30 ga; from Kaṇṇanūr Dēvaramma-seṭṭi, 12 ga; . . . .

Three usual imprecatory verses.

That the dharma here made may endure as long as sun and moon has it been engraved in a śāsana. Great good fortune. Śrī, Śrī.

---

[1] *i.e.* śrīmat Śāntikīrtti-dēva.

[2] It is a matter of special interest to note the existence of this sisterhood of Jain holy women mentioned in this inscription—Ādi-Śrī-Avvagaḷ, Bhujabali-Śrī-Avvagaḷ and so on, each probably attached to some temple. They may have been widows who had adopted a religious life.

[3] ? Bodyguards.

11

Date 1695 *A.D.*

Be it prosperous.

Adored be Śambhu, beauteous with the chāmara-like crescent moon kissing his lofty head ; the original foundation-pillar of the city of the three worlds.

I praise the right tusk of the sportive Boar,—may it protect us,—on which the Earth, uplifted by it, was like a spot.

Be it well. In the year 1615 of the victorious increasing Śālivāhana era, the year named Śrīmukha, the 12th of the bright fortnight of Pushya, Kṛishṇappa-Nāyaka, the son of Vēnkaṭādri-Nāyaka and grandson of Kṛishṇappa-Nāyaka of Bēlūr, of the Kāśyapa-gōtra and Āpastamba-sūtra, caused to be written and given to Yōgapaiya, the son of Puṭṭarasaiya and grandson of Subrahmaṇya-dēva, of the Vaśishṭa-gōtra, Āsvalāyana-sūtra, and Rik-śākha, a deed of gift of a village as follows :—Within the Bēlūr country, which formerly the rājādhirāja rāja-paramēśvara-śrī-vīra-pratāpa śrī-vīra-Kṛishṇa-Rāya-Dēva-mahārāya bestowed on our great-great-grandfather, a Gōvinda to the ocean, perfumed with camphor, in war a Bhīma, boon lord of Maṇināgapura, obtainer of a powerful kingdom, Yara-Kṛishṇappa-Nāyakaraiya—in the Nirugunda-stala of Tungi-nāḍ in Arakalgōḍ, the village of Kaṭṭepura—situated east of Koṇiganahaḷḷi, west of the land to the south of the Hēmāvatī river, and north of Niluvāgilu,—together with Hirumanahaḷḷi,—to the east of Ippugaḷale.

We, Kṛishṇappa-Nāyaka (descent, as above, repeated) to Yōgapaiya (descent, as above, repeated) having given the village of Kaṭṭepura, together with Hirumanahaḷḷi, in the said tithi, at the auspicious time of the Makara-sankramana, with presentation of a coin and pouring of water, that, acquiring the eight rights of full possession belonging to this village, namely, present profit, future profit, hidden treasure, underground stores, springs, minerals, actualities and possibilities, you, your offspring and descendants, as long as sun and moon endure, with power of gift, exchange or sale, may continue to enjoy them in comfort, Kṛishṇappa-Nāyaka, the son of Vēnkaṭādri-Nāyaka and grandson of Kṛishṇappa-Nāyaka, of the Kāśyapa-gōtra and Āpastamba-sūtra, to Yōgapaiya, the son of Puṭṭarasaiya and grandson of Subrahmaṇya-dēva, of the Vaśishṭha-gōtra, Āsvalāyana-sūtra and Ṛik-śākha, have caused this deed to be written and given.

The just witnesses to this :—Sun and moon, wind and fire, sky, earth and water, heart and mind, day and night, morning and evening,—these know the deeds of a righteous man.

Of giving or protecting a gift, than giving, protecting a gift is better ; by giving, svarga is obtained ; by protecting a gift, the eternal state. Than giving oneself, to protect another's gift is twice as meritorious ; by taking away another's gift one's own gift becomes fruitless. Land given by oneself is a daughter, that given by one's father is a sister, that given by another is a mother ; therefore land given must not be abandoned. An only sister to all kings in the world, neither to be enjoyed nor taken in marriage, is land given to a Brāhman.

(Signed) Śrī-Kṛishṇa.

12

Date 1782 *A.D.*

Linga-Rājēndra-Vaḍeyar

Vi

Śidhalingappa, deputy (guru) of Koḍagu, caused the repairs to be made in the year Śārvari, the 13th of the bright fortnight of Kārtīka.

The śrīmad-rājādhirāja rāja-paramēśvara prahuḍa-pratāpa apratima-vīra-narapati, seated on the jewelled throne of the Koḍagu samsthāna, ruling the empire of the world; of the Bhāradvāja-gōtra, Āśvalāyana-sūtra and Rikshabhānukādhyāya; of the Vīra-Śaiva religion; Appājēndra-Vaḍeyar's son, Linga-Rājēndra-Vaḍeyar—

Adored be Śambhu, beauteous with the chāmara-like crescent moon kissing his lofty head, the original foundation-pillar of the city of the three worlds.

Be it well—the 4881st[year] of the victorious increasing Kali (era) having expired, the year Vikāri being current, on the 10th of the dark fortnight of Māgha, Wednesday, at 7½ hours of the daylight,—submitted to the will of Śiva (*i.e.* died).

At this time of his becoming subject to Śiva, the moon to the waters of the womb of that Mahārāja (*i.e.* his son), Vīra-Rājēndra-Vaḍeyar, being in his presence, performed the funeral rites,—and, according to his orders, had his tomb made in Mahādēvapura, had a temple built and the god Basavēśvara consecrated above the tomb, and had a maṭha of the Murige sect erected. And, to provide for the worship at all times of the gaṇas and of this god, assigned this Mahādēvapura land, in the year Nala, on the 1st of the bright fortnight of Chaitra, Friday, setting up (boundary) stones, stamped with the linga, to the villages of Chikka-Harade, Jambūru, Bēlūru, and Basavanahaḷḷi,—and caused a deed of the gift to be written and given.

The repairs were begun in the year Śārvari, on the 13th day of the bright fortnight of Kārtika, and completed in the year Śubhakṛitu, on the 10th of the bright fortnight of Vaiśākha, Monday.

13

Date 1796 *A.D.*

At the feet of Niranjana-dēva of the Abbi maṭha, deputy of Śāntavīra-svāmi, the deputy of the Pākōḍu Mahanta-svāmi Mallikārjuna-svāmi, disciple of the Murigi-svāmi.

Adored be Śambhu, beauteous with the chāmara-like crescent moon kissing his lofty head, the original foundation-pillar of the city of the three worlds.

Be it well. In the year 1718 of the victorious increasing Śālivāhana era, the year Nala being current, on the 1st day of the bright fortnight of Chaitra, Friday (8 April 1796),—When, dedicated by the lotus hands of the svāmi of the Sidhapura maṭha, who was follower of the doctrine of those enthroned in the upper cave at Śivaganga and of the Vīra-Śaiva religion; the śrīmad-rājādhirāja rāja-paramēśvara prahuḍa-pratāpa vipratima-vīra-narapati, seated on the jewelled throne of the Koḍagu samsthāna, was ruling the empire of the world;—of the Bhāradvāja-gōtra, Āśvalāyana-sūtra, and Rukshabhānukādhyāya, Appājēndra-Vaḍeyar's grandson, Linga-Rājēndra-Vaḍeyar's son, Vīra-Rājēndra-Vaḍeyar wrote and presented a renewed deed of gift as follows:—

Whereas the two villages which formerly, in the year 1650 of the Śālivāhana era, the year Kīlaka, on the 2nd day of the bright fortnight of Kārttika, Wednesday (23 October 1728), our senior grand-uncle (grandfather's elder brother) Doḍḍa-Vīrappa-Vaḍeyar,—in addition to the two villages Hosaḷḷi and Jigaṭṭaḷḷi which had formerly come to the Abbi-maṭha of Yadava-nād,—when Doḍḍa-Virūpāksha-svāmi paid a visit to Maḍikēri, holding his feet and making petition, in order to obtain merit as long as sun and moon endure, newly presented to the Abbi-maṭha the Bāchaḷḷi village, having a ground-rent of 16 varaha; and these three villages, Hosaḷḷi, Jigaṭṭaḷḷi and Bāchaḷḷi, had been made over to the Abbi maṭha, with the erection of (boundary) stones stamped with the linga, in the presence of the people of the four (boundary) villages.

On this 1st day of the bright fortnight of Chaitra, Friday,—in order that our father and all ancestors may attain to the eternal Śiva-lōka,—we have written a renewed gift of the land on a copper plate and presented it.

And within the four boundaries of these three villages, Hosaḷḷi, Jigaṭṭaḷḷi, and Bāchaḷḷi, which belong to the Abbi maṭha, the eight rights of full possession, namely, hidden treasure, underground stores, springs, timber, minerals, present profit, future profit, actualities and possibilities, etcetera,—the whole of that land, as an offering to Śiva, in order that, performing the worship of the gaṇas and continuing the work of merit as long as sun and moon endure, at the time of Śiva-pūjā blessings may be continually invoked with the hymn of benediction (saying)—

Recollection of former births, dominion of the world, the glory of good fortune, surpassing beauty,
Faith in thee, knowledge, long life, (objects of) desire,—(of these) be thou giver to me, Śankara, from age to age—

have we written and given this renewed gift of land.

Witnesses thereto :—Sun and moon, wind and fire, sky, earth and water, heart (or conscience) and Yama, day and night, and the two twilights ; these know the deeds of a righteous man.

Than making a gift oneself, to protect another's gift is twice as meritorious : by taking away another's gift one's own gift becomes fruitless.

The said grant of land was according to order written on Friday by the private secretary Śambhaiya.

14

Date 1796 *A.D.*

At the feet of Śāntavīra-svāmi, deputy of the Koḍali Mahanta-svāmi, the deputy of Mahā-Murigā-svāmi.

Adored be Sambhu, beauteous with the chāmara-like crescent moon kissing his lofty head, the original foundation-pillar of the city of the three worlds.

Be it well. In the year 1718 of the victorious increasing Śālivāhana era, the year Nala being current, on the 1st day of the bright fortnight of Chaitra, Friday (8 April 1796),—When, dedicated by the lotus hands of the crown svāmi of the Siddapura maṭha, who was follower of the doctrine of those enthroned in the upper cave at Śivaganga, and of the Vīra-Śaiva religion ; the śrīmad-rājādhirāja rāja-paramēśvara prahuḍa-pratāpa apratima-vīra-narapati, seated on the jewelled throne of the Koḍagu samsthāna, was ruling the empire of the world ;—of the Bhāradvāja-gōtra, Āśvalāyana-sūtra, and Rukshabhānukādhyāya,—Appājēndra-Vaḍeyar's grandson, like the moon in raising the waters in the womb of Linga-Rājēndra-Vaḍeyar,—Vīra-Rājēndra-Vaḍeyar, as an offering for Śiva, granted a deed of gift as follows :—

When the svāmi visited this Mahādēvapura maṭha, performing obeisance to him with the eight members and holding his feet, in order to obtain merit as long as sun and moon endure, he wrote and made over *uttār* land as follows :—as an offering for Śiva, to the maṭha 700 bhaṭṭis of paddy, the produce of this land having a bijavari of 17 bhaṭṭis ; and to the maṭha for extra expenses, the ground rent of the villages marked out by the erection of stones with the stamp of the linga and presented, as follows :—from Chikka Harade and Jambūru villages, whose bijavari of 43 bhaṭṭis has a ground rent of 39 varaha, deducting the former grants for pura-varga, dēva-mānya, and bhūta-uttāra, altogether 6½ varaha for bijavari of 6½ bhaṭṭis, the ground rent of the remaining free land, 36½ varaha for bijavari of 36½ bhaṭṭis ; from Bēlūru, belonging to Thenka-nāḍ-mande in Yaḍava-nāḍ, with Guduguru in Basavanahaḷḷi, the two villages having a ground rent of 50 varaha for bijavari of 50 bhaṭṭis, deducting the former grants for pura-varga, dēva-mānya, bhūta-uttāra, and nāyi-maṇṇu, altogether a ground rent of 17½ varaha for 17½ bhaṭṭis, the ground rent of the remaining free land, 32½ varaha for a bijavari of 32½ bhaṭṭis. Total, from the 4 villages, after deducting the former grants, ground rent of free land coming to the maṭha,—69 varaha, and 700 bhaṭṭis of produce.

Having presented this in this tithi, with the erection of stones stamped with the linga, in the presence of the people of the four villages,—with the desire that father and all other ancestors may attain to the eternal Śiva-lōka, there are given, within the four boundaries of these villages marked out by the erection of stones stamped with the linga, the eight rights of full possession, namely, hidden treasure, underground stores, springs, timber, minerals, present profit, future profit, actualities and possibilities, etcetera; and the whole of that land, as an offering to Śiva, in order that performing the worship of the gaṇas, at the time of Śiva-pūjā may be recited the hymn of blessing (saying)—

Recollection of former births, dominion of the world, the glory of good fortune, surpassing beauty,
Faith in thee, knowledge, long life, (objects of) desire,—(of these) be thou giver to me, Śankara, from age to age,—

has been writen and given this grant of land.

Witnesses thereto:—Sun and moon, wind and fire, sky, earth and water, heart (or conscience) and Yama, day and night, and the two twilights; these know the deeds of a righteous man.

Than making a gift oneself, to protect another's gift is twice as meritorious: by taking away another's gift one's own gift becomes fruitless.

Approval to the gift of land in my own hand,

(Signed) śrī-Vi.

15

Date 1808 *A.D.*

Kali expired 4909.

16

Date 1815 *A.D.*

In the year Yuva, the 5th of the bright fortnight of Jēshṭha; the Virakta-maṭha ot Chilaḷa Shāka-svāmi.

17

Date 1820 *A.D.*

Be it well. In the year 1739 of the victorious increasing Śālivāhana era, the year Īśvara, on the 2nd of the dark fortnight of Jēshṭha, Sunday, (1st June 1817), the 1,796,392nd Kali day,—on this auspicious day,—like a pārijāta to the milk ocean the Chandra-vamśa, born in the Bhāradvāja-gōtra, of the Āśvalāyana-sūtra and Rik-śākha, proficient in supporting the Vīra-Śaiva religion, seated on the illustrious jewelled and beautiful throne in the ancient Kshīra-nagara [1] in the auspicious Koḍagu-samsthāna, a sun in unequalled valour and glory, of uninterrupted splendour, of a fame which illuminated all the points of the compass, a Yudhishṭhira in upholding all manner of royal virtues,—the mahārāja-Appāji-Rājēndra's grandson, Linga-Rājēndra-Vaḍeyar's son, śrī-Linga-Rājēndra-Vaḍeyar, reflecting that by the

---

[1] Hālēri.

performance in this world of good deeds must be obtained the perfection of fruit in both this world and the next, and that with that object he should cause to be set up a Śiva-linga as an act ensuring the acquisition of the highest merit, so resolved in his mind,—And on that day, in an auspicious moment, having commenced the erection of a beautiful new Ōṁkārēśvara temple, a lotus ornament to the earth, which with its skilfully designed manṭapas, etcetera, might be called a royal lotus,—from that time to the year Vikrama, the 12th of the bright fortnight of Chaitra, Sunday, (26th March 1820), or 2 years 9 months and 25 days,—on that auspicious 1,797,421st Kali day,—having completed all the preparations for this great wonder, he caused to be set up the fortune-bestowing Śiva-linga named Ōṁkārēśvara, and satisfied his desires;—that is to say, through the power bestowed by the great mercy of the holy Chandraśēkhara, the said divine purpose fulfilling every wish of the mind, the setting up of the Śiva-linga was perfectly accomplished.

Whoso with devotion praise the holy Mahēśvara, to them at all times whatever merit may be obtained will itself become perpetual: which, that it may be known to all people, has this śāsana been written. Be it prosperous.

Yearly, for the gods Ōṁkārēśvara, Kumārēśvara, and śrī-Nandīśvara, to be continued in perpetuity as long as sun and moon endure, for the daily service, for the offering of food, for the perpetual lamp, for the general service, for the five lunar observances, and for the salaried servants, are granted 1,221 one thousand two hundred and twenty-one Kanṭhirāyi varaha; which money, with remission on grain, cloths and other articles, to be granted every year from the palace-divān's office treasury for the support of religion, being appointed to be spent on the services,—it is directed that at the three seasons divine worship be carried on according to the śāstras without intermission, that a daily inquiry be held, and that the accounts and papers of this temple be examined annually.

Such is the decree for the allowance. By order. The Kali year 4922, the year Vikrama, the 22nd of the true Jēshṭha, Monday.

(Signed) śrī-Linga-Rājēndra-Vaḍeyar.

. . . . . .

18

Date 1831 *A.D.*

In the year Khara, on the 1st of the dark fortnight of Kārttika,—Channaiya's guru Rājaiya's younger brother's son Channa, for the worship of incense and lights to the god Mallikārjuṇa,—having made obeisance to Vī(ra-Rājēndra)-Vaḍeyar,—presented as described

Set up at sunrise.

19

Date 1831 *A.D.*

. . . the 1st of the dark fortnight,—the devotional copper-tablet that Vīra-Vaḍeyar set up at the Aigaḷa-maṭha of the [Hālēri] land in (memory of) the courage of Hālēri Mamadaiarasa's ? son.

20

Date 1831 *A.D.*

In the auspicious year named Khara, on the 10th of the bright fortnight of Āsvīja,—to Siddalinga-svāmi of the Yeḍatore-maṭha.

21

Date 1831 *A.D.*

The holy god Gangādhara.

Vīra-Rājēndra-Vaḍeyar.

22

Date 1841 *A.D.*

In the Śālivāhana-śaka year 1763, the year Śārvari, the raiyats of the Kiggaṭṭu ten nāḍs have through their faith repaired the temple of the god Rāmēśvara of Irpi on the Lakshmantīrtha (river).

23

Date 1842 *A.D.*.

Sōmaśēkhara Śiva-yōgīśvara, (spiritually) born from the lotus hands of Śāntavīra-svāmi, deputy of the holy Murigi-svāmi, in the Kali year 4643 expired, the year Sōbhanakṛitu, on the 2nd of the bright fortnight of Kārttika, Monday, under the constellation Rōhini, before 7 o'clock in the morning, erected the *kalaśa* over this throne.

24

Date 1597 *A.D.*

. . . . Be it well. In the year 1519 of the victorious Śālivāhana era, the year Hēvilamba, on the 5th of the bright fortnight of Aśvayūja, Tuesday,—of the . . . . . gōtra, Āśvalāyana-sūtra and Ruk-śākha, Nanjarāyapaṭṭaṇa Śrīkanṭha-Rājaya's son Rudragaṇa made to . . . . . . a grant of land at Gaṇagūr, in order that his father and mother . . . . . . and forefathers might attain to a station in Kailāsa. Whoso destroys the village granted (is guilty of) . . . . his father and mother, and (incurs the anger) of (the ruler) of Nanjarājapaṭṭaṇa . . . . Fortune.

25

Date 1824 *A.D.*

Vi

Maharaja Veer Rajender Wadeer [1]

Be it well. In the year 1743 of the victorious Śālivāhana era (= 1822 A.D.), the year Ishu, on the 11th of the bright fortnight of Pālguna, Sunday, the 1,798,128th Kali day, on this auspicious day,—When, a tree of paradise from the milk ocean the Lunar race, born in the Bhāradvāja-gōtra, of the Āśvalāyana-sūtra and Ṛik-śākhā, fully conversant with the Vīra-Śaiva creed, seated on the beautiful throne resplendent with clustres of jewels in the immaculate Kshīranagara [2], situated in the fortunate Koḍagu samsthāna, eclipsing by the glory of his valour the brightness of the sun, an Ākhaṇḍala (Indra) of unbroken (*akhaṇḍa*) wealth, celebrated with a fame which pervaded all the points of the compass, in possessing all distinguished royal virtues a Yudhishṭhira,—the Mahārāja Linga-Rājēndra-Vaḍeyar's grandson, Linga-Rājēndra-Vaḍeyar's son, śrī-Vīra-Rājēndra-Vaḍeyar, with justice, mercy and rectitude was ruling the empire of the world, at all times devoted to meditation on

---

[1] In English capital letters.

[2] Hālēri.

Mahādēva ;—after some time, the elephants in his country having increased beyond bounds, were causing destruction to the fruits and crops raised by men for their sustenance, killing wayfarers, and doing damage to the houses,—so, when the subjects respectfully petitioned that they were unable to bear these calamities, considering in his mind that it is the duty of a king to put down the evil and uphold the good, he prayed to Gaurīdhava (Śiva) to give him power to remove these troubles, and having gained the help of Sāmba-Śankara's (Śiva's) supreme favour, from that date to the year Tāraṇa (= 1824 A.D.), the 12th of the dark fortnight of Chaitra, Monday,—2 years, 1 month and 25 days,—to the 1,798,913th Kali day,—during those days, going among the herds of rutting elephants ranging in the midst of the forests by means of his painted chariot like a lion, he made good the pronunciation of *gaja* (elephant) in the popular form *aja* (goat).

The number of elephants which by the valour and power of his arm he in various ways brought to an end, and of those which by his orders trained soldiers captured alive with chains, is as follows:—In the year Chitrabhānu (1822 A.D.), on the 10th of the dark fortnight of Āshāḍha, in Nanjarāyapaṭṭaṇa tālōk, elephants killed 6, captured 9; on the 7th of the dark fortnight of Srāvaṇa, in the same tālōk, elephants killed 42, captured 22; on the 5th of the bright fortnight of Adhika Āśvayuja, in the same tālōk and in Uluguli-Mūḍigēri-nāḍ, elephants killed 47, captured 15; on the 11th of the same bright fortnight, in Nanjarāyapaṭṭaṇa tālōk, Horūr-Nūrokkal-nāḍ and Uluguli-Mūḍigēri-nāḍ, elephants killed 34, captured 6; on the 11th of the bright fortnight of Nija Āśvayuja, in Nanjarāyapaṭṭaṇa tālōk, elephants killed 20, captured 6; in the year Svabhānu (1823 A.D.), on the 5th of the bright fortnight of Nija Chaitra, in Koḍagu-Srīrangapaṭṭaṇa, elephants killed 4, captured 18; on the 3rd of the bright fortnight of Vaiśākha, in Beṭṭiyatta-nāḍ and Channanakōṭe, elephants killed 21, captured 41; in the year Tāraṇa (1824 A.D.), on the 12th of the dark fortnight of Chaitra, in Kiggaṭṭu-nāḍ, elephants killed 10, captured 40; on thirty other days, elephants killed 49, captured 24;—altogether, in thirty-eight days, elephants killed by his own hand 233, captured alive by hand by trained soldiers according to order 181;—total of both 414.

In this manner the desires of all being accomplished, astonishment was expressed as follows:—In the forests, herds of elephants, towering like mountains, hid the sun as when the sky is overcast with storm-clouds, and roamed about trumpeting; but with seven-tongued weapons (fire-arms) like thunderbolts he slew them in a moment, while men captured alive stout and lofty rutting elephants as if they were mice,—this was indeed a marvel.

26

Date 1544 *A.D.*

In the year 1466 of the auspicious Śālivāhana era, the year Krōdhi, on the 1st of the bright fortnight of Chaitra,—śrīman mahā-maṇḍalēśvara Changālva-Srīkaṇṭharasu granted to Lingaṇṇ-oḍēr-dēva the land belonging to Bagutanakōṭe, free of all imposts. Whoso destroys this free grant will be in a dreadful hell.

27

Date about 1220 *A.D.*

(Very much effaced).

. . . . Munivarāditya . . . . had Herūr built . . . . Ālapa of Herūr did this and Changāluva had it decorated. Munivarāditya sending for Malala . . . appointed him as *paṭṭaṇa-svāmi* . . . .

28

Date 944 *A.D.*

(The greater part is effaced).

Be it well. In Saka 866, the year Krōdhi, ... ma, cutting off his head, died. His family . . . . . gave . . . . . Whoso destroys this has slain tawny cows on the banks of the Ganges and killed a Brāhman. Būchaga's mother, as a memorial of the death of her son, had this set up. Bavanayya wrote it.

29

Date 1857 *A.D.*

In order to repair and construct anew as a Śivālaya the ancient stone temple of Mahādēva on the Kunda hill in Beṭṭiyattu-nāḍ, where Īśvara appeared,—the Takka-mokastaru of this nāḍ, with all the people, and also the Takka-mokastaru of Kakkēri village in Ammati-nāḍ, having agreed together, began the work in the year 1776 of the Śālivāhana era, (1854 A.D.), the Kali year 4955, the year named Ānanda, on the 18th of the month Tulā, the 15th of the bright fortnight of Kārttika, Thursday, at an auspicious moment, on the expiry of the 1,810,060th Kali day.

And for the restoration of this great (sacred) place, Maneppaṇḍra . . . . . having provided a fund, as an offering to Īśvara,—list of people who rendered service :— Kaṇḍeya-rāvuta . . . . . śānabhāga Brāhmaṇa-Venkapaiya, subhedār Koḍandēra-Mudaiya, and pārupatyagār Maneppaṇḍra-Puchaiya assisted by having . . . . . made. Koḍandēra-Mēdaiya assisted by having the door-posts made. Saṇvaṇḍra-Bōḷaiya, Maṇiṇde-Timmaiya-gavuḍa, and Chinne-gauḍa's (son) Channappa assisted with the god's water-pipe, curtain and stairs. The jahāgīrdār of Kunda-grāma, Hayāt-Khān-sābi, assisted with the Nandīśvara in front.

In this manner all the people united, and by the favour of Śiva completed the work of restoring this Śivālaya in the year named Paingala (1857 A.D.), on the 15th of the bright fortnight of Vaiśākha, Friday, at an auspicious moment.

To those who performed this service . . . will be welfare (*saukhya*) in this world, and salvation (*mukti*) in the next.

30

Date ? about 1050 *A.D.*

. . . . when Koḍangāla . . . son was ruling—Biḻiya-seṭṭi, falling with devotion at the feet of all the yatis, gained this glory of the gods.

Prosperity to the Jina śāsana. The lord of Maduvanga-nāḍ, Kiviriyayya, kept the vow for twelve (days) in the Changala basadi and expired. His sons Bāki and Buki set up this.

31

Date ? about 1050 *A.D.*

Prosperity to the śāsana of the Jinēndras, a destroyer of sin, a sun in dispersing the darkness the doctrines of evil sects.

Be it well. Fortune . . . . . . desiring the other world, benefactress of others, ... without hesitation deciding 'I will obtain *mukti*,' taking leave of her relatives, she gained the tomb,—the wonder of all, Jakkiyabbe. The *mantraki* of

Chandiyabbe-gāvuṇḍi, *śrāvaki* of Kastūri-bhaṭṭāra, Jakkiyabbe performed *sanyasanam* and expired. Her husband, the chief *śrāvaka* Eḍayya. Fortune.

32

Date 1278 *A.D.*

(*Very much effaced all down the middle of the stone.*)

Be it well. Fortune. In the year 1201 of the . . . Śakas [1], the year Bahudhānya, on the . . . of the dark fortnight of Vaiśākha, for the god Mallikārjjuna of Malapanahaḷḷi a grant of lands was made by Hiriya-Vīraṇṇa and Chika-Vīraṇṇa. (Details of the lands. Usual imprecations.)

33

Date ? 1176 *A.D.*

Be it well. When śrīman mahā-maṇḍaḷēśvara Vīra-Chōḷa-Koṅgāḷuva-Dēva was ruling the kingdom of the world:—Tāyi [2]-Padumala-Dēvi, Sōmala-Dēvi, Tōḷūr Duddarasa, Balleya-daṇḍanāyaka, and Haḍiyeṟa Kirikaṇa,—all these being present, in the year Manmatha, the month Kumbha, Sunday, the 10th, he granted in the Muḷḷu-nāḍ Seventy, for the children's children of Aṇṇattamma [3] to raise and receive customs dues as follows :—good ox, free; headman's fee—for each hamlet in Ganahūr, 5 *haṇa*; tribute money—for each hamlet in Ganahūr, 5 *haṇa*; king's tax, and pandal money, free; except the Ganga fixed rent, tax on income and gifts, forced labour, demand, fines for . . . . . . and all such, free.

Whoso speaks of failing in the grant made by Vīra-Chōḷa Koṁgāḷva-Dēva is guilty of slaughtering cows and Brāhmans on the banks of the Ganges, and of Brāhman murder.

In the Seventy, 5 *gula* of *bhatta* will be given for each house to Gangōja and Būchaṇa.

34

Date 1064 *A.D.*

Be it well. Of the hundreds of years elapsed since the time of the Śaka king, the 986th, the year Krōdhi, being current, on the 9th of the dark fortnight of Chaitra in that year, Tuesday, under the Pūrvvā-Bhādrapada nakshatra, at the rise of Mīna (Pisces) :—

Be it well. Having crossed completely over the deep ocean of nectar, the *āgama* which issued from the lotus mouth of the holy Arhad-paramēśvara parama-bhaṭṭāraka, whose lotus feet are illumined by the rows of gems set in the crowns of all the gods and demon lords,—śrīmad Guṇasēna paṇḍita-dēva gained the abode of Mōksha-Lakshmī.

His guru, skilled in unfolding the essence of the *siddhānta*, Pushpasēna-vratīndra; his eminent sangha, the Nandi-sangha; lord of the Draviḷa-gaṇa of the great Aruṅguḷ-āmnāya; proficient in the supreme *ārhantya* and other the three jewels, all the great science of grammar, *āgama* and others, and the six established systems of logic;—thus was the vratipati Guṇasēna-āryya, praised of āryyas.

---

[1] The original seems to be *udbhayat Syakara vorusha*. Perhaps meant for *jayābhyudaya-Śaka-varusha.*

[2] Mother :—the queen mother.

[3] This seems to be the name of a person, as though *aṇṇa* means elder brother, and *tamma*, younger brother, when combined they do not double the *t* as here, nor take the singular termination. It is also unlikely that provision was being made by so many donors for the grandchildren of the elder and younger brothers of all of them.

35

Date 1058 *A.D.*

Written by Dharmma-seṭṭi [1]. Be it well. In the 980th Śaka year, the year Vilambi, at the time of the uttarāyaṇa-sankrānti,—śrī-Rājēṁdra-Koṁgāḷva, for the basadi his father had had made, granted in Hāruvanahaḷḷi, Arakanahaḷḷi, and Niḍuta *gōḍu* 3 khaṇḍuga, and similar grants in other villages (named), with the oil from one oil mill. Śrī-Rājādhirāja-Koṁgāḷva's mother, Pōchabbarasi, had (the grant) made to her guru Guṇasēna-paṇḍita-dēva, of the Draviḷa-gaṇa, Nandi-sangha and Arungaḷ-ānvaya, and given with pouring of water.

Whoso takes away land given by himself or by another is born a worm in ordure for sixty thousand years.

36

Date about 1070 *A.D.*

(Nearly all defaced.) A memorial to some one who died,—perhaps Pṛithuvī-Koṁgāḷva's queen.

37

Date about 1050 *A.D.*

Be it well. Srī-Rājādhirāja-Komgāḷva's mother Pōchabbarasi, lay disciple of Guṇasēna-paṇḍita-dēva of the Draviḷa-gaṇa, Nandi-sangha and Arungaḷ-ānvaya, had this basadi made.

Great good fortune.

38

Date about 1050 *A.D.*

Be it well. Srī-Rājēndra-Chōḷa-Koṁgāḷva's son Rā[jādhirāja]-Koṁgāḷva gave, with pouring of water, ... as a dwelling place to his guru Guṇasēna-paṇḍita-dēva, of the Tivuḷa-gaṇa, Arungaḷ-ānvaya and Nandi-sangha. Great good fortune. Śrī. Śrī.

39

Date 1390 *A.D.*

Be it well. Fortune. In the 1313th Śaka year, the year Pra[mō]dūta, on the 3rd of the bright fortnight of Vaiśākha, Sunday,—of the śrī-Mūla-sangha, Dēśi-gaṇa, Pustaka-gachchha and Koṇḍakundānvaya, the Āryya Śubhēndu's offspring Vījayakīrtti-dēva's beloved disciple Bāhubali-dēva having obtained this temple, restored it :

Śrī-Rājā[dhirāja], through Koṁgāḷva-Rugmiṇi-Dēvi's queen's bodyguard Vijaya-dēva, that it might stand fast in order that merit might be to his mother . . . son, that Pōchabbarasi had set up, and granted for it the village of Nulabihaḷḷi in Aṇilavāḍi (and other lands, whose boundaries are given in detail, much effaced), with oil from one oil mill, to continue as long as moon and sun. . . . .

(And) the joy of all people, reading the record of the dedication, with the view of continuing it, the king Vīra-Harihara, who had been in many fights,—to the guardian of those who come into the king's shelter, a cage of adamant to refugees, servant of the bearer of the

---

[1] The writer's name usually comes at the end, but was put at the top perhaps for want of space at the bottom.

conch, discus and ? club, Gonkā-Raḍḍi-nāyaka,—whom Guṇḍappa-daṇṇāyaka had noticed (for his bravery)—gave Muḷḷu-nāḍ of his own favour.—(And) Siddha-gauḍa assembled the subjects, and giving to Aṇṇādēvi's Kumāranahaḷḷi the name of Bhīmāpura, set up stones at the four boundaries, and presented it, with pouring of water. And giving to Kāragōḍ the name Aṇ[ṇa]ngapura, presented it, with pouring of water, to Pārśvanātha. Also lands (specified) for gifts, grazing, etc. Arjuna wrote the śāsana. Imprecations.

40

Date 1216 *A.D.*

Be it well. Fortune. In the 1138th Śaka year, the year Dhātu, the 15th of the bright fortnight of Jēshṭa, Tuesday,-Immaḍi-A . . . ya-Rāya's army chaplain (*kaṭakāchāryya*) Vidyādhara-Būchidēvarasa expired . . . .

41

Date about 1030 *A.D.*

The holy footprints of Guṇasēna-paṇḍita's gurū Pushpasēna-siddhānta-dēva.

42

Date about 1050 *A.D.*

Be it well. The Nāga well which Guṇasēna-paṇḍita-dēva caused to be dug as *dharmma* for the town.

43

Date 1077 *A.D.*

Fortune. In the 999th Śaka year, the year Pingala, ... when śrī-Rājēndra-Chōḷa-Koṁgāḷva was ruling the kingdom:—his crowned queen Padmala-Dēvi having died, ... from strong emotion, he and his wife . . . .

44

Date about 1080 *A.D.*

Uttama-Chōḷa-Seṭṭi . . . . with a sword cutting off his head, died.

45

Date 1296 *A.D.*

Ōm. Obeisance. Be it well. In the reign of—with all titles, the maṇḍalika-Nārāyaṇa, the champion who put to flight Maleya, a cage of adamant to refugees,—śrī-Harihara-Dēva Chōḷa-Dēva,—in the year Durmmukhi, on the 5th of the bright fortnight of Chaitra, Monday,—when Beluhu-nāḍ Godduṁbāḍi, Muḷivarāditya-nāḍ Mallikārjjuna, Niḍita Meṇasa, and others the whole nāḍ, uniting, marched to the Muḷḷūr fort and besieging it, were scaling the fort,—Boppa-gauḍi's (son) Malleya, fighting the Muḷḷūr fort, hewing down the barrier and slaying, fell in the crooked entrance. On his falling, the three hundred men of the villages, especially of Māsāvi, uniting, gave as a *vīra-sēse* for him 3 paddy-fields in the Mākōve land.

of the Mullūr paddy-fields, and 5 paddy-fields in Hiḍijagala; these eight paddy-fields Boppa-gauḍi's (sons) Mālaiya and Mādaiya having exchanged for the new *amāni* tank and 9 ga, the Māsāvi village united and made over to them, free of all imposts. These boundaries are fixed.

This stone was made by Kengolali Bāchāchāri's son Bairōja. The Kopaṇa-tīrttha *sēnabōva*, Sāteya, wrote the letters of this śāsana. Great good fortune. Śrī. Śrī.

46

Date 1004 *A.D.*

Be it well. The sun in the sky the Chōḷa-kula which was like the stem of the tree of paradise the Solar race, the friend of the virgin daughter of Kavēra (that is, the Kāvērī river) devoted to removing the sins of all people,—the great Chōḷa king Rājakēsarivarmma-Permmānaḍigaḷ,—to Manija, who in the battle of Panasoge had massed (his forces) and fought, saying I will not return till they are completely put down, so that those who opposed him died,—of his great grace, saying to bind a *paṭṭa* on him and give him a nāḍ,—sent word to Panchavan-mārāya, who bound on him a *paṭṭa* (inscribed with the title) as *Kshatriya-sikhā maṇi Koṅgāḷva*, and gave him Mālavvi [now Mālambi].

To this, gāvuṇḍa-Rāchamma's family are witnesses,—Kaṇṇavangala Āditya-gāvuṇḍa, and . . gaḻani Nanniya Mēru, Keḻane . . . cha-gāvuṇḍa, Nallūr Eṟeyanga-gāvuṇḍa, (*the rest is effaced*).

47

Date 1756 *A.D.*

In the year Dhātu, on the 5th of the bright fortnight of Āśvīja,—śrīmat Vēnkaṭādri-Nāyaka's (son) Krishṇappa-Nāyaka granted to Mālambi Rāche-gauḍa the land-rent of 12 ga. Twelve varaha have we given.

48

Date about 1050 *A.D.*

Be it well. When śrī-Komgāḷva was ruling the kingdom:—Komaraya and Sundaraya, when the cows of . . . . were carried off, attacked those who drove them away, and . . . .

(Images of Sundaran and Komaran, with the names attached).

49

Date 1070 *A.D.*

[1] Be it well. In the 993rd Śaka year, the year Sādhārana, on new-moon day of the month Chaitra,—śrīmad Rājēndra-Prithuvī-Komgāḷva granted fifty khaṇḍugas of land in the rice fields east and west under the Gaurati tank of Suḻligōḍu for the enjoyment of the priest of the god Vīra-Siddhēśvara of Hoshavaḻḻi, and made them over with pouring of water. Also Rājavallabha-seṭṭi gave 40 gadyāṇas for the tank, and *āḍavala* gadyāṇa 1½. Whoso fails in this has slaughtered cows. Whoso seizes on land given by himself or by another, is born a worm in ordure for sixty thousand years.

[1] One line and a half at the top, beginning with *Svasti*, is too illegible to make out its purport. It was perhaps a subsequent addition.

50

Date 1070 *A.D.*

Be it well. In the 993rd Saka year, the year Sādhāraṇa, on new-moon day of the month Chaitra,—when srī-Rājēndra-Prithuvi-Koṁgāḷva was ruling the kingdom :—for the great god Vīra-Siddhēśvara of Hoshavaḷḷi he gave money and bought land in Posavaḷḷi Nīragāvuṇḍa's field, and gave ten khaṇḍugas *āḍavalam*. Whoso fails in this has slaughtered cows.

51

Date ? 1106 *A.D.*

In the fortunate year Pārtthiva, on the 10th of the bright fortnight of Phālguna, Thursday,—Annadāni-arasa had this sluice built. The builders were Venkataiya and Malaiya. Bomarasaiya's writing. The god Basalinga was made in the time of Nanna-gauḍa.

52

Date ? about 1290 *A.D.*

In the year . . . . , on the 10th of the bright fortnight of Vaiśākha, Tuesday,—an act of grace granted for the southern Guṇḍa-nāḍ Seventy :—If to . . . . there is no male, it will go to a female and to female children. Whoso causes failure in this charity commits sin and has fallen into Naraka. He is guilty of slaughtering cows on the banks of the Ganges and of the murder of a Brāhman.

The great minister Paḍivala-Bānammarāja's son Heggaḍe-Nākana wrote it. Great good fortune . . . . Vajjaragāla Bayala-nāḍ Bammōja made the śāsana.

53

Date ? 1055 *A.D.*

When . . . . was ruling the kingdom of the world :— . . . . -daṇḍanayaka, with others, of whom he was the chief, remitted the dues and gifts of the . . . ku-nāḍ Seventy for Voḍeyappa and Honnapaya, and the money tribute . . . . all dues . . . . . . in the year Manmatha, on the . . . . of Jēshṭa, Friday, with the dues and gifts were granted as a favour . . . . Koṁgāḷva-Dēva.

54

Date about 1300 *A.D.*

(The first part is gone.) Details of certain lands granted ; and the tribute for Gōpāladēva's army, house-tax, *solage*, forced labour,—freedom from all these, of his own will, did he give. In token of approval, that Malli-Dēva Harihara-Dēvarasa's signature :—

śrī-Chenna-Sadāśiva.

55

Date about 1280 *A.D.*

(The first part is gone.) When . . . . Dēvarasa was ruling the kingdom of the world :—Chikkeya-Nāyaka having fallen in the fight at the boundary of Gaṭṭabāḍi in Yaḍavu-nāḍ,—for Chikkeya-Nāyaka's children, that Malli-Dēvarasa and Harihara-Dēvarasa, with all the . . . . of Tenka-nāḍ . . . .

56

Date? 1044 *A.D.*

The tomb of Prabhāchandra-dēva, the beloved eldest disciple of . . . Śubhachandra-dēva, of the śrī-Mūla-sangha, Dēśiya-gaṇa, Pustaka-gachcha, Koṇḍakundānvaya, and Ingulēśvara-baḷi. He obtained release (died) in the year Tāraṇa, on the fifth of the bright fortnight of Chaitra, Friday.

57

Date 1095 *A.D.*

Be it well. In the 1017th Śaka year, the year Yuva, the second of the bright fortnight of the month Śrāvaṇa, Sunday,—the śrīman mahā-maṇḍalēśvara, chief lord of Tripura, sun to the lotus the Balīndra-kula, champion of the Four-faced (Brahmā), a cage of adamant to refugees, a lion to the elephant his enemies, a Bhīma of the powerful, a Rāma in war, a pleasure garden of the Malepas (or hill chiefs), praised by the eulogists, plunderer of foreign territory, his father's warrior, his head at the feet of Śiva, an ocean of truth, a saw to the heart of his enemies, a Rakkasa in war with kings,—with these and many other titles,—Duddharasa, born to Hiṭṭeyarasa and Junjala-Dēvi, being of great might and valour, possessed of fresh youth, the beloved of Vijaya-Lakshmī (the goddess of victory), protecting Maleya, terrifying and driving away his enemies, casting them out of their forts, an incarnation of prowess (or a Vīrabhadra), the Kali-yuga Yama,—protecting and ruling Saṁhatha-nāḍ, Pākuvāḍi and other places,—having fifteen horses, fifty male servants, two hundred and fifty strong men, forty-five retainers of good family, and a retinue of many subjects guards relatives and landed proprietors,—on the application of his lawful wife Chikala-Dēvi, ... having the Rāja(samudra) tank built, and the . . . . erected, having set up a *chatram* for holy Brāhmans, having caused rice fields to be made at the river, and brightening many acts of *dharmma*,—when he gained the Śiva-lōka (died), his brother Jūjarasa, out of friendship performing his obsequies, had this vīra-śāsana written by Moḷate Duddha-malla, minister for peace and war, and sēnabhōva Rājimayya's son Bamma-dēva. Whoso contemns the rice fields that Duddharasa thus caused to be made, has slain cows and Brāhmans in Bāṇarāsi. Great good fortune. Śrī. Śrī.

58

Date? 1380 *A.D.*

In the year Raudri, on the fifth of the bright fortnight of Jēshta, Sunday,—the Handra . . dūr Pāri . . . paid a visit,—Śrī-Mānika-dēva. Great good fortune. Śrī. Śrī.

59

Date? 1297 *A.D.*

Be it well. When śrīman mahā-maṇḍalēśvara, ... Nārāyaṇa, ... Harihara-Dēva. . . . . . was ruling :—in the year Hēvalambi, on the fifth of the first half of the month Māgha, the *nakshatra* being Aśvini, Thursday,—the regulation formerly made by Harihara . . . . . for property accruing to a female in Kundūr was as follows :—It will belong to a female, to female children and to children of female slaves. (Here follow a number of names)—These gauḍas and others gave this regulation by śāsana to the towns of this nāḍ, for as long as sun and moon endure. Sēnabōva Jinayya wrote it. Malōja engraved the stone. . . . .

60

Date ? about 900 *A.D.*

Teyalayya Jūbu, washing his feet, gave Baraṛi to Eṛeya[ra]sa as an agrahāra. Moreover, Chaṭṭayyaṁ Dhāraka-Balaha Koṅgaṇivarmmaṁ, washing his feet, gave . . . . . . to Ponnamaṇṇa. . . . .

61

Date ? about 1095 *A.D.*

(Very much effaced). . . . . . Be it well. The śrīman mahā-maṇḍalēśvara, Tribhuvanamalla Vīra. . . . . Changālva. . . . . to the mahā-ma[ṇḍalēśvara] . . . . ditya-dēva. . . . .

62

Date ? about 1100 *A.D.*

Be it well. With all titles, srīmat Shaṇmēdō-Kōkam, the Kaliyuga Brahma, ascended (to heaven).

63

Date ? 1348 *A.D.*

In the year Sarvadhāri, on the 5th of the dark fortnight of Chaitra, Sunday,—Gauli-Nanjarappaya and his elder brother granted this *gauḍike* to Hānagal Linge-gauḍa.

64

Date ? about 1350 *A.D.*

śrīmat Bilu-gauḍa and Aṇaba-gauḍa gave this village to the four — Bayiru ka, Yirāma, Nāgajyaya, and Kempaṇa.

65

Date 1175 *A.D.*

Śrī. In the year Jaya, on full moon day in the bright fortnight of Phālguna, Thursday,—when Hoysaṇa bhujabala śrī-Vīra-Ballāla-Dēvarasa was ruling the kingdom of the world:—to Māyaṇṇa, son of Bīraya of the Kasapa...—gavuḍas of Siriyūr in the west of Biluhu-nād were granted the eight rights of full possession, such as, hidden treasure, underground stores, springs, minerals, and future profit, of the god Mallikārjuna of Sirivūr, together with the *kāluga*, by a śāsana, with pouring of water. Whoso destroys this will incur the guilt of slaughtering cows on the bank of the Ganges. Great good fortune. Śrī, śrī, śrī.

The guardian of those who take shelter. Śrī.

66

Date about 1755 *A.D.*

(Sanskrit). May it be prosperous. Sending for the best of the *paramahamsa sannyāsis*, the great Yōgi named Kaivalya, ever solely devoted to wisdom,—the Bēlūr king Kṛishṇa gave him an elephant and the Mūdravaḷḷi village, as an auspicious offering to Kṛishṇa. If it be asked, for what reason was it given? (*stops here*).

67

Date ? 1360 *A.D.*

In the year Vikāri, on the 5th of the bright fortnight of Phālguṇa, Saturday.—Trinamēra-Dēvaṇṇa having gone below the Ghāṭs and . . . . . . —Hulukōḍ Chikkaṇṇaya Bomma-gauḍa's *biragal*. Kalina-Bōja engraved it. Śrī . . . . . . Demmaya and Chikkaṇṇaya . . . . .

68

Date 1731 *A.D.*

Śrī. Be it well. In the 1652nd year of the victorious increasing Śālivāhana era, the year Sādhārana, on the 2nd of the dark fortnight of Māgha, Friday—in the presence of Manjunātha-svāmi of Kuḍuma, for the service of the god. Hāvēri Vīrap-oḍēr gave, free of all imposts, Heggaḍahaḷḷi and Sirangāḷa, and had (boundary) stones set up to the 29 hamlets belonging to the two places, and gave them.

69

Date 1731 *A.D.*

The sign of Manjunātha-svāmi of Kuḍuma.—(*ḍamaruga* and *triśūla.*)

70

Date about 1175 *A.D.*

Be it well. When the refuge of all worlds, the favourite of earth and fortune, the mahārājādhirāja, paramēśvara, parama-bhaṭṭāraka, sun in the sky the Yādava-kula, crest-jewel of perfection, Rāja of the Malerājas, champion among the Malapas, gaṇḍa-bhēruṇḍa, unshaken in war, unassisted brave, single-handed hero, Śanivāra-siddhi, Giridurgga-malla, destroyer of Magara-Rāya. . . . . . śrī-Vīra-Hoysaṇa [Vīra-Ballāḷa-Dēva was ruling]:—

71

Date ? about 1700 *A.D.*

Be it well. Śrī. Sirivangala Mācha-gāvuṇḍa Siriyama-tandi *vīra[gal]*. Mācha-goṇḍa's son Kāva-goṇḍa set up the stone. Mariyōja's work. Fortune.

72

Date ? about 1300 *A.D.*

There are six lines, but the whole of the letters have been so nicked as to be illegible.[1]

73

Date ? about 1700 *A.D.*

The stone station of the Jōgi of the westerns.
The western royal stone.
Obeisance to the Jōgi of the westerns.

74

Date about 910 *A.D.*

Be it well. Śrī-Eṟeyapa's . . . . while saying the end of the battle is good, died, and obtained a *kalnāḍ*. Whose destroys this, incurs the guilt of destroying cows and Bāṇārasi. One *bāḻu* free from taxes.

Great good fortune. Śrī.

75

Date ? 1264 *A.D.*

Be it well. Śrīman mahā-maṇḍalēśvara, subduer of Chaṭṭu, in firm character Rāma, supporter of Satyarāya, in solid adamant Rudra, guardian of refugees, śrīmad Vīra-Munivarāditya Gōkula-dēvarasa:—

In the year Raktākshi, the month Kanyā,—when the Tengu-nāḍaka seized the cows of Yaḷaghaḷi—his brave servant Mēlāḷi's infuriated wife Bidaḍe, wrestled with, overpowered, and threw him down, the rope to his legs;—and received a nose-jewel (as reward).

---

[1] From its appearance this inscription might have supplied some information of value. It may have been for this reason it was defaced.

ಕೊಡಗು ದೇಶದ ಶಾಸನಗಳು

TEXT AS IN THE ORIGINAL

1

ಮಡಿಕೇರಿಯಲ್ಲಿ ಸರ್ಕಾರದ ಖಜಾನೆಯಲ್ಲಿ ಸಿಕ್ಕಿದ ತಾಮ್ರ ಶಾಸನ.

೩ ಪತ್ರಗಳು - ಪೂರ್ವದ ಹಳಗನ್ನಡಕ್ಷರ.

೧ ನೇ ಪತ್ರದ ಹಿಂಭಾಗ.

1 ಓ ಸ್ವಸ್ತಿ ಜಿತಮ್ಭಗವತಾ ಗತಘನಗಗನಾಭೇನ ಪದ್ಮನಾಭೇನ ಶ್ರೀಮದ್ಜಾಹ್ನವೀಯಕು

2 ಲಾಮಲಾವ್ಯೋಮಾವಭಾಸನಭಾಸ್ಕರಃ ಸ್ವಖಡ್ಗೈಕಪ್ರಹಾರಖಣ್ಡಿತ ಮಹಾಸಿಲಾಸ್ತಮ್ಭಲಬ್ಧಬಲ

3 ಪರಾಕ್ರಮೋದಾರಣೋರಿಗಣವಿದಾರಣೋಪಲಬ್ಧಬ್ರಣವಿಭೂಷಣವಿಭೂಷಿತಕನ್ವಾಯನ

4 ಸಗೋತ್ರಸ್ಯ ಶ್ರೀಮಾನ್ಕೊಙ್ಗಣಿಮಹಾಧಿರಾಜ ॥ ತತ್ಪುತ್ರಪಿತುರನ್ವಾಗತಗುಣಯುಕ್ತೋವಿ

5 ದ್ಯಾವಿನೆಯಪಿಹಿತವೃತ್ತಃ ಸಮ್ಯಕ್ಪ್ರಜಾಪಾಳನಾಮಾತ್ರಾಧಿಗತರಾಜ್ಯಪ್ರಯೋಜನವಿದ್ವತ್ಕ

6 ವಿಕಾಞ್ಚನನಿಕಾಷೋಪಲಭೂತೋ ನೀತಿಸಾಸ್ತ್ರಸ್ಯ ವಕ್ತೃಪ್ರಯೋಕ್ತೃ ಕುಸಲಸ್ಯ ದತ್ತಕಸೂತ್ರ

7 ವೃತ್ತಿಪ್ರಣೇತಾ ಶ್ರೀಮಾನ್ಮಾಧವಮಹಾಧಿರಾಜ ॥ ತತ್ಪುತ್ರಪಿತೃಪೈತಾಮಹಾಗುಣಯುಕ್ತೋನೇಕ

8 ಚಾತುರ್ದನ್ತಯುದ್ಧನಾಪ್ತಚತುರುದಧಿಸಲಿಲಸ್ವಾದಿತಯಸ ಶ್ರೀಮದ್ಹರಿವರ್ಮ್ಮಮಹಾಧಿರಾಜ ॥ ತ

9 ತ್ಪುತ್ರ ॥ ದ್ವಿಜಗುರುದೇವತಾಪೂಜನಪರೋ ನಾರಾಯಣಚರಣಾನುದ್ಧ್ಯತ ಶ್ರೀಮದ್ವಿಷ್ಣುಗೋಪಮ

೨ ನೇ ಪತ್ರದ ಮುಂಭಾಗ.

10 ಹಾಧಿರಾಜ ॥ ತಸ್ಯ ಪುತ್ರ ॥ ತ್ರ್ಯಯಮ್ಬಕಚರಣಾಂಭೋರುಹರಜಃಪವಿತ್ರೀಕೃತೋತ್ತಮಾಙ್ಗಸ್ವಭುಜ

11 ಬಳಪರಾಕ್ರಮಕ್ರಯಾಕ್ರೀತರಾಜ್ಯಕಲಿಯುಗಬಳಪಂಕಾವಸನ್ನವೃಷೋದ್ಧರಣನಿತ್ಯಸನ್ನದ್ಧ ಶ್ರೀಮಾನ್ಮಾಧ

12 ವಮಹಾಧಿರಾಜ ॥ ತಸ್ಯ ಪುತ್ರ ॥ ಶ್ರೀಮದ್ಕದಂಬಕುಲಗಗನಗಭಸ್ತಿಮಾಲಿನಕೃಷ್ಣವರ್ಮ್ಮಮ

13 ಹಾಧಿರಾಜಸ್ಯಪ್ರಿಯಾಭಾಗಿನೇಯೋ ವಿದ್ಯಾವಿನೆಯಾತಿಸಯಪರಿಪೂರಿತಾನ್ತರಾತ್ಮ ನಿರವಗ್ರಹಪ್ರಧಾನಸೌ

14 ರ್ಯ್ಯವಿದ್ವತ್ಸುಪ್ರಥಮಗಣ್ಯ ಶ್ರೀಮಾನ್ಕೊಙ್ಗಣಿಮಹಾಧಿರಾಜ ಅವಿನೀತನಾಮಧೇಯದತ್ತಸ್ಯ

15 ದೇಸಿಗಗಣಂಕೊಣ್ಡಕುನ್ದಾನ್ವಯಗುಣಚನ್ದ್ರಭಟಾರ ಸಿಷ್ಯಸ್ಯ ಅಭಣನ್ದಿಭಟಾರತಸ್ಯ ಸಿಷ್ಯಸ್ಯ

16 ಸೀಳಭದ್ರಭಟಾರಸಿಷ್ಯಸ್ಯ ಜಯಣನ್ದಿಭಟಾರಸಿಷ್ಯಸ್ಯ ಗುಣಣನ್ದಿಭಟಾರಸಿಷ್ಯಸ್ಯ ಚನ್ದಣನ್ದಿಭಟಾರ
ಗೆರ್ಗ ಅಷ್ಟಾ ಅ

17 ಸೀತಿಉತ್ತರಸ್ಯ ತ್ರಯೋಸತಸ್ಯ ಸಂವತ್ಸರಸ್ಯ ಮಾಘಮಾಸಂ ಸೋಮವಾರಂ ಸ್ವಾತಿನಕ್ಷತ್ರ ಸುದ್ಧಪಞ್ಚಮಿ
ಅಕಾಳ

18 ವರ್ಷಪೃಥುವೀವಲ್ಲಭಮನ್ತ್ರತಳವನನಗರಶ್ರೀವಿಜಯಜಿನಾಲಯಕ್ಕೆ ಪೂನಾಡುಘಾಸಹಸ್ರ ಎಡೆನಾಡುಸ

19 ಪ್ತರಿಮಧ್ಯೇ ಬದಣೆಗುಪ್ಪೆನಾಮ ಅವಿನೀತಮಹಾಧಿರಾಜೇನದತ್ತೇನಪಡಿಯ ಆಪೊಳಂ ಊರೂ

೨ ನೇ ಪತ್ರದ ಹಿಂಭಾಗ.

20 ರೊಳ್ಪನ್ನಿರ್ಕ್ಕಣ್ಡುಗಜ್ಗೆಯ್ದು ಅಮ್ಬಲಿಮಣ್ಣುಂ ತಳವನಪುರದೊಳ್ತಳವಿತ್ತಿಯಮಣ್ಪೊಗಗೆಟಿಯೊಳ್ಪ

21 ನ್ನಿರ್ಕ್ಕಣ್ಡುಗಂಪಿರಿಕೆರೆಯೊಳಂರಾಜಮಾನಂ ಅನುಮೋದನಪನ್ನಿರ್ಕ್ಕಣ್ಡುಗಂಮನೋಹರಂದತ್ತಂ ಬದಣೆ
ಗುಪ್ಪೆ

22 ಗ್ರಾಮಸ್ಯ ಸೀಮಾನ್ತರಂ ಪೂರ್ಬ್ಬಸ್ಯಾಂ ದಿಸಿ ಕೆಂಜಿಗೆಮೊಅಡಿ ಎಗಜಸಲೆಯೊಕರಿವಳ್ಳಿಯ ಕೊಟ್ಟಗರಬ

23 ದಣೆಗುಪ್ಪೆಯ ತ್ರಿಸನ್ಧಿಯಸತ್ತಿಕೊಅಡು ಆಗ್ನೇಯದಿನತ್ತಬನ್ದು ಕಾಗಣೆತಟಾಕಂ ಪುನದಕ್ಷಿಣಸ್ಯಾಂ

24 ದಿಸಿ ಬಹುಕ್ಷುಕಿಯಬೆಳ್ಕಣೆ ವೃಕ್ಷಮು ಪುನಪಶ್ಚಿಮಮೊಕಟೆಸನ ಬಹುಮೂಲಿಕಪನ್ತಿಯೆ ಪುನಬ

25 ದಣೆಗುಪ್ಪೆಯ ಕೊಟ್ಟಗರಮತ್ತಿಗಿಯ ತ್ರಿಸನ್ಧಿಯ ಕೊಡಚಿಪಣ್ಡಿಗಾಲೆ ಪುನನೈರಕ್ರ್ಯದೆ ಸನ್ದುಕಥೆಕವೃಕ್ಷ

26 ಮೆ ಪುನ ಪಶ್ಚಿಮಸ್ಯಾಂ ದಿಸಿ ಪೆಱ್ದಿಜ್ಜಿಲ್ವೃಕ್ಷಮೆ ಸಾನ್ತೆಜೆತಿಯ ವಟವೃಕ್ಷಮೆ ಪುನತೊರೆವಳ್ಳಮೆ ಉತ್ತ ರಾಮುಖ

27 ದೆಸೆನ್ದಬಾಹುಮೂಲಿಕಪನ್ತಿಯೆಜಮ್ಮುಪಡಿಯತಟಾಕಮೆ ಪುನವಾಯುವ್ಯದೆ ಗಟೆಚಿಂಚವೃಕ್ಷಮೆ ಪುನಬದಣೆ

28 ಗುಪ್ಪೆಯವಱಿಗಿಯಕೊಳೆಯನೂರದಾಸನೂರತ್ರಿಸನ್ದಿಯನೆರ್ಗ್ಗಿಲಗುಂಬೆವಿಡುವೆಳಂಗೆಪುನಗಜಪೆತಿ

29 ಯೆಗ್ರಾಮ ಉತ್ತರದಿಸಿ ಕಾಯ್ನವೊಱಡಿಎ ಇಱೆದುಕೆಂಬರೆಯೆ ಪುನಪೂರ್ಬ್ಬಮುಖದೆಸೆನ್ದಬಹುಮೂ ಲಿಕಪ

೨ ನೇ ಪತ್ರದ ಮುಂಭಾಗ-

30 ನ್ತಿಯೆ ಪುನಕಡಱತ್ತಿಗಾಲವಟವೃಕ್ಷಮೆ ಪುನ ಇಶಾನದೆಬದಣೆಗುಪ್ಪೆಯ ದಾಸನೂರಪ್ರೊಜ್ಜಿದ ತ್ರಿಸನ್ದಿಯ

31 ತಟಾಕಮೆ ಕೊಡಿಗಟ್ಟಚಿಞ್ಚವೃಕ್ಷಮೆ ಕೆಂತಱಮ್ಬಿನದಿಃಶೆಇಂ ಪೂರ್ಬ್ಬದೆಕೂಡಿತ್ತುಸೀಮಾನ್ತರಂ ॥ ತಸ್ಯ ಸ್ಸಾಕ್ಷಿಣಾ

32 ಗಙ್ಗರಾಜಕುಲ ಸಕಲಾಸ್ಥಯಿಕಪುರುಷಪೆರ್ಬ್ಬಕ್ಕವಾಣಮಱಗರೆಯಸೆನ್ದ್ರಕಗಂಜಿನಾಡನಿರ್ಗ್ಗುನ್ದಮಣಿ ಯು

33 ಗುರೆಯನನ್ಯಾಲಸಿಂಬಾಲಾದಪಭೃತ್ಯಯಾಂ ॥ ದೇಃಸಸಾಕ್ಷಿತಗಡೂರಕುಱುಗೋವರುಗಣಿಗನೂರತಗಡರು ಆಲ್ತೊ

34 ಡತೆನನ್ದಕರುಂ ಉಮ್ಮತ್ತೂರಬೆಳ್ಳರರುಂ ಆಳಗೆಯರುಂ ಬದಣೆಗುಪ್ಪೆಯ ಝುಂಸೆನ್ನಬೆಳ್ಳರರುಪೆರ್ಗ್ಗಿವಿ ಯೆಪಂ ॥

35 ಸ್ವದತ್ತಂಪರದತ್ತಾಂಗ್ವಾ ಯೋಽಹರೇಥವಸುನ್ಧರೀ ಷಷ್ಟಿಂವರ್ಷಸಹಸ್ರಾಣಿ ವಿಷ್ಠಾಯಾಂಜಾಯತೇಕ್ರಿಮಿ॥ವ

36 ಸುಭಿವಸುಧಾಭುಕ್ತಂ ರಾಜಭಿಸ್ಸಕರಾಜಭಿ ಯಸ್ಯಯಸ್ಯಯೆದಾಭೂಮಿ ತಸ್ಯತಸ್ಯತದಾಫಳಂ ॥ ದೇವ

37 ಸ್ವನ್ನುವಿಷಂಘೋರಂ ನವಿಷಂವಿಷಮುಚ್ಯತೇ ವಿಷಮೇಕಾಕಿನಂಹನ್ತಿ ದೇವಸ್ವಪುತ್ರಪೌತ್ರಿಕಂ ॥ ಸಾಮಾ ನ್ಯೋಯಂ ಧ

38 ರ್ಮ್ಮಹೇತುಂ ನೃಪಾಣಾಂ ಕಾಲೇಕಾಲೇ ಪಾಲನೀಯೋ ಭವದ್ಭಿ ಸರ್ಬ್ಬಾನೇತಾಂಭಾಗಿನ ಪಾರ್ತ್ಥಿವೇ ನ್ದ್ರಾಭೂಯೋಭೂಯೋ

39 ಯಾಚತೇ ರಾಮಭದ್ರಾ ॥ ವಿಸ್ವಕರ್ಮ್ಮಲಿಖಿತಂ ॥ ೨

2

ಕಿಗ್ಗಟ್ನಾಡಿನಲ್ಲಿ ಬಿಳಿಯೂರ ಗ್ರಾಮದ ಕಡಂಗದಲ್ಲಿಬಿದ್ದಿರುವ ಶಿಲಾ ಶಾಸನ

1 ೨ ಭದ್ರಮಸ್ತುಜಿನಶಾಸನಾಯಸಕನೃಪ
2 ತೀತಾಕಾಲ ಸಂವತ್ಸರಂಗಳೆಣ್ಟುನೂಱೊಮ್ಬತ್ತನೆಯವರ್ಷ
3 ಮ್ಪ್ರವರ್ತ್ತಿಸುತ್ತಿರೆ ಸ್ವಸ್ತಿಸತ್ಯವಾಕ್ಯ ಕೊಂಗುಣಿವರ್ಮ್ಮಧರ್ಮ್ಮಮ
4 ಹಾರಾಜಾಧಿರಾಜಕೊವಳಾಲಪುರವರೇಶ್ವರನನ್ದಗಿರಿನಾಥ ಶ್ರೀಮ
5 ತ್ಪೆರ್ಮ್ಮನಡಿಯರಾಜ್ಯಾಭಿಷೇಕಂಗೆಯ್ದು ಪದಿನೆಣ್ಟನೆಯವರ್ಷದೆನ್ದುಪಾ
6 ಲ್ಗುಣಮಾಸದ ಶ್ರೀಪಞ್ಚಮಿಯನ್ದು ಶಿವಣನ್ದಿಸಿದ್ಧಾನ್ತದ ಭಟಾರ
7 ರಶಿಷ್ಯರ್ಸರ್ವ್ವಣನ್ದಿದೇವರ್ಗ್ಗೆ ಪೆಣ್ನೆಗಡಙ್ಗದ ಸತ್ಯವಾಕ್ಯಜಿನಾಲ
8 ಯಕ್ಕೆ ಪೆದ್ದೊಱೆಗರೆಯಬಿಳಿಲೂರ್ಪನ್ನಿರ್ಪಳ್ಳಿಯುಮಂಸರ್ಬ್ಬಪಾದವರಿ
9 ಹಾರಪೆರ್ಮ್ಮನಡಿಕೊಟ್ಟೊತೊಮ್ಬತ್ತಱಸಾಸಿರ್ಬ್ಬರುಮಯ್ನೂಮನ್ತರುಂಬೆದ್ದೊ
10 ಱೆಗರೆಯಎಳ್ಪದಿಮ್ಬರುಂ ಎಣ್ತೊಕ್ಕಲುಂ ಇದಕ್ಕೆ ಸಾಕ್ಷಿ ಮಳೆಸಾಸಿ
11 ರ್ವ್ವರುಮಯ್ನೂರ್ವ್ವರುಂಮಯ್ದಮರಿಗರುಂ ಇದಕ್ಕೆ ಕಾಪು ಇದನಱೆದೊಂ
12 ಬಾರಣಾಸಿಯುಮಂಸಾಸಿರ್ಬ್ಬಪಾರ್ಬ್ಬರುಮಂಸಾಸಿರಕವಿಲೆಯುಮಂಅ
13 ಱೆದೊಂಪಞ್ಚಮಹಾಪಾತಕನಕ್ಕುಂಸೆಜ್ಜೋಜನಲಿಖಿತ್ತಂ
14 ಬೆಳಲೂರು ಎಣ್ಟುತ್ತುಗದ್ಯಾಣಪೊನ್ನುಂ ಎಣ್ಟುನೂಱಬತ್ತ
15 ಮುಂ ತಱುವ್ರೊಂ

3

ಅದೇ ನಾಡಿನಲ್ಲಿ ಕೊತ್ತೂರು ಗ್ರಾಮದ ಲಕ್ಕುಂಡ ಕಾಡಿನಲ್ಲಿರುವ ಶಿಲಾಶಾಸನ

1 ಸ್ವಸ್ತಿ ಸತ್ಯವಾಕ್ಯಕೊಂಗುಣಿವರ್ಮ್ಮ
2 ಧರ್ಮ್ಮಮಹಾರಾಜಾಧಿರಾಜಂಕುವ
3 ಳಾಲಪುರವರೇಶ್ವರಂ ನನ್ದಗಿರಿನಾಥಂ
4 ಶ್ರೀಮತ್ಪೆರ್ಮ್ಮನಡಿಗಳ್ ಜೆಸಲ
5 ಎಱೆಯಜ್ಞಗಾವುಣ್ಡನಮಗಂಗೆಪೆರ್ಮ್ಮಾ
6 ಡಿವಟ್ಟಂಗಟ್ಟಿಬಿಟ್ಟಸ್ತಿತಿಕ್ರಮಮಾ
7 ವುದೆನ್ದೊಡೆಸಿದ್ಧಾಯದಪೊಣ್ನಾಳ್ಪತ್ತು
8 ಗದ್ಯಾಣಪೊನ್ನುಂಬಿಟ್ಟಿಯಭ
9 ತ್ತದೊಳ್ ನೂಱುಭತ್ತಮುಮಂಎಲ್ಲಾ
10 ಕಾಲಕ್ಕಂಸಾಸನವಾಗೆಬಿ
11 ಟ್ಟರ್ ಬೂವಯ್ಯನಕ್ಕರಂಮಂಗಳಂ
12 ಎಱೆಯಂಗಂಗೆಕಲ್ಲಾಡುಮಹಾಶ್ರೀ

4

ಅದೇ ನಾಡಿನಲ್ಲಿ ಪೆಗ್ಗೂರ ಗ್ರಾಮದಲ್ಲಿರುವ ಶಿಲಾಶಾಸನ

1 ಸ್ವಸ್ತಿ ಸಕನೃಪಕಾಳಾತೀತಸಂವತ್ಸರಸತಙ್ಗ ೮೯೯ ತ್ತನೆಯ ಈಸ್ವರಸಂವ
2 ತ್ಸರಂಪ್ರವರ್ತ್ತಿಸೆ ॥ ಸ್ವಸ್ತಿ ಸತ್ಯವಾಕ್ಯಕೊಙ್ಗಣಿವರ್ಮ್ಮಧರ್ಮ್ಮಮಹಾ
3 ರಾಜಾಧಿರಾಜಾ ಕೊಳಾಳಪುರವರೇಶ್ವರ ನನ್ದಗಿರಿನಾಥ ಶ್ರೀಮತ್
4 ರಾಚಮಲ್ಲಪೆರ್ಮ್ಮನಡಿಗಳ್ ತದ್ವರ್ಷಾಭ್ಯನ್ತರಪಾಲ್ಗುಣಸುಕ್ಲಪಕ್ಷದ ನ
5 ನ್ದೀಸ್ವರಂತಲ್ಪದೆವಸವಾಗೆ ಸ್ವಸ್ತಿಸಮಸ್ತವೈರಿಗಜಘಟಾಟೋಪ
6 ಕುಂಭಿಕುಂಭಸ್ತಳಸ್ಫುಟಿತಾನರ್ಘ್ಯಮುಕ್ತಾಫಳಗ್ರಹಣಭೀಕರಕರಾಸೆ
7 ನಿವಾಸಿತದಕ್ಷಿಣದೋರ್ದ್ದಣ್ಡಮಣ್ಡಿತ ಪ್ರಚಣ್ಡಂ ಅಣ್ಣನಬಣ್ಟಬ
8 ಡವರರನಣ್ಟಂ ಶ್ರೀಮತ್ ರಕ್ಕಸಬೆದ್ದೊಱೆಗರೆಯನಾಳುತ್ತಿರೆಭದ್ರಮ
9 ಸ್ತು ಜಿನಶಾಸನಾಯ ಶ್ರೀ ಬೆಳ್ಗೊಳನಿವಾಸಿಗಳಪ್ಪ ಶ್ರೀ ಬೀರಸೇನಸಿ
10 ದ್ಧಾನ್ತದೇವರವರಶಿಷ್ಯರ್ ಶ್ರೀ ಗೋಣಸೇನಪಣ್ಡಿತಭಟ್ಟಾರಕರವರ
11 ಶಿಷ್ಯರ್ ಶ್ರೀಮತ್ ಅನನ್ತವೀರ್ಯ್ಯಯ್ಯಂಗಳ್ಪೆಗ್ಗೂರದೊರುಂಪೊ
12 ಸವಾದಗಮುಮನಭ್ಯನ್ತರಸಿದ್ಧಿಯಾಗೆ ಪಡೆದರದರ್ಕ್ಕೆಸಾ
13 ಕ್ಷಿತೊಂಭತ್ತುಸಾಸಿರ್ಬ್ಬರುಮಯ್ನೂರ್ವ್ವರುಂಬೆದ್ದೊಱೆಗರೆ
14 ಯೆಪ್ಪದಿಂಬರುಮೆಣ್ಟುಕ್ಕಲುಮಿದಂಕಾವನನ್ಗಲ್ಪವರ್ಮ್ಮಲೆಪರು
15 ಮೆಯ್ನೂರ್ವ್ವರುಮಯ್ದು ಮಾರಿಗರುಂ ಶ್ರೀಪುರುಷ [1] ಮಹಾರಾಜನ
16 ದತ್ತಿಯನಾವೊನೊರ್ಬ್ಬನಱಿದೊಂ ಬಾಣರಾಸಿಯುಂ ಸಾಸಿರ್ಬ್ಬಬ್ರಾಹ್ಮ
17 ಣರುಂ ಸಾಸಿರಕವಿಲೆಯುಮನಱಿದ ಪಞ್ಚಮಹಾಪಾತಕನಕ್ಕುಂ
18 ಇದನಾರೊರ್ಬ್ಬರ್ಕಾದರವರ್ಗೆಪಿರಿದು ಪುಣ್ಯಂ ಚನ್ದಣನ್ದಿಯಯ್ಯನ ಲಿಖಿತಂ
19 ಪೆಗ್ಗೂರದೂರಬಸದಿಯ ಶಾಸನಂ

5

ಮಡಿಕೇರಿಯಲ್ಲಿ ಸೆಂಟ್ರಲ್ ಸ್ಕೂಲಿನ ಬಾಗಿಲಲ್ಲಿ ತಂದು ಇಟ್ಟಿದ್ದ ಶಿಲಾಶಾಸನ

1 ಸ್ವಸ್ತಿ ಶ್ರೀ ಶಕವರಿ
2 ಷ ೯೨೧ ನೆಯ ಸಾ
3 ವ್ಯೇರಿಸಂ
4 ವತ್ಸರ
5 ದಪಾಲ್ಗು
6 ಣಮಾಸ
7 ದಪುಣ್ಣಮೆ ಉತ್ತರೆಭಾ
8 ದ್ರಪದ ಅರ್ಕ್ಕವಾರದೆನ್ಪ
9 ಗಣಗೂರಬಿರ್ಗಾಮು
10 ಣ್ಡನಮಗಂಹಞ್ಜ [ದ]
11 ರ್ಮಸೆಟ್ಟಿಕುಣಿನ್ದೋರೊಳೆಗೆಗೇದು
12 ಕಾಲಂತಿಱಿದ್ದೂಕಾಲೂರಂಮಾ
13 ಡಿಮುಳ್ಳೂನ್ನಾಡಬೊಕನಹ
14 ಳ್ಳಿಯಹಕಾದಿವಾಡಿಯಗೆ
15 ರಹಳ್ಳಿ - - ಯು -
16 ಳೆಯುನಾಡಕೂಡಲೂರು
17 ಮಂತನ್ನಭುಜಬಲದಿನ್ದ
18 ಪಡೆದುಮೊದಲ್ಕಾಲುಶಿ
19 ಯಂಮಿನ್ದುರಾಮೇಶ್ವರಮಠ
20 - - ಬತ್ತುಕಳ್ಚಿಳಂಗಳೆಲೂಧ
21 [ರ್ಮ್ಮ]ಕ್ಕೆಬಿಟ್ಟಮಣ್ಣಾಬಣ್ಡಗ
22 ಈಧರ್ಮ್ಮವನಳಿದಂಕವಿಲ
- - - - - -

[1] or ? ಶ್ರೀಪುರದ, as in first edition, and IA, vi, 102.

6

ಯೇಳುಸಾವಿರ ಶೀಮೆಯೆಲ್ಲಿ ನಿಡುತ-ಗ್ರಾಮದಲ್ಲಿರುವ ವೀರಕಲ್ಲು

ಸ್ವಸ್ತಿ ಶ್ರೀ ಜಯಾಭ್ಯುದಯಶಕವರುಷ ೧೧೭೭ ನೆ ರಾಕ್ಷಸ ಸಂ । ವೈಶಾಖ ಶುದ್ಧ ೧೧ ಶಿ ಶ್ರೀಮತ್ ಪ್ರತಾಪ ಚಕ್ರವರ್ತಿ ಹೊಯ್ಸಣ ಭುಜಬಲ ಶ್ರೀ ವೀರನರಸಿಂಹರಾಯನ...ಕಾಲದಲ್ಲಿ ಕಹಿಗೋಡಿನ ಬೀರಗವುಡನ ಮಗ ಸೋಮ್ಮಯೆನು ಬೊಗುಳಿತ್ತಾ ಬುಂಬಿಯೆನಾಯಕನು ತಾಉ ದೂತ ಬೀಮ್ಮಯ ಸೋಮಯ್ಯನೊಡನೆ ಯತ್ತಿಸೂಗಿಕಾಡಿದಲ್ಲಿ ಬಿದ್ದನು । ಆ ಸೋಮ್ಮಯೆನು ದೇವಲೋಕಕ್ಕೆ ಸಲ್ಲಬೇಕೆನ್ದು ಆತನೋಟನ ಹುಟ್ಟಿದ ಮಾರಿಗವುಡನು ಆ ಸೋಮಗವುಡನ ಮಗ ಮಾಯಿಗನು ಪರಿಪಾಯಮಾಡಿಸಿದ ಬೀರಗಲ್ಲು ಮಂಗಳ ಮಹಾ ಶ್ರೀ ಶ್ರೀ ಶ್ರೀ

7

ಅದೇ ಗ್ರಾಮದಲ್ಲಿರುವ ಮತ್ತೊಂದು ವೀರಕಲ್ಲು

ಸ್ವಸ್ತಿ ಶ್ರೀವಿಜಯಾಭ್ಯುದಯಶಕವರುಷ ೧೨೦೭ ಪಾರ್ಥಿವ ಸಂ । ರದೆ ವೈಶಾಖ ಶುಧ ೧೫ ಶ್ರೀಮತ್‌ಪ್ರತಾಪ ಚಕ್ರವರ್ತಿ ಹೊಯ್ಸಣ ಭುಜಬಲ ಶ್ರೀ ವೀರನಾರಸಿಂಹದೇವರಸರ ರಾಜ್ಯಾಭ್ಯುದಯ ಕಾಲದಲ್ಲು ಕಹಿಗೋಡಿನ ಮಾರತಮ್ಮನು ತನ್ನ ಕೊಚನ ಪ್ರತಿತ್ತು ಮತ್ಸರವಿರೋಧಂಗಳ ಕೂಡಿ ಕಾಳಗದಲ್ಲು ಕಾದಿ ಬಿದ್ದನು । ಆ ಮಾರತಮ್ಮನು ದೇವಲೋಕಕ್ಕೆ ಸಲಬೇಕೆನ್ದು ಆತನ ತಮ್ಮ ಮಲೆಯನಾಯಕ ಆ ಮಾರತಮ್ಮನ ಮಕ್ಕಳು ಸೋಮಣ್ಣ ವೀರಗಲ್ಲು ಮಂಗಳ ಮಹಾ ಶ್ರೀ ಶ್ರೀ ಶ್ರೀ

8

ಪಾಡಿನಾಲ್ಕುನಾಡ ತಾಲ್ಲೂಕು ಬೆಂಗನಾಡು ಕುಯಂಗೆರಿನಾಡ ಪಾಲೂರ ಗ್ರಾಮದ ಮಹಾಲಿಂಗೇಶ್ವರ ದೇವಸ್ಥಾನದಲ್ಲಿರುವ ಶಿಲಾ ಶಾಸನ

ಪ್ರಮಾಣ 4′4″ × 2′9″.

ಗ್ರಂಥ ಮತ್ತು ಅರವಕ್ಷರ

1 ஸ்வஸ்திஶ்ரீ | விநாயகம் விஶேஷஜ்ஞம்
2 [illegible]
3 [illegible] | ஸ்வஸ்திஶ்ரீ
4 ஶ்ரீ [illegible]
5 [illegible]
6 [illegible] செய்த ஶிலாஶாஸநம்
7 [illegible]
8 [illegible]
9 [illegible]
10 [illegible]
11 [illegible] வொன்று செய்த ஶிலாஶா
12 [illegible]
13 [illegible]
14 [illegible] கொன்று
15 [illegible]
16 [illegible] கொன்றவ
17 [illegible]
18 [illegible]
19 [illegible]
20. [illegible]

21 [illegible]
22 [illegible]
23 [illegible]
24 [illegible]
25 [illegible]
26 [illegible]

9

ಪಾಡಿನಾಲ್ಕು ನಾಡ ತಾಲ್ಲೂಕು ತವುನಾಡು ಸಂಪಜಿನಾಡ ಭಾಗಮಣ್ಡಲ ಗ್ರಾಮದ
ಭಗಂಡೇಶ್ವರದೇವಸ್ಥಾನದಲ್ಲಿರುವ ಶಿಲಾ ಶಾಸನ

ಪ್ರಮಾಣ 4'6" × 2'8".

ಗ್ರಂಥ ಮತ್ತು ಅರವಕ್ಷರ

1 [illegible]
2 [illegible]
3 [illegible]
4 [illegible]
5 [illegible]
6 [illegible]
7 [illegible]
8 [illegible]
9 [illegible]
10 [illegible]
11 [illegible]
12 [illegible]
13 [illegible]
14 [illegible]
15 [illegible]
16 [illegible]
17 [illegible]
18 [illegible]
19 [illegible]
20 [illegible]
21 [illegible]
22 [illegible]
23 [illegible]
24 [illegible]
25 [illegible]
26 [illegible]
27 [illegible]
28 [illegible]
29 [illegible]
30 [illegible]
31 [illegible] . . [illegible] எழுத்து ||

10

ಅಂಜನಗಿರಿಯಲ್ಲಿರುವ ಶಿಲಾ ಶಾಸನ

ಪ್ರಮಾಣ 5′5″ × 2′4″.

1 ಶ್ರೀ ಶಾನ್ತಿನಾಥಾಯ ನಮಃ ॥ ನಿರ್ವಿಘ್ನಮಸ್ತು ॥ ಶುಭಮಸ್ತು ॥
2 ಶ್ರೀಮತ್ಪರಮಗಂಭೀರಸ್ಯಾದ್ವಾದಾಮೋಘಲಾಂಛನಂ । ಜಿಯಾತ್ತ್ರೈಲೋಕ್ಯನಾಥ
3 ಸ್ಯ ಶಾಸನಂ ಜಿನಶಾಸನಂ ॥ ಸ್ವಸ್ತಿ ಶ್ರೀ ಮೂಲಸಂಘ ದೇಶಿಗಣ ಪುಸ್ತಕ ಗ
4 ಚ್ಛ ಕುಂಡಕುಂದಾನ್ವಯದೆಯಿಂಗುಳೇಶ್ವರವಳಿಯ ಶ್ರೀಮದ್ಬೆಳುಗುಳ ಪುರವರಾ
5 ಧೀಶ್ವರ ಗುಮ್ಮಟ ಜಿನೇಶ್ವರನಾದ ಪದ್ಮಮತ್ತಮಧುಕರಾಯಮಾನರಾದ ತ
6 ತ್ಕಾಲ ಧರ್ಮ ಪ್ರವರ್ತ್ತಕರಾದ ಧರ್ಮ್ಮಾಚಾರ್ಯ್ಯರ ಬಿರುದಾವಲಿ ಯೆಂತೆಂದೊಡೆ ।
7 ಪಂಡಿತ ಪುಂಡರೀಕ ಕುಲಮಂ ಪರಿಬೋಧಿಸಿಯುರ್ವ್ವಿಕೊರ್ಮ್ಮ ಉದ್ದಂಡ ಕುವಾದಿ
8 ವೃತ್ತಮಮನೋಡಿಸಿ ಕೂಡೆ ದಿಗಂಬರ ಪ್ರಭಾಮಂಡನ ವೃತ್ತಮೆಂತಳೆದು ಭವ್ಯರಥಾ
9 ಂಗ ಮನೋಮುತಾವಗಂಸಂಚಿತದೇವಸೂರ್ಯ್ಯನೆಸೆದಂನಯವಾಗ್ಮರುಚಿಯಿಂನಿರಂತರಂ ॥
10 ಸ್ವಸ್ತಿ ಶ್ರೀಮದರಾಯರಾಜಗುರುಮಂಡಲಾಚಾರ್ಯ್ಯ ಮಹಾವಾದ ವಾದೀಶ್ವರ
11 ರಾಯವಾದಿಪಿತಾಮಹ ಸಕಲ ವಿದ್ವಜ್ಜನ ಚಕ್ರವರ್ತ್ತಿಗಳುಂ ಬಲ್ಲಾಳರಾಯಜೀವರಕ್ಷಪಾ
12 ಲಕಾದ್ಯನೇಕಬಿರುದಾವಲೀವಿರಾಜಮಾನರುಮಪ್ಪಶ್ರೀಮಚ್ಚಾರುಕೀರ್ತ್ತಿಪಂಡಿತದೇವರು
13 ಗಳ ಪ್ರಶಿಷ್ಯರಾದ ತಚ್ಛಿಷ್ಯ ಶ್ರೀಮದಭಿನವಚಾರುಕೀರ್ತ್ತಿಪಂಡಿತದೇವರುಗಳ ಪ್ರಿಯ
14 ಶಿಷ್ಯರಾದ ತಸ್ಯಾಗ್ರಜಶಿಷ್ಯ ಶ್ರೀಮಚ್ಚಾರುಕೀರ್ತಿಪಂಡಿತದೇವರುಗಳ ಸತೀರ್ತ್ಥ್ಯರಾದ ಶ್ರೀ
15 ಮಚ್ಛಾಂತಿಕೀರ್ತ್ತಿದೇವರುಗಳು ಶಕವರ್ಷ ॥ ೧೭೬೬ ಸಂದ ವರ್ತ್ತಮಾನ ಕ್ರೋಧಿಸಂವತ್ಸ
16 ರದ ಕಾರ್ತಿಕ ಶುಧ ೧೫ ಲೂಬರಸಿದ ಶಿಲಾಶಾಸನದ ಕ್ರಮವೆಂತೆಂದೊಡೆ ತಂಮ ಗುರು
17 ಶ್ರೀಮದಭಿನವಚಾರುಕೀರ್ತ್ತಿಪಂಡಿತದೇವರುಗಳು । ಕಲಿಕಾಲಧರ್ಮ್ಮತೀರ್ತ್ಥ
18 ಪ್ರವರ್ತ್ತನ ನಿಮಿತ್ತವಾಗಿ ಸುವರ್ಣ್ಣವತಿನದಿಯಿಂದ ಸ್ವಯಂಪ್ರತ್ಯಕ್ಷರಾಗಿ ಶಾನ್ತಿತೀ
19 ರ್ತ್ಥೇಶ್ವರನು ಅನಂತನಾಥಸ್ವಾಮಿಯು ಶಕವರುಷ ೧೭೫೨ ನೆಯ ವಿಕೃತು ಸಂವತ್ಸ
20 ರದ ಚೈತ್ರದಲು ಬಿಜಿಮಾಡಲಾಗಿ ಅಂಜನಗಿರಿಯ ಅಗ್ರನಿವಾಸಿಯಾಗಿದ್ದ
21 ಶಾಂತಿನಾಥಸ್ವಾಮಿಯ ಬಸದಿಗೆ ಬಿಜಿಮಾಡಿಸಿ ಗಿರಿಯಗ್ರದಲ್ಲಿ ದಾರುಮಯದ ಬ
22 ಸದಿಯಮಾಡಿಸಿ ಖರ ಸಂವತ್ಸರದ ಚೈತ್ರಮಾಸದಲ್ಲಿ ಸ್ವಾನುಜರಾದ ಕೋಣಸನಗರದ
23 ಶಾಂತೋಪಾಧ್ಯಾಯರ ಕಯ್ಯಿಂದ ಪ್ರತಿಷ್ಟೆಯಮಾಡಿಸಿ ಶಿಲಾಮಯವಾದ ಬಸ
24 ದಿಯಮಾಡಿಸೆನ್ದು ಬುದ್ಧಿಗತಿಸಲಾಗಿ ಅಲ್ಲಿಂದ ಮುಂದೆ ಕ್ರೋಧಿ ಸಂವತ್ಸರದ ಕಾ
25 ರ್ತಿಕ ಶು ೧೫ ನೆಲೆಗೆ ಕಲು ಗೆಲಸಹಾಲಧಾರೆಗಳ ನಡಸಿದ ವಿವರ ನಂಜರಾಯ
26 ಪಟ್ಟಣಕ್ಕೆ ಸಲುವ ಬೆಂಮತ್ತಿಬೂತನಹಳಿಮಗನಕೆರೆಯಸಮ[ಸ್ತ]ಹಲರಿಂ ಕಲುಗೆ
27 ಲಸಕ್ಕೆ ಸಂದ ಹೊಂನ್ನು ಗ ೨೦೦ ಹನಸೋಗೆಯ ಆದಿಶ್ರೀ ಅವ್ವಗಳು ಅಂಮನಕೊಸಹ
28 ಳ್ಳಿಯ ಭುಜಬಲಿ ಶ್ರೀಅವ್ವಗಳಿಂದ ಗರ್ಬ್ಭಗೃಹವಗ್ಯವಲ್ಲಿ ಕಲುಗೆಲಸಕ್ಕೆ ಸಂದದು ಗ ೩೦ ಹೊಂನು
29 ತಂಮಗುರು ಶ್ರೀಮಚ್ಚಾರುಕೀರ್ತ್ತಿಪಂಡಿತ ದೇವರುಗಳಿಗೆ ತಾವಿತ್ತಂಡಕ್ಕೆ ಮೂಟಿ
30 ಹಾಲದಾಗೆ ಮಧ್ಯಭಾಗಿಲಲಿ ಪ್ರೊಂದುಹೊತ್ತಿನ ನೈವೇದ್ಯಕ್ಕೆ ಕೆಲಸಂಮದುಗ ೫೦ ಆಹಾರದಾ
31 ನಕ್ಕೆ ಕೆಲಸಂದೆದುಗ ೫೦ । ಶುಭಕೃತು ಸಂವತ್ಸರದ ಫಾಲ್ಗುನ ಶು ೧೫ ಲು ಅಂಜನ
32 ಗಿರಿಯ ಶಾಂತೀಶ್ವರಗೆ ಬಿದಗೆ ಸೀತಾಳಮಳಿಗೆಯ ಸಮಸ್ತಹಲರು ಕಂನಡಿ
33 ಗಹಲರು ನಾನಾದೇಸಿಯ ಹಲರು ಮಾಡಿದ ಧರ್ಮ್ಮ । ನಾಳು ಕಟ್ಟದ ಕಾಲು ನಡೆ
34 ವೊಂದಕ್ಕೆ ಗ ೦೯೧ ವನು ಆಹಾರದಾನಕ್ಕೆ ಕೊಡುವೆಉ ಯೆಂದು ಬರಸಿದ ಈ
35 ಧರ್ಮಶಾಸನ ಯೀ ಧರ್ಮಕ್ಕೆ ತಪ್ಪಿದವರು ಗೋಬ್ರಾಹ್ಮರನ್ ಕೊಂದ ದೋಷಕ್ಕೆ ಹೋವ
36 ರು ॥ (ಯೆಡಪಾರ್ಶ್ವ)
37 ಶಕ ವರುಷ
38 ೧೭೬೪ ನೆ
39 ಯ ಶುಭಕೃತು
40 ಸಂವತ್ಸರದ

41 ಚೈತ್ರ ಶುದ್ಧ ೧೩
42 ಬುಧವಾರ ವ್ಯ
43 ಷಭಲಗ್ನದಲ್ಲಿ
44 ಮೋಚಿ ತಂಡ
45 ದೇಹಾರಗಳು
46 ಕುಲ ಪ್ರತಿಷ್ಟ
47 ಯಾಯಿತ್ತು ॥
48 ದಾನಶಾಲೆಗೆ
49 ಹಳ್ಳಿವಯಲ
50 ಗದ್ದೆಯ ಕ್ರಯದ
51 ಮೊಲ್ಯ ಗ ೩೦
52 ಕೊಲಾಯರು ಹೊ
53 ಸಗದ್ದೆಗೈದುದ
54 ಕ್ಕೆ ಕೊಟ್ಟುದು ಗಂ
55 ಉಭಯಂ ವೆಚ್ಚ
56 ಗ ೧೨೦ ಕ್ಕೆ ಆದಾ
57. ಯ ಶ್ರೀಮಚ್ಚಾ
58 ರುಕೀರ್ತಿ ಪಂಡಿತ
59 ದೇವರುಗಳ ಶಿಷ್ಯ
60 ರು ಗುನಸೊಗೆಯಅ
61 ದಿ ಶ್ರೀ ಅವ್ವೆಗಳುಗೆ
62 ಬುಜಬಲಿ ಶ್ರೀ
63 ಅವ್ವೆಗಳಿಂ ಗ ೨೪
64 ಬಸವೆಟ್ಟಣದ ಅನ
65 ಂತಮತಿ ಅವೆಗಳು
66 ನೇ [ಮಿ] ಶ್ರೀ ಅವ್ವೆಗಳಿಂ ಸ
67 ಂದೆದು ಗ ೨೪ ಮು
68 ದ್ದಿ ಸೆಟ್ಟಿಯವಿಜಿ
69 ಯ ಶ್ರೀ ಅವ್ವೆಗಳಿ
70 ಂಸಂದೆದು ಗ ೧೦
71 ಮುಲುಗನಹಳಿಯ
72 ಆದ್ಯೆಕ್ಕಗಳಿಂಸಂ
73 ಗ ೧೨ ಹಾರುವ
74 ಸೆಟ್ಟಿಯ ವಿಜಯ
75 ಣಾ ಶೆಟ್ಟಿರಿಂ ಗ ೩೦
76 ಕಂಣನೂರ ದೇವರಂ
77 ಮ ಶೆಟ್ಟಿಯರಿಂ ಗ ೧೨
78 ಅಸುಂಡಿಯ ಅರಸ

(ಬಲ ಪಾರ್ಶ್ವ)

79—106

ಧರ್ಮ ಶ್ಲೋಕಗಳು

107 ಈ ಮಾಡಿದ ಧ
108 ರ್ಮ್ಮಉ ಆಚ
109 ಂದ್ರಾರ್ಕ್ಕ ಸ್ಥಾ
110 ಯಿಯಾಗಿ ನಡೆ
111 ಯಲಿ ಯೆಂದು
112 ಬರಸಿದ ಧರ್ಮ್ಮ
113 ಶಾಸನಕ್ಕೆ ಮಂ
114 ಗಲ ಮಹಾ
115 ಶ್ರೀ ಶ್ರೀ

11

ಕಟ್ಟೆಪುರದಲ್ಲಿರುವ ತಾಮ್ರ ಶಾಸನ

ಶುಭಮಸ್ತು ॥ ನಮಸ್ತುಂಗಶಿರಶ್ಚುಂಬಿ ಚಂದ್ರಚಾಮರಚಾರವೇ ತ್ರೈಲೋಕ್ಯನಗರಾರಂಭಮೂಲಸ್ತಂಭಾಯ ಶಂಭವೇ ॥ ವನ್ದೇಲೀಲಾವರಾಹಸ್ಯ ದಂಷ್ಟ್ರದಣ್ಡಸಪಾತು ನಃ ಉಧೃತಾ ಮೇದಿನೀ ಯೇನ ಕಲಂಕಮಿವಯತ್ರಸಾ ॥ ಸ್ವಸ್ತಿ ಶ್ರೀ ವಿಜಯಾಭ್ಯುದಯಸಾಲಿವಾಹನಶಕವರುಷಗಳು ೧೬೧೫ ನೆಯ ಶ್ರೀಮುಖನಾಮ ಸಂವತ್ಸರದ ಪುಷ್ಯ ಶು ೧೨ ಲು ಕಾಶ್ಯಪಗೊತ್ರದ ಆಪಸ್ತಂಬ ಸೂತ್ರದ ಬೇಲೂರಕೃಷ್ಣಪ್ಪನಾಯಕರ ಪೌತ್ರರಾದ ವೆಂಕಟಾದ್ರಿನಾಯಕರ ಪುತ್ರರಾದ ಕೃಷ್ಣಪ್ಪನಾಯಕರು ವಸಿಷ್ಠಗೋತ್ರದ ಆಶ್ವಾಯನ ಸೂತ್ರದ ಋಕ್ಶಾಖಾಧ್ಯಾಯನರಾದ ಸುಬ್ರಹ್ಮಣ್ಯ ದೇವಗಳ ಪೌತ್ರರಾದ ಪುಟ್ಟರಸೈಯನ ಪುತ್ರರಾದ ಯೋಗಪ್ಪೈಯಗೆ ಬರಿಸಿಕೊಟ್ಟ ಗ್ರಾಮದಾನಶಾಸನ ಕ್ರಮವೆಂತೆಂದರೆ ಪೂರ್ವದಲ್ಲಿ ಶ್ರೀಮದ್ರಾಜಾಧಿರಾಜರಾಜಪರಮೇಶ್ವರ ಶ್ರೀ ವೀರಪ್ರತಾಪ ಶ್ರೀವೀರಕೃಷ್ಣರಾಯದೇವ ಮಹಾರಾಯರವರು ನಮ್ಮ ವೃದ್ಧಪಿತಾಮಹರಾದ ಸಿನ್ಧುಗೋವಿನ್ದ ಹಿಮಕರಗನ್ಧಧವಲಾಂಕಭೀಮಮಣಿನಾಗಪುರವರಾಧೀಶ್ವರ ಬಲ್ಲೀಯದ ಸಪ್ತಾಂಗಹರಣರಾದ ಯರಕೃಷ್ಣಪ್ಪನಾಯಕರ್ಯ್ಯೆಯನವರಿಗೆ ಪಾಲಿಸ್ತ ಬೇಲೂರಶೀಮೆಗೆ ಸಲುವ ಅರಕಲ್ಗೋಡವಲಿತದ ತುಂಗನಾಡ ನೀರುಗುಂದಸ್ತಲದಲ್ಲಿ ಕೋಣಿಗನಹಳ್ಳಿಗೆ ಪೂರ್ವ ಹೇಮಾವತಿನದಿಗೆ ದಕ್ಷಿಣದ ಜಮಿನಿಗೆ ಪಶ್ಚಿಮ ನಿಲುವಾಗಿಲಿಗೆ ವುತ್ತರವಾದ ಕಟ್ಟೆಪುರದಗ್ರಾಮ ಯಿಪ್ಪುಗಳಲಿಗೆ ಪೂರ್ವವಾದ ಹಿರುಮನಹಳ್ಳಿ ಸಹಾ ಕಾಶ್ಯಪಗೋತ್ರದ ಆಪಸ್ತಂಬಸೂತ್ರದ ಕೃಷ್ಣಪ್ಪನಾಯಕರ ಪೌತ್ರರಾದ ವೆಂಕಟಾದ್ರಿನಾಯಕರ ಪುತ್ರರಾದ ಕೃಷ್ಣಪ್ಪನಾಯಕರು ವಸಿಷ್ಠಗೋತ್ರ ಅಶ್ವಾಯನ ಸೂತ್ರದ ಋಕ್ಶಾಖಾಧ್ಯಾಯನರಾದ ಸುಬ್ರಹ್ಮಣ್ಯದೇವಗಳ ಪೌತ್ರರಾದ ಪುಟ್ಟರಸೈಯನ ಪುತ್ರರಾದ ಯೋಗಪ್ಪೈಯಗೆ ಕಟ್ಟೆಪುರದಗ್ರಾಮ ಹಿರುಮನಹಳ್ಳಿ ಸಹ ಯಿತತ್ಥಾತಿಥಿ ಮಕರ ಸಂಕ್ರಮನ ಪುಣ್ಯಕಾಲದಲ್ಲಿ ಸುರಣ್ಯೋದಕದಾನಧಾರಾಪೂರ್ವಕವಾಗಿ ಕೊಟ್ಟೆವಾಗಿ ಯಿ ಗ್ರಾಮಕ್ಕೆ ಸಲುವ ಅಕ್ಷಿನಾಗಾಮಿನಿಧಿನಿಕ್ಷೇಪ

ಜಲಪಾಷಾನ ಸಿದ್ಧಸಾಧ್ಯಂಗಳೆಂಬ ಅಷ್ಟಭೋಗ ಸ್ವಾಮ್ಯವನ್ನು ಆಗುಮಾಡಿಕೊಂಡು ನಿಮ್ಮ ಸಂತಾನಪರಂಪರಾ ಆಚಂದ್ರಾರ್ಕಸ್ಥಾಯಿಗಳಾಗಿ ದಾನಾದಿ ವಿನಿಮಯ ವಿಕ್ರಯಗಳಿಗೆ ಯೋಗ್ಯವಾಗಿ ಸುಖದಲ್ಲಿ ಅನುಭವಿಸಿಕೊಂಡು ಯಿಹದುಯೆಂದು ಕಾಶ್ಯಪಗೋತ್ರದ ಆಪಸ್ತಂಬಸೂತ್ರದ ಕೃಷ್ಣಪ್ಪನಾಯಕರ ಪೌತ್ರರಾದ ವೆಂಕಟಾದ್ರಿನಾಯಕರ ಪುತ್ರರಾದ ಕೃಷ್ಣಪ್ಪನಾಯಕರು ವಸಿಷ್ಟಗೋತ್ರದ ಆಶ್ವಾಯನ ಸೂತ್ರದ ಋಕ್ಶಾಖಾಧ್ಯಾಯನರಾದ ಸುಬ್ರಹ್ಮಣ್ಯದೇವಗಳ ಪೌತ್ರರಾದ ಪುಟ್ಟರಸ್ಯೆಯನ ಪುತ್ರರಾದ ಯೋಗಪ್ಪಯ್ಯಗೆ ಬರಿಸಿಕೊಟ್ಟ ಶಾಸನ ॥ ಯಿದಕ್ಕೆ ಧರ್ಮಸಾಕ್ಷಿಗಳು ಆದಿತ್ಯಚಂದ್ರಾವನಿಲೋನಲಶ್ಚ ಧ್ಯೌರ್ಭೂಮಿರಾಪೋ ಹೃದಯಂ ಮನಶ್ಚ ಅಹಶ್ಚರಾತ್ರಿಶ್ಚವುಭೇಚಸನ್ಧ್ಯೇ ಧರ್ಮಶ್ಚ ಜಾನಾತಿ ನರಸ್ಯವೃತ್ತಂ ॥ ದಾನಪಾಲನಯೋರ್ಮಧ್ಯೇ ದಾನಾತ್ ಶ್ರೇಯೋನುಪಾಲನಂ ದಾನಾತ್ ಸ್ವರ್ಗಮವಾಪ್ನೋತಿ ಪಾಲನಾದಚ್ಯುತಂ ಪದಂ ॥ ಸ್ವದತ್ತಾದ್ವಿಗುಣಂ ಪುಣ್ಯಂ ಪರದತ್ತಾನುಪಾಲನಂ ಪರದತ್ತಾಪಹಾರೇಣ ಸ್ವದತ್ತಂ ನಿಷ್ಫಲಂಭವೇತ್ ॥ ಸ್ವದತ್ತಾ ಪುತ್ರಿಕಾ ಧಾತ್ರೀ ಪಿತೃದತ್ತಾ ಸಹೋದರೀ ಅನ್ಯದತ್ತಾ ಸ್ವಮಾತಾಚ ದತ್ತಭೂಮಿಂ ಪರಿತ್ಯಜೇತ್ ॥ ಯೇಕೈವಭಗಿನೀ ಲೋಕೇ ಸರ್ವೇಷಾಮೇವ ಭೂಭುಜಾಂ ನ ಭೋಗ್ಯಾನಕರಗ್ರಾಹ್ಯಾವಿಪ್ರದತ್ತಾವಸುಂಧರಾ ॥ ಶ್ರೀಕೃಷ್ಣ-

12

ಮಹಾದೇವಪುರದ ತಾಮ್ರ ಶಾಸನ

ಎ

ಲಿಂಗ ರಾಜೇಂದ್ರವಡೆಯರು ಕೊಡಗಿನ ಚರಮೂರ್ತಿಗಳಾದ ಶಿಧಲಿಂಗಪ್ಪದೇವರು।
ಶಾರ್ವರಿ ಸಂವತ್ಸರದ ಕಾರ್ತಿಕ ಶುಧ ೧೩ ಯು ಮಂದವಾರದಲ್ಲು ಜೀರ್ಣೋದ್ಧಾರಮಾಡಿಸಿದ್ದು ।

ಶ್ರೀಮದ್ರಾಜಾಧಿರಾಜ ರಾಜಪರಮೇಸ್ವರ ಪ್ರಹುಡಪ್ರತಾಪ ಅಪ್ರತಿಮ ವೀರನರಪತಿ ಕೊಡಗಿನ ಸಂಸ್ಥಾನದ ಶ್ರೀ ರತ್ನಸಿಂಹಾಸನಾರೂಢರಾಗಿ ಪ್ರಿಥ್ವೀ ಸಾಮ್ರಾಜ್ಯಂ ಗೈಯುತ್ತಿದ್ದ ಭಾರದ್ವಾಜಗೋತ್ರದ ಆಶ್ವಲಾಯನ ಸೂತ್ರದ ರುಕ್ಷಭಾನುಕಾಧ್ಯಾಯ ವೀರಶೈವಮತಸ್ತರಾದ ಅಪ್ಪಾಜೇಂದ್ರವಡೆಯರವರ ಪುತ್ರರಾದ ಲಿಂಗರಾಜೇಂದ್ರವಡೆಯರು ।

ನಮಸ್ತುಂಗಶಿರಶ್ಚುಂಬಿ ಚಂದ್ರಚಾಮರ ಚಾರವೇ । ತ್ರೈಲೋಕ್ಯನಗರಾರಮ್ಭಮೂಲಸ್ತಂಭಾಯ
ಶಂಭವೇ ॥

ಸ್ವಸ್ತಿ ಶ್ರೀ ವಿಜಯಾಭ್ಯುದಯ ಕಲಿ ಸಂದ ೪೮೮೧ ನ ವರ್ತಮಾನಕ್ಕೆ ಸಲ್ಲುವ ವಿಕಾರಿಸಂವತ್ಸರದ ಮಾಘ ಬಹುಳ ೧೦ ಯು ಬುಧವಾರ ದಿವಿಗಳಿಗೆ ಶ್ರೀಗ ಶಿವಾಧೀನವಾದ್ದು।

ಯಿಾ ಶಿವಾಧೀನವಾಗುವ ತತ್ಕಾಲದಲ್ಲು ಯಿಾ ಮಹಾರಾಜರ ಗರ್ಭಾಬ್ಧಿಸುಧಾಕರಾಯಮಾನರಾದ ವೀರರಾಜೇಂದ್ರವಡೆಯರು ಸನ್ನಿಧಾನದಲ್ಲು ಯಿದ್ದು ಸತ್ಕರ್ಮವನ್ನು ವಿಚಾರಿಸಿ ಅಪ್ಪನಪ್ರಕಾರ ಮಹಾದೇವಪುರದಲ್ಲು ಕ್ರಿಯಸಮಾಧಿಯನ್ನು ಮಾಡಿಸಿ ದೇವಸ್ಥಾನವನ್ನು ಕಟ್ಟಿಸಿ ಆಸಮಾಧಿಮೇಲೆ ಬಸವೇಶ್ವರದೇವರ ಪ್ರತಿಷ್ಠೆಯನ್ನು ಮಾಡಿಸಿ ಮುರಿಗೆ ಸಂಪ್ರದಾಯದ ಮಠವನ್ನು ಕಟ್ಟಿಸಿ ಸದಾಕಾಲದಲ್ಲು ಗಣಾರಾಧನೆ ಯಿಾ ದೇವತಾರಾಧನೆ ವೃದ್ಧಿಕ್ಕೆ ಯಿಾ ಮಹಾದೇವಪುರ ಭೂಮಿ ಚಿಕ್ಕಹರದೆ ಜಂಬೂರ ಬೇಲೂರು ಬಸವನಹಳ್ಳಿ ಗ್ರಾಮಕ್ಕೆ ಸಹ ಲಿಂಗಮುದ್ರೆ ಶಿಲಾಪ್ರತಿಷ್ಠೆಯನ್ನು ಮಾಡಿಸಿ ನಲಸಂವತ್ಸರದ ಚೈತ್ರ ಶುಧ ೧ ವು ಭಾರ್ಗವಾರದಲ್ಲು ವಪ್ಪಿಸಿ ದಾನಶಾಸನವನ್ನು ಬರದುಕೊಟ್ಟು ಯಿಧೆಯಾಗಿ ಜೀರ್ಣೋದ್ಧಾರ ಆದ್ದು ಶಾರ್ವರಿಸಂವತ್ಸರದ ಕಾರ್ತಿಕ ಶುಧ ೧೩ ದಿವಸ ಪ್ರಾರಂಭ ಶುಭಕೃತು ಸಂವತ್ಸರದ ವೈಶಾಖ ಶುಧ ೧೦ ಗುರುವಾರಕ್ಕೆ ಆಕೈರು ಆಗಿಯಿಧೆ-

13

ಯಡವನಾಡ ಅಬ್ಬಿಮಠದ ತಾಮ್ರ ಶಾಸನ

ಮುರಿಗಿ ಸ್ವಾಮಿಯವರ ಪಾದಕ ಮಲ್ಲಿಕಾರ್ಜುನಸ್ವಾಮಿಯ ಪಾಕೋಡು ಮಹಂತ ಸ್ವಾಮಿಯವರ ಚರಮೂರ್ತಿಗಳಾದ ಶಾಂತವೀರಸ್ವಾಮಿಯವರ ಚರಮೂರ್ತಿಗಳಾದ ಅಬ್ಬಿಮಠದ ನಿರಂಜನದೇವರ ಪಾದಕ್ಕೆ-

ನಮಸ್ತುಂಗ ಶಿರಸ್ಚುಂಬಿ ಚಂದ್ರಚಾಮರ ಚಾರವೇ। ತ್ರೈಲೋಕ್ಯನಗರಾರಂಭ ಮೂಲಸ್ತಂಭಾಯ ಶಂಭವೇ ॥

ಸ್ವಸ್ತಿ ಶ್ರೀ ವಿಜಯಾಭ್ಯುದಯ ಶಾಲಿವಾಹನ ಶಕವರುಷ ೧೭೧೮ನೆ ವರ್ತಮಾನಕ್ಕೆ ಸಲ್ಲುವ ನಲಸಂವತ್ಸರದ ಚೈತ್ರ ಶು ೧ ಭಾರ್ಗವಾರದಲ್ಲು ಶಿವಗಂಗಮೇಲಿನ ಗವಿಸಿಂಹಾಸನಾರೂಢರ ಸಾಂಪ್ರದಾಯಸ್ತರಾದ ಶಿಧಪುರದ

ಮಠದ ಸ್ವಾಮಿಯವರ ಕರಕಮಲಸಂಜಾತರಾದ ವೀರ ಶೈವಮತಸ್ತರಾದ ಶ್ರೀಮದ್ರಾಜಾದಿರಾಜ ರಾಜ ಪರಮೇಶ್ವರ ಪ್ರಹುಡ ಪ್ರತಾಪ ಅಪ್ರತಿಮ ವೀರನರಪತಿ ಕೊಡಗಿನ ಸಂಸ್ಥಾನದ ಶ್ರೀ ರತ್ನಸಿಂಹಾಸನಾರೂಢರಾಗಿ ಪ್ರಿಥ್ವೀ ಸಾಮ್ರಾಜ್ಯಂ ಗೈವುತ್ತಿರಲು ಭಾರದ್ವಾಜಗೋತ್ರದ ಆಶ್ವಲಾಯನಸೂತ್ರ ರುಕ್ಷಭಾನುಕಾಧ್ಯಾಯಗಳಾದ ಅಪ್ಪಾಜೇಂದ್ರವಡೆಯರವರ ಪೌತ್ರರಾದ ಲಿಂಗರಾಜೇಂದ್ರವಡೆಯರವರ ಪುತ್ರರಾದ ವೀರರಾಜೇಂದ್ರವಡೆಯರವರು ಬರದು ಪಪ್ಪಿಸ್ತ ಜೀರ್ಣ್ಣೋರ್ದ್ಧಾರದ ದಾನಶಾಸನದ ಕ್ರಮವೆಂತೆಂದರೆ– ಸ್ವಾಕು ಶಾಲಿವಾಹನ ಶಕವರುಷ ೧೬೫೦ ನೆ ಕೀಲಕಸಂವತ್ಸರದ ಕಾರ್ತ್ತಿಕ ಶುದ್ಧ ೨ ಬುಧವಾರದಲ್ಲು ಹಿರೆ ಅಜ್ಜಯನವರಾದ ದೊಡ್ಡವೀರಪ್ಪವಡೆಯರವರು ಯಡವನಾಡು ಅಬ್ಬಿಮಠಕ್ಕೆ ಪ್ರಾಕುನಡದು ಬರುತ್ತಿದ್ದ ಗ್ರಾಮ ಹೊಸಳ್ಳಿಗ್ರಾಮ ವಂದು ಜಿಗಟ್ಟಳ್ಳಿಗ್ರಾಮ ವೆಂದು ವುಭಯಗ್ರಾಮ ಯೆರಡು ಯಿದಲ್ಲದೆ ದೊಡ್ಡ ವೀರೂಪಾಕ್ಷಸ್ವಾಮಿಯವರು ಮಡಿಕೇರಿಗೆ ಚಿತ್ತೈಸಲಾಗಿ ಪಾದವಿಡಿದು ಬಿನ್ನಹಮಾಡಿಕೊಂಡು ಆಚಂದ್ರಾರ್ಕವಾಗಿ ಧರ್ಮಬರಬೇಕೆಂದು ನೂತನವಾಗಿ ಅಬ್ಬಿಮಠಕ್ಕೆ ಬಿಟ್ಟುಕೊಟ್ಟ ಗ್ರಾಮ ಬಾಚಳ್ಳಿ ಗ್ರಾಮ ವಂದಕ್ಕೆ ಕಂದಾಯ ಗ ೧೬ ಹದಿನಾರು ವರಹ ಸಹ ಹೊಸಳ್ಳಿ ಗ್ರಾಮ ೧ ಜಿಗಟ್ಟಳ್ಳಿ ಗ್ರಾಮ ೧ ಬಾಚಳ್ಳಿ ಗ್ರಾಮ ೧ ಅನ್ತುಗ್ರಾಮ ೩ ರ ಚತುಶ್ಸೀಮೆಯೊಳ್ಗೆ ಕಟ್ಟನಲ್ಲಿ ಯಿರುವ ನಿಧಿನಿಕ್ಷೇಪಜಲತರು ಪಾಷಾಣ ಅಕ್ಷೀನ ಆಗಾಮಿ ಸಿದ್ಧಸಾಧ್ಯಂಗಳೆಂಬ ಅಷ್ಟಭೋಗತೇಜಸ್ವಾಮ್ಯ ಮುನ್ತಾದ ಆಸಕಲಭೂಮಿಯನ್ನು ಶಿವಾರ್ಪಿತವಾಗಿ ಗಣಾರಾಧನೆಯನ್ನು ನಡಿಸಿಕೊಂಡು ಆಚಂದ್ರಾರ್ಕವಾಗಿ ಧರ್ಮವನ್ನು ನಡಿಸ್ತ ಶಿವಪೂಜಾಕಾಲದಲ್ಲು ಆಶೀರ್ವಾದ ಶ್ಲೋಕ। ಜಾತಿಸ್ಮರತ್ವಂ ಪ್ರಿಥ್ವೀಪತಿತ್ವಂ ಸವುಭಾಗ್ಯಲಾವಣ್ಯಮತೀವರೂಪಂ । ತ್ವದ್ಭಕ್ತಿವಿದ್ಯೇಪರಮಾಯುರಿಷ್ಟಂ ತ್ವಂದಕ್ಷಮೇ ಶಂಕರ ಜನ್ಮಜನ್ಮನಿ ॥ ಯಂಬ ಆಶೀರ್ವಾದವನ್ನು ಮಾಡುತ್ತಾಯಿರಬೇಕೆಂಬದಾಗಿ ಬರದು ಪಪಿಸ್ತ ಜೀರ್ಣೋರ್ದ್ಧಾರದ ಭೂಸಾಧನಕ್ಕೆ ಸಾಕ್ಷಿಗಳು–ಆದಿತ್ಯಚನ್ದ್ರೌ ಅನಿಲೋನಲಶ್ಚ ದ್ಯಾವುರ್ಭೂಮಿರಾಪೋಹೃದಯಂ ಯಮಶ್ಚ । ಅಹೋರಾತ್ರಿಶ್ಚ ಉಭಯೆಶ್ಚ ಸಂಧ್ಯಾಧರ್ಮಶ್ಚ ಜಾನಾತಿನರಸ್ಯವೃತ್ತಿಃ ॥ ಸ್ವದತ್ತಾದ್ವಿಗುಣಂಪುಣ್ಯಂ ಪರದತ್ತಾನುಪಾಲನಂ । ಪರದತ್ತಾಪಹಾರೇಣ ಸ್ವದತ್ತಾಂನಿಶ್ಫಲಂಭವೇತ್ ॥ ಯಂಬ ಭೂಸಾಧನಕ್ಕೆ ಅಪ್ಪಣೆಪ್ರಕಾರ ಬಾರ್ಗವಾರ ಬರದಾತ ಖಾಸರಹಸ್ಯದ ಶಂಭೈಯ.

ಶ್ರೀ ವಿ ॥

14

ಮಹಾದೇವಪುರದಲ್ಲಿರುವ ತಾಮ್ರ ಶಾಸನ

ಶ್ರೀಮನ್ಮಹಾಮುರಿಗಾಸ್ವಾಮಿಗಳವರ ಚರಮೂರ್ತ್ತಿಗಳಾದ ಕೊಡಲಿಮಹಂತಸ್ವಾಮಿಗಳವರ ಚರಮೂರ್ತ್ತಿಗಳಾದ ಶಾಂತವೀರಸ್ವಾಮಿಯವರ ಪಾದಕ್ಕೆ—

ನಮಸ್ತುಂಗಶಿರಶ್ಚುಂಬಿ ಚಂದ್ರಚಾಮರಚಾರವೇ। ತ್ರೈಲೋಕ್ಯನಗರಾರಂಭಮೂಲಸ್ತಂಭಾಯ ಶಮ್ಭವೇ ॥

ಸ್ವಸ್ತಿ ಶ್ರೀವಿಜಯಾಭ್ಯುದಯ ಶಾಲಿವಹನ ಶಕವರ್ಷ ೧೭೧೮ ನೆ ವರ್ತಮಾನಕ್ಕೆ ಸಲ್ಲುವ ನಳಸಂವತ್ಸರದ ಚೈತ್ರಶುದ್ಧ ೧ ಭಾರ್ಗವಾರದಲ್ಲು ಶಿವಗಂಗೆಮೇಲನ ಗವಿಸಿಂಹಾಸನಾರೂಢರ ಸಾಂಪ್ರದಾಯಸ್ತರಾದ ವೀರಶೈವಮತಸ್ತರಾದ ಸಿದ್ಧಾಪುರದ ಮಠದ ಪಟ್ಟದ ಸ್ವಾಮಿಯವರ ಕರಕಮಲ ಸಂಜಾತರಾದ ಶ್ರೀಮದ್ರಾಜಾಧಿರಾಜ ರಾಜಪರಮೇಶ್ವರ ಪ್ರಹುಡ ಪ್ರತಾಪ ಅಪ್ರತಿಮ ವೀರನರಪತಿ ಕೊಡಗಿನ ಸಂಸ್ಥಾನದ ಶ್ರೀರತ್ನ ಸಿಂಹಾಸನಾರೂಢರಾಗಿ ಪೃಥ್ವೀ ಸಾಮ್ರಾಜ್ಯಂ ಗೈಯ್ಯುತ್ತಿರಲು ಭಾರದ್ವಾಜ ಗೋತ್ರದ ಆಶ್ವಲಾಯನ ಸೂತ್ರದ ರುಕ್ಷಭಾನುಕಾಧ್ಯಾಯಗಳಾದ ಅಪ್ಪಾಜೇಂದ್ರವಡೆಯರವರ ಪವುತ್ರರಾದ ಲಿಂಗರಾಜೇಂದ್ರವಡೆಯರವರ ಗರ್ಭಾಬ್ಧಿಸುಧಾಕರಾಯಮಾನರಾದ ವೀರರಾಜೇಂದ್ರವಡೆಯರವರು ಶಿವಾರ್ಪನಕ್ಕೆ ಸಮರ್ಪಿಸಿದ ದಾನಶಾಸನದಕ್ರಮವೆಂತೆಂದರೆ। ಮಹಾದೇವಪುರಮಠಯಿದಕ್ಕೆ ಸ್ವಾಮಿಯವರು ಚಿತ್ತೈಸಲಾಗಿ ಸಾಷ್ಟಾಂಗಪ್ರಣಾಮಿಶಿ ಪಾದವಿಡಿದು ಆಚಂದ್ರಾರ್ಕವಾಗಿ ಧರ್ಮಬರಬೇಕೆನ್ದು ಬರದುಪಪ್ಪಿಸಿದ ವುತ್ತಾರದ ಭೂಮಿವಿವರ। ಶಿವಾರ್ಪನದಬಗ್ಯೆ ಮಠಕ್ಕೆ ಮೇಲುಪೆಟ್ಟದ ಬಗ್ಯೆ ಲಿಂಗಮುದ್ರೆ ಶಿಲಾಪ್ರತಿಷ್ಟೆಯನ್ನುಮಾಡಿಸಿ ಬಿಟ್ಟುಕೊಟ್ಟ ಗ್ರಾಮಗಳಿಂದ ಬರುವ ಕನ್ದಾಯದ ವಿವರ ಚಿಕ್ಕಹರದೆ ಜಂಬೂರು ಗ್ರಾಮಕ್ಕೆ ಬಿಜಭಟ್ಟಿ ೪೪ ಕ್ಕೆ ಕಂದಾಯ ೩೯ ವರಹ ಪ್ರಾಕಿನ ವುತ್ತಾರ ಯಿಾ ಗ್ರಾಮದ ಪುರವರ್ಗದೇವಮಾನ್ಯ ಭೂತವುತ್ತಾರಸಹ ಬಿಜಭಟ್ಟಿ ೬ ॥ ಗೆ ೬ ॥ ವರಹ ಹೋಗಲಾಗಿ ಶುದ್ಧನಿನ್ತ ಭೂಮಿಬಿಜವರಿ ಭಟ್ಟಿ ೩೬ ॥ ಕಂದಾಯ ೩೬ ॥ ವರಹ ಯಡವನಾಡುಪಲಿತ್ತದ ತೆಂಕನಾಡುಮಂಡೆಗೆ ಶೇರಿದ ಬೇಲೂರು ಬಸವನಹಳ್ಳಿ ವಳಗಣ ಗುಡುಗೂರು ಸಹ ಗ್ರಾಮ ೨ ಕ್ಕೆ ಬಿಜವರಿಭಟ್ಟಿ ೫೦ ಕ್ಕೆ ಕಂದಾಯ ೫೦ ವರಹಕ್ಕೆ ಪ್ರಾಕಿನವುತ್ತಾರ ಯಿಾ ಗ್ರಾಮದ ಪುರವರ್ಗದೇವಮಾನ್ಯಭೂತವುತ್ತಾರ ಗವುಡುಂಬಲಿನಾಯಿಮನ್ನು ಸಹ ಖಂಡಿಗ ೧೩ ॥ ಗೆ ಕಂದಾಯ ೧೩ ॥ ಹೋಗಲಾಗಿ ಶುದ್ಧನಿಂತದ್ದು ಬಿಜಭಟ್ಟಿ ೩೭ ॥ ಗೆ ಕಂದಾಯ ೩೭ ॥ ವರಹ ಅಂತುಗ್ರಾಮ ೪ ಕ್ಕೆ ಪ್ರಾಕಿನವುತ್ತಾರ ಹೋಗಲಾಗಿ ಶುದ್ಧನಿಂತ

ದ್ದು ಯಿಾ ಮಠಕ್ಕೆ ಬರುವ ಕಂದಾಯ ೬೯ ವರಹ ಭೆತ್ತಭಟ್ಟೆ ೩೦೦ ಬೆಳೆಯು ಚವು ಗ್ರಾಮದೇವರ ಮುನ್ದಿಟ್ಟು ಲಿಂಗ ಮುದ್ರೆ ಶಿಲಾಪ್ರತಿಷ್ಟೆಯನ್ನು ಮಾಡಿಸಿಕೊಟ್ಟು ಯಿಾ ತಿಥಿಯಲ್ಲೂ ಪಿತ್ರಾದಿ ಸಮಸ್ತಪಿತೃಗಳಿಗು ಅಕ್ಷಯ ಶಿವಲೋಕ ಪ್ರಾಪ್ತಿಯಾಗಬೇಕು ಯೆಂಬ ಅಪೇಕ್ಷೆಯಿಂದ ಭೂಸಾಧನವನ್ನು ಬರದು ವಪ್ಪಿಸ್ತೇವಾಗಿ ಯಿಾ ಗ್ರಾಮಕ್ಕೆ ಚವುಕಟ್ಟು ಲಿಂಗಮುದ್ರೆ ಶಿಲಾಪ್ರತಿಷ್ಟೆವಳಗಾದ ನಿಧಿನಿಕ್ಷೇಪಜಲತರು ಪಾಷಾಣ ಅಕ್ಷೀನ ಆಗಾಮಿಸಿದ್ಧ ಸಾಧ್ಯಂಗಳೆಂಬ ಅಷ್ಟಭೋಗತೇಜಸಾಮ್ಯಮುನ್ನಾದ ಆಸಕಲ ಭೂಮಿಯನ್ನು ಶಿವಾರ್ಪಿತವಾಗಿ ಗಣಾರಾಧನೆಯನ್ನು ಮಾಡಿಸಿಕೊಂಡು ಶಿವಪೂಜಾಕಾಲದಲ್ಲು ಆಶೀರ್ವಾದ ಶ್ಲೋಕ—ಜಾತಿಸ್ಮರತ್ವಂ ಪೃಥ್ವೀಪತಿತ್ವಂ ಸವುಭಾಗ್ಯಲಾವಣ್ಯಮತೀವ ರೂಪಂ। ತ್ವದ್ಭಕ್ತಿವಿದ್ಯೇಪರಮಾಯುರಿಷ್ಟಂ ತ್ವಂದೆಹ್ಯಮೇ ಶಂಕರ ಜನ್ಮ ಜನ್ಮನಿ॥ ಯೆಂಬ ಆಶೀರ್ವಾದವನ್ನು ಮಾಡುತ್ತ ಯಿರಬೇಕೆಂಬದಾಗಿ ಬರದು ವಪ್ಪಿಸ್ತ ಭೂಸಾಧನಕ್ಕೆ ಸಾಕ್ಷಿಗಳು – ಆದಿತ್ಯ ಚಂದ್ರೋ ಅನಿಲೋ ನಲಶ್ಚ ದ್ಯೌರ್ಭೂರ್ಮಿರಾಪೋ ಹೃದಯಂ ಯಮಶ್ಚ ಅಹಶ್ಚ ರಾತ್ರಿಶ್ಚ ವುಭೆಯಶ್ಚ ಸಂದ್ಯಾ ಧರ್ಮಸ್ಯ ಜಾನಾತಿ ನರಸ್ಯ ವೃತ್ತಃ॥ ಸ್ವದತ್ತಾದ್ವಿಗುಣಂ ಪುಣ್ಯಂ ಪರದತ್ತಾನುಪಾಲನಂ ಪರದತ್ತಾಪಹಾರೇಣ ಸ್ವದತ್ತಂ ನಿಷ್ಫಲಂ ಭವೇತ್ ಯೆಂಬ ಭೂಸಾಧನಕ್ಕೆ ಸ್ವಹಸ್ತಾವಪ್ಪಿತಾ ಶ್ರೀ ವಿ॥

15

ಗದ್ದಿಗೆಯ ಮೇಲೆ

ಕಲಿ ಸನ್ದ ೪೯೧೯

16

ದೆನಗಲ್ಲಿನಲ್ಲಿರುವ ಶಿಲಾಶಾಸನ

ವಿರಾಜಪುರದ ಮಠ

ಇವಸಂವತ್ಸರದ ಜೇಷ್ಟ ಶುಧ ೫ ರಲ್ಲು ಚೇಲಳಷಾಕಸ್ವಾಮಿಗಳ ವಿರಕ್ತಮಟ್ಟ

17

ಮಡಿಕೇರಿಯಲ್ಲಿ ಓಂಕಾರೇಶ್ವರ ದೇವಸ್ಥಾನದ ತಾಮ್ರಶಾಸನ

ಸ್ವಸ್ತಿ ಶ್ರೀವಿಜಯಾಭ್ಯುದಯ ಶಾಲಿವಾಹನ ಶಕವರ್ಷ ೧೭೩೯ ನೆ ಯಿಾಶ್ವರಸಂವತ್ಸರದ ಜೇಷ್ಟಬಹುಳ ಬಿದಿಗೆಯು ಭಾನುವಾರಕ್ಕೆ ಕಲಿದಿನ ೧೮೭೬೫೩೦ ನೆ ಯಿಾ ಶುಭದಿವಸದಲ್ಲಿ ಚಂದ್ರವಂಶಕ್ಷೀರಪಾರಾವಾರಪಾರಿಜಾತಾಯಮಾನರಾದ ಭಾರದ್ವಾಜಗೋತ್ರಸಂಜಾತರಾದ ಆಶ್ವಲಾಯನ ಸೂತ್ರ ಋಕ್ಶಾಖಿಗಳಾದ ವೀರ ಶೈವಮತ ಧುರೀಣ ಪ್ರವೀಣರಾದ ಶ್ರೀಮತ್ಕೊಡಗು ಸಂಸ್ಥಾನ ಸಂಸ್ಥಿತ ಸಮಾದ್ಯಕ್ಷೀರನಗರಮಧ್ಯಪರಿಭ್ರಾಜಮಾನ ಮಣಿಗಣಖಚಿತ ಚಾರುಸಿಂಹಾಸನಾರೂಢರಾದ ಅಪ್ರತಿಮಪ್ರತಾಪಪ್ರಕಾಶ ಪ್ರಹಸಿತಮಾರ್ತಾಂಡಮಂಡಲರಾದ ಅಖಂಡಾಖಂಡವೈಭವಸಮೇತರಾದ ಸಕಲದಿಗಂತರಾಲವಿದ್ಯೋತ್ತಮ ಸಮಾನಕೀರ್ತಿ ಪ್ರಖ್ಯಾತರಾದ ಸಮಸ್ತ ಪ್ರಶಸ್ತ ರಾಜಧರ್ಮಾವಧಾರಣ ಯುಧಿಷ್ಠಿರರಾದ ಮಹಾರಾಜ ಅಪ್ಪಾಜಿರಾಜೇಂದ್ರರವರ ಪೌತ್ರರಾದ ಲಿಂಗರಾಜೇಂದ್ರವಡೆಯರವರ ಪುತ್ರರಾದ ಶ್ರೀ ಲಿಂಗರಾಜೇಂದ್ರವಡೆಯರವರು ಯಿಾ ಲೋಕದಲ್ಲಿ ಸುಕೃತಕ್ರಿಯೆಗಳನ್ನು ವಿರಚಿಸಿದರೆ ಇಹಪರಮೆರಡರಲ್ಲಿಯೂ ಶಾಶ್ವಿತಫಲಭರಿತರಾಗಿ ಯಿರಬೇಕು ತತ್ಕಾರಣದಿಂದ ಮಹತ್ತಾದ ಪುಣ್ಯಫಲಪ್ರದಾಯಕವಾಗಿ ಯಿರವೆಂಥಾ ಶಿವಲಿಂಗಪ್ರತಿಷ್ಠಾಪನಉ ಕರ್ತವ್ಯವೆಂದು ಚಿತ್ತದಲ್ಲಿ ನಿಶ್ಚೈಶಿ ತದ್ದಿವಸ ಶುಭಮುಹೂರ್ತದಲ್ಲಿ ಆಸೆದ್ರುಶಶ್ರೀಕಾಶಲಮಣ್ಟಪಾವಿ ಯುಕ್ತ ರಾಜಕಮಲಾಕರಾಖ್ಯಾಪದ್ಮಕರಾಭಿರಾಮನೂತನೋಂಕಾರೇಶ್ವರ ದೇವಸ್ಥಾನವನ್ನು ಪ್ರಾರಂಭಿಸಿ ತದಾರಭ್ಯ ವಿಕ್ರಮಸಂವತ್ಸರದ ಚೈತ್ರಶುದ್ಧದ್ವಾದಸಿಯು ಭಾನುವಾರದವರಿಗೆ ವರುಷ ೨ ತಿಂಗಳು ೯ ದಿನ ೨೫ ಕಲಿದಿನ ೧೮೭೬೮೨೧ ನೆ ಯೇತದ್ರುಶಸುದಿವಸದಲ್ಲಿ ಅತ್ಯಾಶ್ಚರಕವಾದನ್ಥಾದ್ದನ್ನು ಸಾಮಗ್ರಿಯವಾಗಿ ನಿರ್ಮಿಶಿ ಶ್ರೀಕರವಾಗಿಯಿರುವಂಥ ಓಂಕಾರೇಶ್ವರನಾಮಕ ಶಿವಲಿಂಗವನ್ನು ಪ್ರತಿಷ್ಠಾಪಿಸಿ ಸನ್ತುಷ್ಟಚಿತ್ತರಾದ್ದು ಹ್ಯಾಗೆನ್ದರೆ ಶ್ರೀಮಚ್ಚಂದ್ರಶೇಖರನ ಪರಮಕೃಪಾನುಗ್ರಹಸಾಮರ್ಥ್ಯದಿಂದ ಸಕಲಮನೋರಥ ಪ್ರದವಾಗಿಯಿರುವಂಥ ಯೇತದ್ದೇವತಾಯತ್ನ ಶಿವಲಿಂಗಪ್ರತಿಷ್ಠಾಪನಉ ನಿರ್ವಿಘ್ನದಿಂದ ವಿರಚಿತವಾಯಿತು ಯಾರು ಭಕ್ತಿಯಿಂದ ಶ್ರೀ ಮಹೇಶ್ವರನ ಭಜಿಸುತ್ತಾರೋ ಅವರಿಗ ಸರ್ವತ್ರ ಅನಿಕರಸಾಧ್ಯವಾಗಿ ಯಿರುವಂಥ ಶುಭಫಲಉ ಸ್ವಯಮೇವ ಸಾಧ್ಯವಾಗುತ್ತದೆ ಯೆಂದು ಸರ್ವಜನಪರಿಜ್ಞಾನಾರ್ಥವಾಗಿ ಬರಸಿಯಿರುವಂಥ ಶಾಸನ॥ ಶುಭಮಸ್ತು॥

ಅಂತುವೆರುಷ ೧ ಕ್ಕೆ ಓಂಕಾರೇಶ್ವರಗಣಾಧೀಶ್ವರಕುಮಾರೇಶ್ವರ ಶ್ರೀನಂದೀಶ್ವರ ದೇವರಿಗೆ ಸಹ ಆಚಂದ್ರಾರ್ಕವಾಗಿ ಶಾಶ್ವಿತದಿಂದೆ ನಡದುಬರತಕ್ಕಬಗ್ಗ್ಯೆ ನಿತ್ಯಕಟ್ಲೆ ಅಮೃತಪಡಿನಂದಾದೀಪ ವಿಶೇಷಕಟ್ಲೆ ಪಂಚಪರ್ವಸಂಬಳಗಾರ ಜನಕ್ಕೆ ಸಹ ಅಪಣೆಕೊಡಿಸಿ ಯಿರುವ ಕಂಠೀರಾಯಿ ೧೨೨೧ ವಂದುಸಾವಿರ ಯಿನ್ನೂರ ಯಿಪ್ಪತ್ತೊಂದುವರಹಕ್ಕೆ ಹಣದಿಂದ ಜಿನಿಶಿಜಾಳಿಮುಂತಾದರಿಂದ ಉತ್ತಾರವನ್ನು ಧರ್ಮಸಂಗ್ರಹದಬಗ್ಗ್ಯೆ ಅರಮನೆ ದಿವಾನ್‌ಕಚೇರಿ ಸಸ್ತಾಂತ್ರದಿಂದ ಪ್ರತಿ ಸಂವತ್ಸರದಲ್ಲು ಕೊಡಿಸಿಕೊಟ್ಟು ಸೇವಾರ್ಥವಾಗಿ ವಿನಿಯೋಗಕ್ಕೆಂದು ನೇಮಿಸಿಯಿರುವಂಥವರಿಂದ ಕಾಲತ್ರಯದಲ್ಲು ಶಾಸ್ತ್ರಪ್ರಕಾರ ದೇವತಾಸೇವೆಯನ್ನು ಸಾಂಗವಾಗಿ ಮಾಡಿಸುತ್ತ ದಿನಂಪ್ರತಿ ವಿಚಾರಿಸಿಕೊಂಡು ವರುಷಂ ಪ್ರತಿ ಯಿಾ ದೇವಸ್ಥಾನದ ಲೆಕ್ಕಪಕ್ಕಮುಂತಾದ್ದನ್ನು ಜಡ್ತಿತಗದು ಕೊಳ್ಳುತ್ತ ಬರುವದಾಗಿ ಯೆಂಬ ತಸ್ತೀಕು ನಿರೂಪಕ್ಕೆ ಅಪ್ಪಣೆ ಪ್ರಕಾರ ಕಲಿವರ್ಷ ೪೯೨೨ ನೆ ವಿಕ್ರಮಸಂವತ್ಸರದ ನಿಜಜೇಷ್ಠ ತಾರೀಕು ೨ ನೆ ಭಾನುವಾರ ॥

ಶ್ರೀಲಿಂಗರಾಜೇಂದ್ರ ವಡೆಯರವರು ॥

18

ಕಿಚ್ಚೆಟ್ಟದಲ್ಲಿರುವ ಶಿಲಾಶಾಸನ

ಖರ ಸಂವತ್ಸರದ ಕಾರ್ತಿಕ ಬ ೧ ರಲ್ಲು ಚಂನ್ನೈನ ಗುರುಉ ರಾಜೈಯ್ಯನವರ ತಮ್ಮನ ಕುಮಾರ ಚನ್ನ ಮಲ್ಲಿಕಾರ್ಜುನದೇವರಿಗೆ ದೂಪದೀಪ ಆರಾಧನೆಗೆ ವಿ ॥ ವಡೆಯರ ನಮುಸ್ಕಾರಮಾಡಿ ಕೊಟ್ಟ ವಿವರ ಉದೆಯಕಾಲದಲಿ ಸ್ತಾಪನೆ ಮಾಡಿದ್ದು-

19

ಇಗ್ಗೊಡ್ಲಿನಲ್ಲಿರುವ ಶಿಲಾಶಾಸನ

……………ದೆಕ ಬಉಳ ೧ ನೆ ಯಲ್ಲು ವೀರವಡೆಯರು ಹಾಲೇರಿ ಮುಮ್ಮೈ ಅರಸಿನವರ ಕುವರ ವೀರಯಲ್ಲಿ ಮಾಡಿದ ಭಕ್ತಿತಾಂಬ್ರ (ಹಾಲೇರಿ) ಭೂಮಿಯ ಐಗಳಮತಕ್ಕೆ-

20

ದೆನುಗಲ್ಲಿನಲ್ಲಿರುವ ಶಿಲಾಶಾಸನ

ಶ್ರೀಮತು ಖರನಾಮ ಸಂವತ್ಸರದ ಆಶ್ವೀಜ ಶುದ್ಧ ೧೦ ರಲ್ಲು ಯೆಡತೂರೆ ಮುಟ್ಟದ ಶಿದ್ದಲಿಂಗಸ್ವಾಮಿಯವರಿಗೆ-

21

ಮಯುಮುಡಿಯೆಲ್ಲಿರುವ ಶಿಲಾಶಾಸನ

ಶ್ರೀಗಂಗಾಧರದೇವರು ॥ ವೀರರಾಜೇಂದ್ರ ವಡೆಯರವರು

22

ಇರ್ಪಿಯಲ್ಲಿರುವ ಶಿಲಾಶಾಸನ

ಶಾಲಿವಾಹನ ಶಕವರ್ಷ ೧೭೬೫ ನೇ ಶಾರ್ವರಿ ಸಂವತ್ಸರದಲ್ಲು ಕಿಗ್ಗಟ್ಟು ಹತ್ತುನಾಡು ರೈಹಿತರು ತಂಮ ಭಕ್ತಿಯಿಂದ ಲಕ್ಷ್ಮಣತೀರ್ಥದ ಬಲಿಯಿರುವ ಇರ್ಪಿನ ರಾಮೇಶ್ವರ ದೇವರ ದೇವಸ್ತಾನವನ್ನು ಜೀರ್ಣೋದ್ಧಾರ ಮಾಡಿಸಿಯಿದ್ದಾರೆ-

23

ಮಹಾದೇವಪುರದಲ್ಲಿರುವ ಶಿಲಾಶಾಸನ

ಶ್ರೀ ಮುರಿಗಾ ಸ್ವಾಮಿಗಳವರ ಚರಮೂರ್ತಿಗಳಾದ ಶಾಂತವೀರಸ್ವಾಮಿಯವರ ಕರಕಮಲಸಂಜನಿತರಾದ ಸೋಮಶೇಖರ ಶಿವಯೋಗೀಶ್ವರರು ಕಲಿಸಂದೆ ೪೬೪೫ ನೆ ಶೋಭನಕೃತು ಸಂವತ್ಸರದ ಕಾರ್ತ್ತಿಕ ಶುದ್ಧ ಬಿದಿಗೆಯು ಗುರುವಾರ ರೋಹಿನಿ ನಕ್ಷತ್ರ ಪ್ರಾತಃಕಾಲ ಗಂಟೆ ೭ ರ ವಳಗೆ ಯಿಾಗದ್ದುಗೆಮೇಲೆ ಕಲಶಸ್ಥಾಪನೆ ಮಾಡಿಸಿದ್ದು

24

ಬೆಟ್ಟಯತ್ತುನಾಡಿನಲ್ಲಿ ಗಣಗೂರು ಗ್ರಾಮದ ಹಳೇಗ್ರಾಮ ನಿವೇಶನದಲ್ಲಿರುವ ಶಿಲಾಶಾಸನ

1 .... ಸ್ವಸ್ತಿ ಶ್ರೀ
2 ವಿಜಯಾಭ್ಯುದಯ ಶಾಲಿವಾಹ
3 ನ ಶಕವರುಷ ೧೫೯೯ ನೆಯ ಹೇವಿಳಂ
4 ಬಿ ಸಂವತ್ಸರದ ಆಶ್ವಯುಜ ಸು ೫ ಭೌಮ ವಾರ
5 ..... ಗೋತ್ರದ ಆಶ್ವಲಾಯನಸೂತ್ರದ ರು ಕು ಶಾಖೆ
6 ನಂಜರಾಯಪಟ್ಟಣದ ಶ್ರೀಕಂಠರಾಜಯ
7 ನ ಪುತ್ರರಾದ ರುದ್ರಗಣಂಗಳು ನಕು ಸಂಚಿ
8 ....ರವರಿಗೆ ಗಣಗೂರು ಮಹಾ
9 ....ಂಗಳು ತಮ್ಮತಂದೆ ತಾಯಿಯಿ
10 ....ದೊವಾ ಪಿತೃಗಳಿಗೆ ಕೈಲಾಸ
11 ಪದವಿ ಆಗಲಿಯಂದು ಕೊಟ್ಟಭೊಮಿದಾ
12 ನ ಕೊಟ್ಟ ಗ್ರಾಮಕ್ಕೆ ಆವನ
13 ....ಅಳಿಪಿದರೆ ತಂದೆತಾಯಿ
14 ....ಜದವನಲ್ಲಿ ನಂಜರಾಯ
15 ....ನಾದದು ಜಮಗೆಯ ಅಮಂದ
16 ......ಅತಯಿನಾಶಿಕೆಯ ಅನತರೂ
17 ....ಶ್ರೀ

25

ಮಡಿಕೇರಿಯಲ್ಲಿ ಕಮಿಷನರ ಕಚೇರಿಯ ಗೋಡೆಗೆ ಕಟ್ಟಿಯಿರುವ ಶಿಲಾಶಾಸನ

ವಿ

MAHARAJA VEER RAJENDER WADEER.

1 ಸ್ವಸ್ತಿಶ್ರೀ ಜಯಾಭ್ಯುದಯ ಶಾಲಿವಾಹನ ಶಕವರ್ಷ ೧೭೪೩ ನೇ ಇಷು ಸಂವತ್ಸರದ ಪಾಲ್ಗುಣಶು ೧೧ ಯು ಭಾನುವಾರ
2 ಕ್ಕೆ ಕಲಿದಿನ ೧೮೭೮೧೦೮ ನೇ ಈ ಶುಭದಿವಸದಲ್ಲಿ ಯಿಂದುವಂಶಕ್ಷೀರಪಾರಾವಾರಪಾರಿಜಾತಾಯ ಮಾನರಾದ।
3 ಭರದ್ವಾಜಗೋತ್ರ ಸಂಜಾತರಾದ ।ಆಶ್ವಲಾಯನಸೂತ್ರಋಕ್‌ಶಾಖಿಗಳಾದ। ವೀರಶೈವಮತಧುರೀಣ ಪ್ರವೀಣರಾದ।
4 ಶ್ರೀ ಮತ್ಕೊಡಗುಸಂಸ್ಥಾನಸಂಸ್ಥಿತಾನವಧ್ಯಕ್ಷೀರನಗರಮಧ್ಯೆಪರಿಭ್ರಾಜಮಾನಮಣಿಗಣಖಚಿತಚಾರುಸಿಂ ಹಾಸ
5 ನಾರೂಢರಾದ। ಅಪ್ರತಿಮಪ್ರತಾಪಪ್ರಕಾಶಪ್ರಹಸಿತಮಾರ್ತಾಂಡಮಂಡಲರಾದ । ಆಖಂಡಲಾಖಂಡವೈಭವ ಸಮೇತರಾದ।
6 ಸಕಲದಿಗಂತರಾಳಸಂದ್ಯೋತಮಾನಕೀರ್ತಿಪ್ರಖ್ಯಾತರಾದ । ಸಮಸ್ತಪ್ರಶಸ್ತರಾಜಧರ್ಮಾವಧರಣಯುಧಿ ಷ್ಠಿರರಾದ । ಮಹಾರಾಜಲಿಂಗರಾ
7 ಜೇಂದ್ರವಡೆಯರ ಪೌತ್ರರಾದ । ಲಿಂಗರಾಜೇಂದ್ರವಡೆಯರವರ ಪುತ್ರರಾದ। ಶ್ರೀ ವೀರರಾಜೇಂದ್ರ ವಡೆಯ ರವರು । ಸಧರ್ಮಸುಶೀಲಸುಚ
8 ರ್ಯದಿಂದ ಪೃಥ್ವೀಸಾಂಮ್ರಾಜ್ಯಂಗೈಯುತ್ತ ಅನುಗಾಲದಲ್ಲು ಮಹಾದೇವಧ್ಯಾನಪರರಾಗಿ ಇರುತಿರುವ ತದನಂತರ ಸ್ವದೇಶದಲ್ಲು ವಾರಣಗಳು
9 ಮಿತಿಮಿಾರಿ ಮಾನವರು ತಂಮ ಉದರಪೋಷಣಾರ್ಥವಾಗಿ ರಚಿಸಿರುವಂಥ ಫಲಪೈರುಗಳನ್ನು ಕರಡು ಮಾಡಿದ್ದರಿಂದಲು ಪಾಂಥಜನರನ್ನು
10 ಹಿಂಸೆಗೈದ್ದರಿಂದಲು ಭವನೋಪದ್ರಗೊಳಿಸಿದ್ದರಿಂದ ಸಹ ಇಂತಪ್ಪ ಬಾಧಿಗಳಿಂದ ನಿಸ್ತರಿಸಲಾರೆವೆಂದು ಪ್ರಜೆಗಳು ಬಿನ್ನೈಸಲಾಗಿ ದುಷ್ಟ
11 ನಿಗ್ರಹ ಶಿಷ್ಟಪರಿಪಾಲನೆ ಯೆಸಗುವಧಾದ್ದು ರಾಜಧರ್ಮವೆಂದು ಚಿತ್ತದಲ್ಲು ಅವಧರಿಸಿ ಯಿದನ್ನು ಪರಿಹರಿ ಸತಕ್ಕ ಸಾಮರ್ಥ್ಯವನ್ನು ಕರುಣಿ
12 ಸಬೇಕೆಂತ ಗೌರೀಧವನಿಗೆ ಪ್ರಾರ್ಥಿಸಲಾಗಿ ತತ್ಸಾಂಬಶಂಕರನ ಪರಮಕೃಪಾನುಗ್ರಹಸಹಾಯವಾದ ಕಾರಣ ತದ್ದಿನದಾರಭ್ಯ ತಾರಣ ಸಂವತ್ಸರದ

13 ಚೈತ್ರ ಬ ೧೨ ಯು ಚಂದ್ರವಾರ ಪರ್ಯ್ಯಂತ ವರುಷ ೨ ತಿಂಗಳು ೧ ದಿನ ೨೫ ಕ್ಕೆ ಕಳಿದಿತ ೧೮೯೮೯೧೩
ಏತಾದೃಶ ದಿವಸದವಳಿಗೆ ಅರಣ್ಯಮಧ್ಯ

14 ದಲ್ಲಿ ಐತರುವ ಮತ್ತಗಜಗಳ ಸಮೂಹಕ್ಕೆ ತದ್ವಾಹನಾಲಂಕಾರಯುಕ್ತದಿಂ ಚಿತ್ರೈಸಿ ಕಂಠೀರವನ
ಪ್ರೋಲ್‌ಪಡಿಪಟ್ಟ ಗಜಗಳೆಂಬ ಉಚ್ಚರಣೆಗೆ

15 ನಾಣ್ನುಡಿ ಕಾಣಿಸಂತೆ ಅಜ ಸದೃಶಂಗೈದು ಸ್ವಸಾಮರ್ಥ್ಯದ ಭುಜಬಲ ಪರಾಕ್ರಮದಿಂದ ವಿಧವಿಧದಲ್ಲುವಿ
ರಾಮಗೈದ ಕುಂಜರಗಳು ಅಪ್ಪಣೆಪ್ರ

16 ಕಾರ ಪಟುಭಟರು ಸಜೀವದಿಂದ ಕೈಸೆರೆ ಹಿಡಿದ ದಂತಿಗಳು ಸಹ ಗಣನೆ ಯೆಷ್ಟೆಂದರೆ ಚಿತ್ರಭಾನು ಸಂವತ್ಸ
ರದ ಆಷಾಢ ಬ ೧೦ ಲ್ಲು ನಂಜ್ರಾಯ

17 ಪಟ್ಟಣ ತಾಲೋಕಿನಲಿ ಲಯವಾದ ಆನೆ ೩ ಕೈಸೆರೆಹಿಡಿದ ಆನೆ ೯ ಶ್ರಾವಣ ಬ ೩ ಲ್ಲು ಸದ್ರಿ ತಾಲೋಕಿನಲಿ,
ಲಯವಾದ ಆನೆ ೭೨ ಕೈಸೆರೆಹಿಡಿದ

18 ಆನೆ ೨೨ ಅಧಿಕ ಆಶ್ವಯುಜ ಶು ೫ ಲ್ಲು ಸದ್ರಿ ತಾಲೋಕಿನಲ್ಲಿ ಉಲುಗುಲಿ ಮೊಡಗೇರಿ ನಾಡಿನಲ್ಲಿ ಸಹ
ಲಯವಾದ ಆನೆ ೭೩ ಕೈಸೆರೆ ಹಿಡಿದಆನೆ ೧೫

19 ಈ ಶು ೧೧ ಲ್ಲು ನಂಜ್ರಾಯ ಪಟ್ಟಣ ತಾಲೋಕಿನಲ್ಲಿ ಹೊರೂರುನೂರೊಕ್ಕಲು ನಾಡಿನಲ್ಲಿ ಉಲುಗುಲಿ
ಮೊಡಿಗೇರಿ ನಾಡಿನಲ್ಲಿ ಸಹ ಲಯವಾದ ಆನೆ

20 ೩೭ ಕೈಸೆರೆ ಹಿಡಿದ ಆನೆ ೬ ನಿಜ ಆಶ್ವಯುಜ ಶು ೧೧ ಲ್ಲು ನಂಜ್ರಾಯಪಟ್ಟಣ ತಾಲೋಕಿನಲ್ಲಿ ಲಯ
ವಾದ ಆನೆ ೨೦ ಕೈಸೆರೆ ಹಿಡಿದ ಆನೆ ೬ ಸ್ವಭಾನಸಂವ

21 ತ್ಸರದ ನಿಜ ಚೈತ್ರ ಶು ೫ ಲ್ಲು ಕೊಡಗು ಶ್ರೀರಂಗಪಟ್ಟಣದಲ್ಲಿ ಲಯವಾದ ಆನೆ ೭ ಕೈಸೆರೆ ಹಿಡಿದ ಆನೆ
೧೮ ವೈಶಾಕ ಶು ೩ ಲ್ಲು ಬೆಟ್ಟೆಯತ್ತ ನಾ

22 ಡಿನಲ್ಲಿ ಚಂನನಕೋಟೆಯಲ್ಲು ಸಹ ಲಯವಾದ ಆನೆ ೨೧ ಕೈಸೆರೆ ಹಿಡಿದ ಆನೆ ೭೧ ತಾರಣ ಸಂವತ್ಸರದ
ಚೈತ್ರ ಬ ೧೨ ಲ್ಲು ಕಿಗ್ಗಟ್ಟ ನಾಡಿ

23 ನಲ್ಲಿ ಲಯವಾದ ಆನೆ ೧೦ ಕೈಸೆರೆ ಹಿಡಿದ ಆನೆ ೭೦ ಯಿತರ ತ್ರಿಂಶದ್ದಿನದಲ್ಲು ಲಯವಾದ ಆನೆ ೭೯ ಕೈ
ಸೆರೆ ಹಿಡಿದ ಆನೆ ೨೭ ಅಂತು ಅಷ್ಟಾತ್ರಿಂ

24 ಶದ್ದಿವಸಕ್ಕೆ ಸ್ವಹಸ್ತದಿಂದ ಲಯವಾದ ಆನೆ ೨೩೩ ಪಟು ಭಟರು ಅಪ್ಪಣೆ ಪ್ರಕಾರ ಪ್ರಾಣಯುಕ್ತವಾಗಿ
ಪ್ರಾಣಗ್ರಹಣವಿಸಗಿದ ಆನೆ ೧೮೧ ಉ

25 ಭಯಂ ಗಜ ೭೧೭ ಯೀ ತೆರದಲ್ಲು ಸಕಲ ಮನೋರಥಪ್ರದವಾಗಲಾಗಿ ವಿಸ್ಮಯಬಟ್ಟದ್ದು ಹ್ಯಾಗೆಯೆಂದರೆ
ವಿಪಿನಗಳಲ್ಲು ಅದ್ರಿಸಮಾನ್ವಿತವಾದ ಕರಿ

26 ಸಮೋಹವ್ರ ದಿನಕರನನ್ನು ಮೇಘಜಾಲ ಮುಚ್ಚುವ ತೆರದಂತೆ ಭೋರ್ಗುಡಿಸು ತಾಗಮಿಸಲಾಗಿ ಶಿಡಿಲಿನೋ
ಪಾದಿ ಯಿರುವಂಥ ಸಹಾ

27 ಚಿತಾಸ್ತ್ರ ಆಯುಧಗಳಿಂದ ತತುಕ್ಷಣದಲ್ಲು ನಿಗ್ರಹಿಸಿದಂಥಾದ್ದು ಸ್ತೋಲೋಂನತವಾಗಿರುವಂಥ ಮದಗಜ
ಗಳನ್ನು ಮೂಶಿಕನಂತೆ

28 ಭಾವಿಸಿ ಮನುಜರು ಪ್ರಾಣಸಮೇತವಾಗಿ ಪರಿಗ್ರಹಿಸಿರುವಂಥ ಆತ್ಯಾಶ್ಚರ್ಯ

26

ಮಡಿಕೇರಿ ತಾಲ್ಲೂಕು ಹೊರೂರು ಮೊಡಗೇರಿನಾಡು ಚೇರಲ ಸಿರಿಮಂಗಲ ಗ್ರಾಮದ ಸರಹದ್ದಿಗೆ ಸೇರಿದ ಮೀನಕೊಲ್ಲಿ ಕಾಡಿನಲ್ಲಿ ಭಕ್ತನಕೋಟೆಯಲ್ಲಿ ಬಿದ್ದಿರುವ ಕಲ್ಲು

ಪ್ರಮಾಣ 7′ 6″ × 2′ 9″.

1 ಶ್ರೀಮತು ಶಾಲಿವಾಹನ ಶಕವರುಷ
2 ೧೭೬೬ ನೆಯ ಕ್ರೋಧಿಸಂವತ್ಸರದ
3 ಚೈತ್ರ ಶು ೧ ಲೂ ಶ್ರೀಮನ್ಮಹಾಮಂಡಲೇ
4 ಶ್ವರ ಚಂಗಾಳ್ವ ಶ್ರೀಕಂಠರಸುಗಳುಲಿಂ
5 ಗಂಣೊಡೇರು ದೇವರಿಗೆ ಬಗುತನಕೋ
6 ಟೆಗೆ ಸಲ್ಲುವ ಭೂಮಿಯನು ಸರ್ವಮಾ
7 ನ್ಯವಾಗಿ ಕೊಟ್ಟರು ಯೀ ಕೊಡಗೆಯುನಳು
8 ಪಿದವರು ರೌರವನರಕದಲ್ಲಿ
9 ಯಿರುವರು

27

ಅದೇ ನಾಡು ಹೆರೂರು ಗ್ರಾಮದ ಸರ್ವೆ ನಂ- $\frac{56}{1}$ ರ ಪೂರುಗುಪ್ಪೆ ಪೈಸಾರಿ ಜಮೀನಿ ದಾರಿಯ ಬಳಿ ಬಿದ್ದಿರುವ ವೀರಕಲ್ಲು.

ಪ್ರಮಾಣ 5′ × 3′ 6″.

(ಮೇಲುಭಾಗ ಪಾರ್ಶ್ವ ಸಹ ಒಡೆದು ಹೋಗಿದೆ)

1 ......ಹರಹಬ
2 ...ಳೆಯಮಾಚಿಗ
3 .. ರಾನೆಗ
4 ...ಸ್ತಿ ಶ್ರೀಮತು
5 ...ಮುನಿವರಾಧಿತ್ಯಂನರೊ-ಉಳಿಯಸೆ
ರೂರ ಎತ್ತಿಕಟ್ಟಿಸಿದ ಕೆ...
6 ...ಧಮಗಂಹೆರೂರಕೋ
7 ...ಕರಮ್ಬಗಹನ್ದಲ
8 ...ಮುದೇವಳ- ಮನೆಗರ್ದ್ದ
9 ...ನಹಣ ಅರಸಣಿಮ ಎ
10 ಣ್ಡಾಲಮನ್ನಣಸಾ
11 ...ಡುಮೆಮುನ್ನ ನೆಲಸ
12 ಟ್ಟುವೆಂದು ಸುಟ್ಟದೆಂನಿಬ
13 ...ಹ ಇಸುವ- ಳ್ದಹೆರೂರ ಆಲಸೆಯಿದಂ
ಚಂಗಾಳುವ ಅಲಂಕರಿಸಿದೆ-
14 ಮುನಿವರಾದಿತ್ಯಮಲಲ
15 ...ಕರಸಿವೆ......ಬಡ
16 .. ಅದುಪಟ್ಟಣಸ್ವಾಮಿಯಸೇ
17 ಯಕೊಣ್ಡುಹೊಸಮು
18 ಕಾವಕ......
19 ...ಗ ಒಪ್ಪಿಗಂ ಎರಬ ..
20 ....
21 ಕಟಿದ್ದಗ...
(ಮುಂದೆ ೩ ಪಂಕ್ತಿಗಳು ಹೋಗಿವೆ)

ಕಲ್ಲಿನ ಎಡಪಾರ್ಶ್ವದಲ್ಲಿ-

25 ...
26 ಲನ...
27 ಳೆಮಾ...
28 ಅಸು ..
29 ದಬುಮಿ..
30 ... .
31 ವೆಚಗರ .
32 ಗಸಕನ್ದವಡ .
33 ಸಯ...ದಕರಿ .
34 ಣಗಹುಲ .
35 ತುಬಡಿವೆ...
(ಮುಂದೆ ಅಸ್ಪಷ್ಟ)

28

ಅದೇ ನಾಡು ಅಂದಗೋವಿಕಲ್ಲೂರು ಸರ್ವೇ ನಂ- 89 ಬಸವೇಶ್ವರದೇವರ ಜೋಡೀ ಭೂಮಿಯಲ್ಲಿನ ವೀರಕಲ್ಲು.

ಪ್ರಮಾಣ 5′ × 3′.

1 ಸ್ವಸ್ತಿಸಕ ೪೬೩
2 ಕ್ರೋಧಿಸಂವತ್ಸರ
....
8 ... . ಮೆತಲೆಗಡಿಪಿಸತ್ತ ಆತನ ಸಂತತಿ...
9 ......ಕೊಟ್ಟ.........
10 ಹಾರ...ಪರ
11 ಕೊಣ್ಡುಸೆಜಿ .....
12 ರಂ . ಗಂಗೆ......
13 ಕವಿಲೆಯನಳಿದ ಬ್ರಹ್ಮತ್ತಿಬೂಚಗನ
14 ಬ್ಯಾತನವು......
15 ಪರೋಕ್ಷವಿ...
16 ಯವೆಮಾ...
17 ಚಿಸಿದಟರೆದೆಂಬಾವಣಯ್ಯ

29

ಕಿಗ್ಗಟ್ಟನಾಡು ತಾಲ್ಲೂಕು ಬೆಟ್ಟಯತ್ತುನಾಡು ಕುಂದದ ಬೆಟ್ಟದ ಮೇಲೆ ಕುಂದದೆಯ್ಯಪ್ಪ ದೇವಸ್ಥಾನದ ಕಂಭದ ಮೇಲೆ

ಶ್ರೀ
1 .... ಈಶ್ವರಪ್ರಸಂನನಾಗಿ......
2 ಬೆಟ್ಟಯತ್ತುನಾಡು ಕುಂದದೆಬೆಟ್ಟದಮೇಲೆ ನೆಲಶಿರು

3 ವಮುಹದೇವರ ಶಿಲಾಮಯವಾದ ಪುರಾಣಗುಡಿ
4 ಯನ್ನು ನವನೆತ್ತವಾಗಿ ಶಿವಾಲಯದಲ್ಲಿ ಜೀರ್ನೋದ್ಧಾರಮಾ
5 ಡುವದಕ್ಕೆ ಯಿನಾಡು ತಕ್ಕ ಮೊಕಸ್ತರೂ ಆದಿಯಾಗಿ ಸವೆ
6 ರ್ೞ ಜನರು ಮತ್ತು ಅವ್ಮತಿನಾಡು ಕಕ್ಕೇರಿಗ್ರಾಮದತ
7 ಕ್ಕಮೊಕಸ್ತರು ಸಹ ಅನುಮತಿಪಟ್ಟು ಶಾಲಿವಾಹನ
8 ಶಕಾಬ್ದವರುಷ ೧೭೩೭ ಕ್ಕೆ ಕಟವರುಷ ೪೯೧೫
9 ನೇ ಆನಂದನಾಮ ಸಂವತ್ಸರದ ತುಲಾಮಾಸ ೧೮ ನೇ
10 ಕಾರ್ತಿಕಶುದ್ಧ ೧೫ ಗುರುವಾರಕ್ಕೆ ಕಲಿಸಂದ ದಿನ ೧೮
11 ೧೮೦೬೦ ದಿನ ಸಂದಶುಭಮೊರ್ತದಲಿ ಪ್ರಾರಂಬ್ಸಿದ ಯಿ
12 ಮಹಾಸ್ತಳ ಜೀರ್ನೋಧಾರದಲ್ಲುಮನೆ...
13 ...ಯಿಶ್ವರಾರ್ಪಿತವೆಂದು ಮುಉಲ್ಯಕೊಟ್ಟು ಸೇವಮಾಡಿದಜನರ
14 ವಿವರ...ಕಂಡೆಯರಾವಂತ......
15 ...ತದಲೂರ...ಮಾಡ್ಸಿದ...
16 ಸಯಿಮಾಡಿದವರುಶಾಣ
17 ಭಾಗರು ಬ್ರಾಂಹ್ಮಣನಂ
18 ಕಪ್ಪೈಯಶುಭ್ರೇದಾರೂಕೊಡಂ
19 ದೇರಮುದ್ದೈಯಃಪಾರುಪತ್ಯ
20 ಗಾರುಮನೆಪ್ಪಂಡ್ರಪುಚ್ಚೈಯ
21 ಬಾಗಿಲುನಿಲಕೆಸಯಮಾಡಿ
22 ಸಿದಕೊಡಂಪೇರಮೇದ್ದೈಯ
23 ದೇವರವಾಣಿವಟತರೆಕಲಾ
24 ಮುಟುಕೆಲಾಸಹಸಾಯಮಾ
25 ಡಿದುಸಂಣ್ವಾಂಡ್ರಬೋಳ್ಳೆಯ್ಯ
26 ಮುಣಂಡೆತಿಂಮ್ಮೈಯಗಳು
27 ಡಚಿಂನೆಗಳುಡನ ಚಂಣಪ್ಪ ನಂಪೀಶ್ವರನ ಪ್ರಸಂನಕ್ಕೆಸಾ
28 ಯಮಾಡಿದು ಕುಂದೆಗ್ರಾಮದ ಜಾಹಗೀರದಾರ್ ಹಯತ್ತ
29 ಕಾನಸಾಬಿ ಯಿಮೇರೆ ಸರ್ವೇ ಜನರು ಕೂಡಿ ಜೀರ್ನೋಧಾರಮಾಡಿ
30 ದಯಿಶಿವಾಲಯದ ಕೆಲಸಲು ಪೈಂಗಳನಾಮಸಂವತ್ರರದ
31 ವೈಶಾಕಶುದ್ಧ ೧೫ ಸುಕ್ರವಾರ ಶುಭಮುಹುರ್ತದಲು ಯಿ
32 ಶಿವಾನುಗ್ರಹದಿಂದ ಪೂರ್ಯೈಸಿಧ ಯಿಸೇವಮಾಡಿದವರಿಗೆ
33 ......ಯಿಹದಲಿ ಸೌಖ್ಯಪರದಲಿಮುಕ್ತಿ

30

ಹತ್ತುಗಟ್ಟುನಾಡು ನಲ್ಲೂರು ಗ್ರಾಮದ ತೀತರಮಾಡು ಮಾದಯ್ಯನ ಮನೆಗೆ ಪಶ್ಚಿಮ ಹಿತ್ತಲ ವತ್ತಿನಲ್ಲಿ ಪರೀಮೆಲೆ

ಪ್ರಮಾಣ 4′ × 1′ 6″.

(ಮೇಲುಭಾಗ ಒಡೆದು ಹೋಗಿಧೆ)

1 ಕೊಡಂಗಾಳ ಎಮಗ...... ....
2 ದಿಳ ಆಚ್ಚಿಡಮೆನ್ದು ಯತಿವರ
3 ಗ್ಗೆರ್ಲ್ಲಂಸಾದರದಿಬೀಚೆನುಸೆ
4 ಟ್ಟೆಯಾವಾದೊಳೆಙಿತಾಚಿ
5 ದನೀಸುರ ಕೀರ್ತ್ತಿಭದ್ರಮ
6 ಸ್ತುಜಿನಶಾಸನಾಯ ಶ್ರೀಮ
7 ಮದುಮಂಗನಾಡದೊರಕಿಠಿರಿ
8 ಯಯ್ಯಂಗಳ್ ಚಾಂಗಳದಬ
9 ಸದಿಯೊಳ್ ಪನ್ನೆರಡಂನೋಂ
10 ತುಮುಡಿಪಿದರ್ ಅವರ ಮಕ್ಕ
11 ಳ್ಬಾಕಿಯು ಬುಕಿಯನಿಜಿಸಿ
12 ದರ್

31

ಅದೇ ಗ್ರಾಮದಲ್ಲಿ ತೀತರವಾಡದ ಮನೇಬಳಿ ಕೆರೆಯಸಮೀಪ ಸರ್ವೇ ನಂ- 117 ರ ಕೆರೆ ಏರೀ ಮೇಲೆ ನಟ್ಟಕಲ್ಲು

ಪ್ರಮಾಣ 3′ 3″ × 1′ 6″.

1 ಭದ್ರಂಭೂಯಾಜ್ಜಿನೇನ್ದ್ರಾಣಾಂಶಾಸನಾ
ಯಾ
2 ಘನಾಶಿನೇಕುತೀರ್ತ್ಥಧ್ವಾನ್ತ ಸಂಘಾತಪ್ರಭ
3 ನ್ನ ಘನಭಾನವೇ ಸ್ವಸ್ತಿ ಶ್ರೀ ಪದಂದೆಧಾನಂ
ಪಾರ
4 ತ್ರಹಿತಕಾರಣಕಂಪರವೋಪಕಾರ
5 ಕಂಕುಡೆತಂದುತಾಜ್ಞಿದಾಯಂತಿಗಮತಿ
6 ಗಂಕೆಭೆಯಾದುದನ್ತಮಳ್ತಡೆಯದೆಮುಕ್ತಿಯ
7 ಂಪಡೆವೆನೆನ್ದು ವಿಚಾರಿಸಿ ಬನ್ಧವರ್ಗ್ಗವಡಂ
8 ಬಡಿಸಿಸಮಾಧಿಯಂಪಡೆದುವಲ್ಲಿ
9 ಯುಮಬ್ಚ್ಚರಿಜಕ್ಕಿಯಬ್ಬೆಯಕಸ್ತೂರಿ
ಭಟ್ಟಾ
10 ರಗ್ಗೆ ಅವರಶ್ರಾವಕಿಜನ್ನಿಯಬ್ಬೆಗಾವು
11 ಣ್ಡಿದಧ್ಯೆರಮಂತ್ರಿಕಿಜಕ್ಕಿಯಬ್ಬೆ ಸನ್ಯಸ
12 ನಂಗೆಯ್ದುಮುಡಿಪಿದಳ್ ॥ ಆಕೆಯಗ
13 ಣ್ಡಪರಮಶ್ರಾವಕ ಎಡಯ್ಯ ಮಂಗಳಂ

32

ನಂಜರಾಜಪಟ್ನ ತಾ ॥ ನಿಡುತ ಹೋಬಳಿ ನಿಡುತದಲ್ಲಿ ಬೀರೇದೇವರ ವನದಲ್ಲಿ ನೆಟ್ಟ ಕಲ್ಲು

ಪ್ರಮಾಣ 2′ 6″ × 1′ 3″.

1 ಸ್ವಸ್ತಿ ಶ್ರೀ......ದ್ಬೆಯೆತ್ಸ್ಯಕರವೊರುಷದ
2 ೧೨೦೧ ಬಹುಧಾಂನ್ಯ ಸಂವತ್ಸರದ ವೈಶಾ
3 ಖ ಬ......ಹಳಯಗು-ಗ...
4 ದವ......ಮಲಪನಹಳ್ಳಿಯ ಮಲ್ಲಿಕಾರ್ಜುನದೇ
5 ವರಪ್ರ...................ಗಡಿನಾಡು ಅ
6 ಣಲಿಪಾ...............ಮೊಳ್ಳನಾಡು ಎ
7 ಕೋಟಿ...............ತಾಮಂತ್ರ್ತಟ್ಟ ಆ
8 ಮಲ್ಲಿಕಾರ್ಜುನದೇವರ......ಹೊರಭೊಮಿಯಜ
9 ......ಣಂ.............ಯಣ್ನಲಕಂಣ
10 ಜಕರಾಮಯ................ಹಿರಿಯವೀರಂ
11 ಣಚಿಕವೀರಂಣ...............ತಿಯೆತಂಡಕ್ಕವು
12 ಆನಾಡವಯಿಂದೆ............ಟ್ಟಗದ್ದೆಬೆದಲು
13 ಬನಸಮುದ್ರದ.........ಕೊ ೧೦ ದೇವರಕೆಹೆ
14 ಯಕೆಳಗೆಕಾರಗದೆ.........ಹುವಿನಗದ್ದೆಕೊ ೧೦
15 ಬನಿಗನಹಳ್ಳಿಯಲು ತಿರುಮಲೆಗೆಉಡಕಟ್ಟಿಸಿದೆ
16 ಕೆಹೆ ಯಕೆಳಗೆಕೊ--ಯೊಳಗೆ ಸೆ ೨ ದೇವರ
17 ಹಿಂದಣಪರೆಯಗದೆ......ಯಂಣೆಗೆ ಸ ೨ ಕೊ ೧
18 ಆ ಹತ್ರಯತೆಂಕಣದಹೊ...ಂಗೆ ಕೊ ೧ ಅಲಿಪಡು
19 ವಹಳ್ಳಗದ್ದ. ಸ ೧ ಕೊಟಕಡಹುಹಿರಿಯಂಣಗೆ ಸ ೧
20 ಕೊಟಕಡಹುವೀರಣ್ನ...ಮಣ್ನ ದೇವನಗದ್ದೆ ಸ ೧ ಮಾ
21 ಕಳಕೆಹೆಯ.........ಸ ೬ ಹಿಡಿ ಜೀಯಕೆ
22 ಹೆಯ...............ಲು ಊರಮುಂದಣ
23 ಕೊ--ತೆಂದೆಡೆ--೦.೧೦೦ ಊರಹಿಂದಣಕೆ
24 -ರಿಕೆ ೬೦೦ ಅಂನ್ತುಬೆದಲು--೩೦೦ ಗದ್ದೆ ಸ ೨೨ ನೂ
25 ಮಲ್ಲಿಗ ಉಡ...ಹಿರಿಯಂಣ್ನ ವೀರಂಣಂಗೆಯೂಸಮ
26 ವಾಗಿ ಅಮೃತಪಡಿಗೆಬಿಟ್ಟ ಧಂರ್ಮ್ಮವಾರು ಅಳಿಪಿದಡೆ

27 ಗಂಗೆಯ ತಡಿಯಲಿ ಕವಿಲೆಯ ಕೊಂದ ಪಾ
28 ...ತಂವಾಪರದತ್ತಂವಾಯೋಹರೇತ ವಸುನ್ಧ
29 ರ್ವ್ಷರಿಷ ಸಹಸ್ರಾಣಾಂ ವಿಷ್ಟಾಯಾಂಜಾಯತೇ...
30 ......ಶಾಸನ......

33

ಅದೇ ಹೋಬಳಿ ನಂದಿಗುಂದೆ ಗ್ರಾಮದಲ್ಲಿ 147 ನೆ ಸರ್ವೇ ನಂಬರ ಸರಕಾರ ಖರಾಬಿನಲ್ಲಿ

ಪ್ರಮಾಣ 6′×2′ 6″.

1 ಸ್ವಸ್ತಿ ಶ್ರೀ ಮನ್ಮಹಾಮಣ್ಡಳೇಸ್ವರಂ ವೀರಚೋಳಕೊಂಗಾಳು
2 ವ ದೇವಪ್ರಿಥಿವೀ ರಾಜ್ಯಂಗೈಯುತ್ತಿರೆತಾಯಿವದೊಮ
3 ಲ ದೇವಿಸೋಮಲದೇವಿ ತೋಳೂರದುದ್ದ ರಸಬಲ್ಲೆಯ
4 ದಣ್ಣಾನಾಯಕನಡಿಯಿಂಅಕಿರಿಕಣಯಿಂತ್ತಿ
5 ನಿಬರುಂ ಮುಂತಾಗಿದ್ದುರ್ ಮನುಮತೆ ಸಂವಛರ
6 ದ ಕುಂಭಮಾಸ ಆದಿವಾರದಸಮಿಯುಂದು ಮು
7 ಳ್ಳುನಾಡೆಪ್ಪತ್ತಕ್ಕಂ ಅಣ್ಣತ್ತಮ್ಮನಮಕ್ಕಳಮಕ್ಕಳ
8 ಗೆತ್ತಯ್ದೊಸಲುಯುದು ಸುಂಕದಬೆಡುಂಗೊಳು
9 ನಲ್ಲೆತ್ತು ಪರಿಹಾರ ಹೆಗ್ಗಡೆಗದ್ಯಾನಗನಹೂರ
10 ಲು ಒಂದು ಹಳ್ಳಿಗೆ ಹಣ ವೈದು ಕಾಣಿಕೆಗದ್ಯಾನ
11 ಗನಹೊರಲೊಂದುಹಳ್ಳಿಗೆಹಣವೈದು
12 ಅರಕೆಜೆ ಹಂದೆಲ ಹಣ ಪರಿಹಾರಗಂಗ
13 ಸಿದ್ಧಾಯ ಹೊಱಗಾಗಿ ಆಯ ದಾಅ ಬಿಟ್ಟೆ ಬೆ
14 ಸಹಡು ವಗೇರಿಗೆ ಪರಿಹಾರವಂ ಬಿಟ್ಟ ।
15 ವೀರಚೋಳ ಕೊಂಗಾಳ್ವ ದೇವಕೊಟ್ಟುದಂತಪ್ಪನು
16 ಡಿದವ ಗಂಗಯ ತಡಿಯ ಕವಿಲೆಯಂ
17 ಬ್ರಾಮ್ಮಣನಂಕೊಂದ ಬ್ರಹ್ಮಾತಿಯಂಕೊಂಡ ॥ ಎ
18 ಪ್ಪತ್ತಜೊಳಗೆ ಮನೆ ಗೈಗುಳ ಭತ್ತಸಲುಯುಮ
19 ಗಂಗೋಜಂಗೆ ಬೂಚಣಂಗೆ ॥

34.

ಅದೇ ಹೋಬಳಿ ಮುಳ್ಳೂರು ಬಸ್ತಿ ಗುಡಿಯಲ್ಲಿ ಪಾರ್ಶ್ವನಾಥ ಬಸ್ತಿಗೆ ದಕ್ಷಿಣ ೧ ನೇ ಕಲ್ಲು

೧ ನೇ ಪಾರ್ಶ್ವ

1 ಸ್ವಸ್ತಿ ಶಕನೃಪಕಾಲಾ
2 ತೀತ ಸಂವತ್ಸರ ಶತಂಗಳ್
3 ೯೪೬ ನೆಯ ಕ್ರೋಧಿಸಂ
4 ವತ್ಸರಂ ಪ್ರರಿವರ್ತ್ತಿಸುತ್ತಿ
5 ರೆತಚ್ಛೈತ್ರಬಹುಳ
6 ನವಮೀಮಙ್ಗಳವಾ
7 ರಂಪೂರ್ವ್ವಭಾದ್ರ
8 ಪದಾನಕ್ಷತ್ರವಿಾ
9 ನೊದೆಯದಲ್ ॥ ಸ್ವಸ್ತಿ
10 ಸಮಸ್ತ ಸುರಾಸುರೇಂ
11 ದ್ರಮಕುಟತಟಘಟಿ
12 ತಮಣಿಮಯೂಖ
13 ರೇಖಾಳಂಕೃತಚಾ

೨ ನೇ ಪಾರ್ಶ್ವ

14 ರುಚರಣಾ
15 ರವಿನ್ದಯು
16 ಗಳಂಭಗವ
17 ದರ್ಹತ್ಪರ
18 ಮೇಶ್ವರಪರ
19 ಮಭಟ್ಟಾರಕ
20 ಮುಖಕಮ
21 ಳವಿನಿರ್ಗತಾ
22 ಗಮಾಮೃತ
23 ಗಂಭೀರಾಂಭೋ
24 ರಾಶಿಪಾರ
25 ಗರಪ್ಪ ಶ್ರೀ
26 ಮದ್ಗುಣಸೇ
27 ನಪಣ್ಡಿತದೇ
28 ವರ್ಮ್ಮಕ್ಷ
29 ಲಕ್ಷ್ಮೀನಿವಾ
30 ಸಕ್ಕಂಸನ್ದ[ರ್]ಱ

೩ ನೇ ಪಾರ್ಶ್ವ

31 ಗುರುಗಳ್ಸಿದ್ಧಾನ್ತತತ್ವಪ್ರ
32 ಕಟನಪಟುಗಳ್ಪ್ರಷ್ಪಸೇ
33 ನವ್ರತೀಂದ್ರವರ್ಗರಸಂಘಿ
34 ನ್ನನ್ದಿಸಂಘಂದ್ರವಿಳಗ
35 ಣಮಹಾರುಬ್ಬುಳಾಮ್ನಾ
36 ಯನಾಥಂಪರಮಾರ್ಹ
37 ನ್ತ್ಯಾದಿರತ್ನತ್ರಯಸ
38 ಕಳಮಹಾಕಬ್ಬ
39 ಶಾಸ್ತ್ರಾಗಮಾದಿಸ್ಥ
40 ರಷಟ್ತರ್ಕ್ಕಪ್ರವೀಣರ್
41 ವ್ರತಿಪತಿಗುಣಸೇನಾ
42 ರ್ಯ್ಯರಾಯ್ಯರ್ಪ್ರಣೋ
43 ತರ್ ॥

35

ಆದೇ ಬಸ್ತೀಗುಡಿಯಲ್ಲಿ ದಕ್ಷಿಣದಲ್ಲಿ ೧ನೇ ಕಲ್ಲು

೧ ನೇ ಪಾರ್ಶ್ವ

1 ಧರ್ಮ್ಮಸೆಟ್ಟಿಬರೆದಂ
2 ಸ್ವಸ್ತಿಶಕವರ್ಷ ೯೭೦
3 ತ್ತನೆಯವಿಳಂಬಿಸಂ
4 ವತ್ಸರದ ಉತ್ತರಾ
5 ಯಣಸಂಕ್ರಾಂತಿ
6 ಯಂದುಶ್ರೀರಾಜೇಂ
7 ದ್ರಕೊಂಗಾಳ್ವಂತಂ
8 ಮಯ್ಯಮಾಡಿಸಿ
9 ದಬಸದಿಗೆ ಕೊ
10 ಟ್ಟಹಾರುವನ
11 ಹಳ್ಳಿಅರಕ
12. ನಹಳ್ಳಿ

೨ ನೇ ಪಾರ್ಶ್ವ

13 ನಿಡುತದ
14 ಗೊಡಲ
15 ಖಣ್ಡು
16 ಗಂ ೩ ಕ ಸ
17 ಕುನಿಯುಂ
18 ಒಳಗೆಜೆ
19 ಯುಂಖಣ್ಡು
20 ಗಂ ೩ ಹೆನ್ನೆ
21 ಲ್ಲೂರಭೂ
22 ಮಿಖಣ್ಡು
23 ಗಂ ೧೦ ಒಂದು
24 ಗಾಣದೆಣ್ಣೆ

೩ ನೇ ಪಾರ್ಶ್ವ

25 ಕಾಜೊಂಗ್ಗಂಡೆಹ
26 ಳ್ಳಿಹಂಗಲ
27 ಬಾನಿ ಖಣ್ಡು
28 ಗಂ ೧೦ ಹು
29 ಣಸೆದಾ
30 ಱುಖಣ್ಡು
31 ಗಂ ೧೦
32 ಗಣಪ
33 ತಿಗೋಡ
34 ಲುಖಣ್ಡು
35 ಗಂ ೩ ಅಸ
36 ಗವೊಳ
37 ಖಣ್ಡುಗಂ
38 ೪

೪ ನೇ ಪಾರ್ಶ್ವ

39 ಶ್ರೀರಾಜಾಧಿರಾ
40 ಜಕೊಂಗಾಳ್ವ
41 ನಬ್ಬೆಪೋಚಬ್ಬರಸಿ
42 ಯತ್ತರ್ಮ್ಮಗುರುಗಳು
43 ದ್ರವಿಳಗಣದನಂ
44 ದಿಸಂಘದರುಂಗಳಾ
45 ನ್ವಯದಗುಣಸೇನ
46 ಪಣ್ಡಿದದೇವರ್ಗ್ಗಮಾ
47 ಡಿಸಿದಾರಾಪೂರ್ವ್ವಕಂ
48 ಕೊಟ್ಟರು ॥ ಸ್ವದತ್ತಂಪ
49 ರದತ್ತಂವಾಯೋಹರೇತಿ
50 ವಸುನ್ಧರಾಂಷಷ್ಟಿರ್ವ್ವ
ರ್ಷ
51 ಸಹಸ್ರಾಣಿವಿಷ್ಟಾ
52 ಯಾಂಜಾಯತೇಕ್ರಿಮಿಃ

36

ಅದೇ ಸ್ಥಳದಲ್ಲಿ ೩ ನೇ ಕಲ್ಲು

1 ....
2 ....ಯಾನಿಘಸತ್ಯಾ
....
5 ಲದೇವಿ ॥ ಭೂತಳ......... .....
6 ವಿನಿರ್ಗತ......ಲೋಕ್ಯವಿಖ್ಯಾತೆ...
7 ....
8 ...ಯಜಾ...ವೋಕ್ಷದ...
9 ....
10 ......ವರ್ಣ್ನ...
....
13 ....ಯ್ದಾಮು
14 ಳಂ...ಪನಿದ...ಮಾಳ.............
15 ...ನುರ್ವ್ವಿಪಾಳಭೂತ...ಬರಸಿದ ಕಾರು
ಣಿಯೂ
16 ದೊವ .....ನವಚನಕಾಯ
17 ವದ್ದಿಗ...ತುಳ್ಳನಬಳ್ಳಿಗಿಯಂಬಂತ್ತಿರಸ...
18 ......ತದಿವಿಜಲೋಕ ॥ ಖಂ
19 .. ಪ್ರಿಥುವೀಕೊಂಗಾಳ್ವನರಸಿ...
(ಇಷ್ಟೇ ಈ ಕಲ್ಲಿನಮೇಲೆ ಕಾಣುವದು)

37

ಅದೇ ಬಸ್ತಿಯಲ್ಲಿ ಪಾರ್ಶ್ವನಾಥ ಬಸ್ತಿಯ ಉತ್ತರ ಗೋಡೇ ಮೇಲೆ

1 ಸ್ವಸ್ತಿ ಶ್ರೀರಾಜಾಧಿರಾಜ ಕೊಂಗಾಳ್ವನಬ್ಬೆ ಪೋಚಬ್ಬರಸಿಯರ್ದ್ರವಿಳಗಣದನನ್ದಿ ಸಂಘದರು
2 ಙ್ಗಳಾನ್ವಯದ ಗುಣಸೇನಪಣ್ಡಿತ ದೇವರಗುಡ್ಡಿಮಾಡಿಸಿದಬಸದಿ ಮಂಗಳ ಮಹಾ

38

ಅದೇ ಬಸ್ತಿಯ ತಳಪಾಮೀ ಕಲ್ಲು

1 ಸ್ವಸ್ತಿ ಶ್ರೀರಾಜೇಂದ್ರಚೋಳಕೊಂಗಾಳ್ವನ ಪುತ್ರ
2 ಶ್ರೀರಾ[ಜಾಧಿರಾಜ] ..ಕೊಂಗಾಳ್ವ......
3 ...ವಾಸಸ್ಥಾನವೆಂತಮ್ಮಗುರುಗ
4 ಳ್ತ್ರವಿಳಗಣದರುಂಗಳಾನ್ವಯದನನ್ದಿ
5 ಸಂಘದಗುಣಸೇನಪಣ್ಡಿತದೇವಗ್ಗೆ ಧಾ
6 ರಾಪೂರ್ವ್ವಕಂಕೊಟ್ಟಂ ಮಂಗಳಮ
7 ಹಾ ಶ್ರೀ ಶ್ರೀ

39

ಅದೇ ಬಸ್ತಿಯಲ್ಲಿ ಚಂದ್ರನಾಥ ಬಸ್ತೀಬಳಿ ಯಿರುವದು

1 ಸ್ವಸ್ತಿ ಶ್ರೀಶಕವರ್ಷ ೧೩೧೩ ನೆಯಪ್ರ [ಮೋ] ದೋತ ಸಂವತ್ಸರದ ವೈಶಾಖ ಸು ೩ ಭಾನವಾ
2 ರದಲ್ಲು ಶ್ರೀ ಮೂಲಸಂಘದೇ ಸಿಗಣಪುಸ್ತಕಗಚ್ಛದ... ಕೊಂಡಕುಂದಾ
3 ನ್ವಯರಾರ್ಯ್ಯ ಶುಭೇನ್ದು ಕಂದ ವಿಜಯಕೀರ್ತಿದೇವರಪ್ರಿಯಶಿಷ್ಯರಪ್ಪಬಾಹುಬ
4 ಲಿದೇವರು ಈ ಸ್ಥಾನಮಂಪಡೆದುದ್ಧಗ್ಸಿದರು ಶ್ರೀರಾಜಾ[ಧಿರಾಜನು] ಕೊಂಗಾಳ್ವರುಗ್ಮಿ
5 ಣಿದೇವಿಯ ದೇವಿಯ ದೇಶಾರದ ವಿಜಯ ದೇವರದ್ವಾರಾ ನೆಲೆನಿಂದೆಂದು ಸ್ವಜನನಿ...ತಪು
6 ತ್ರ...ಆಪೋಚಬ್ಬರಸಿಗೆ ಪುಣ್ಯಾರ್ತ್ಥವಾಗಿ ಪ್ರತಿಷ್ಟೆಯಮಾಡ್ಸಿ ಅಜ್ಞಗಜ್ಜಭೋಗ
7 ಬಿಟ್ಟ ಊರು ಅಣಿಲವಾಡಿಯ ನುಉಬಿಹಳ್ಳಿಯಂ ನಾಡುದೞಿಶಿನಹಳ್ಳಿಮಂ
8 ಳೂರಹಾರುವಹಳ್ಳಿ ಏ ಸೀಮೆ ಮೂಡಹರಿವಹಳ್ಳತೆಂಕ...
9 ಬಡಗಣ ಅಗಳ ನಟ್ಟ ಕಲ್ಲುಪಡುವ ಬೆಟ್ಟಬಡಗಣ ಅ ...ಕಾರೆಗೋದಕ - - - -
10 ಳ್ಳಿಯಸೀಮೆ ಮೂಡನೆಲ್ಲಿಯ ಹೊಳನಟ್ಟ ಕಲ್ಲು ತೆಂಕಬೆಟ್ಟದ.....
11 ಬಡಗಕೆಱೆ ಏರಿ ಈಶಾನ್ಯನಟ್ಟ ಕಲ್ಲುಮುಳ್ಳೂರ ಗದ್ದೆಗಳಗಲವ್ರೋನಿ ಖ ೧
12 ...ಗೞೆಯ ಕೆಳಗೆ ಖ ೨ ಅಗದೊಳು - - ಕೊ ೧೦ ಕನಗೊಡಲ - - ಕೊ ೧೦ - -
13 ಗಾಲಖ ೧ ಕೊಡಗೊಸಲು ಕೊ ೨ ಅಚ್ಚಗದೆ ಕೊ ೧೦ ಲೋಕಗದ್ದೆಕೊ ೧೦ . ...
14 ೧೫ ಸಂಗೆ ಗದ್ದೆ ಖ ೧ ಬೋಳಗದ್ದೆ ಖ ೧ ಕೊ ೯ ಆಲದಕಾಡಿ ಖ ೧ ಕೊ ೧೦ ಅಸರವ
15 ಕ್ಕಿ ಖ ೧ ಕೊ ... ವೆಸಿಕುನಿ ಖ ೧ ನಿಡಿತದ ಗೋಡಲು ಖ ೩ ಮ್ಯಣಸದಲ್ಲಿ ಖ ೧ ಕೊ ೧೦
16 ಹೊನ್ನದೇವಿಯ ಸರಣ ಗೋಡಲು ಖ ೧ ಹೆಣ್ಣಿನಾರ ಭೂಮಿ ಖ ೨ ಒಂದು ಗಾಣದ
17 ಣ್ಣ ಬಿಟ್ಟದು ಆಚನಾಪ್ರಾರ್ಕ್ಕ ಸರ್ವ್ವಜನಾನಂದರ್ ದೀಕ್ಷತೆಯಪಟ್ಟ ಓದಿ ಸವತ್ತಿಸೆಯಾಗವೀ
18 ರಹರಿಹರೋರ್ವ್ವೀಶ ಪಲವರಂಕಾದಿ ರಾಯಮಹೆವ್ರೊಕ್ಕರಕಾವ ಶರಣಾಗತವಜ್ರಪಂಜ
19 ರ ಶಂಖಚಕ್ರ ಗಜದಾರಭ ತ್ಯೆ ಗೊಂಕಾಱಿಡ್ಡಿನಾಯ್ಕಗೆ ಗುಂಡಪ್ಪ ದಣ್ಣಾನಾಯ್ಕರುಕು
20 ರಿತ್ತುಮುಳ್ಳೈ ನಾಡಂ ಕುಡುವಂತರಾದರ್ ಸ್ವಭಾವಾರ್ತ್ಥವಾಗಿ ಸಿದ್ಧಗೌಡ ಪ್ರಜೆಗಳಕ
21 ರೆಕೊಂಡು ಜಂಣಾದೇವಿಯ ಕುಮಾರನಹಳ್ಳಿಯ ಭೀಮಾಪುರವೆಂದು ಪೆಸ
22 ರಿಟ್ಟು ಚತುಸ್ಸೀಮೆಯ ಕಲ್ಲನಟ್ಟುಧಾರಾಪೂರ್ವ್ವಕವಾಗಿ ಕೊಟ್ಟರೂ || ಕಾರ
23 ಗೋಡಂ ಅ[ಂಣಾ]ಂಗಪುರವೆಂದು ಪೆಸರನಿಟ್ಟು ಧಾರಾಪೂರ್ವ್ವಕವಾಗಿ ಪಾರ್ಶ್ವನಾ
24 ಥಂಗಿತ್ತರೂ || [ಕಿ]ರತ್ಯದಂಗಕ್ಕೆ ದಾನಶಾಲೆ ಗೋಮಾಲೆ ಜಯಮಾಳಪುರಿಯಲ್ಲಿ
25 ಗದ್ದೆ ಖ ೩ ಗಣಪತಿ ಗೋಡಲು ಖ ೩ ಹುಣಿಸೆದಾಱು ಖ ೧ ಎಳಂತ್ತಾ
26 ಜ್ಜನ ಶಾಸನಂ || ಶ್ರೀ

*27 ಈಧರ್ಮಕ್ಕೆ ಅಳಿಪಿ
28 ದವರು ಪಶುಸಿಸು
29 ಹೆಣ್ಣು ಗುರುಇವರ
30 ಕೊಂದಕೋಟಿ ಪಾಪದಲಿಹೋ
31 ಪರುಪಂದಿಯತಿಂಬರು

40

ಅದೇ ಚಂದ್ರನಾಥ ಬಸ್ತಿಯ ಎದುರಿಗಿರುವ ಮಂಟಪದಬಳಿ

1 ಸ್ವಸ್ತಿಶ್ರೀಶಕವರ್ಷ
2 ೧೧೩೮ ನೇ ಧಾತುಸಂ
3 ವತ್ಸರದ ಜೇಷ್ಟ
4 ಶು ೧೫ ಮಂ. ವಾ
5 ರದೆಲ್ಲು ಇಂಮಡಿ
6 ಅ..............
7 ....
8 ....ಯರಾಯ
9 ಕಟಕಾಚಾರ್ಯ್ಯರಪ್ಪ...ವಿ
10 ದ್ಯಾಧರಬೂಚಿದೇವರಸರುಮು
11 ಡಿಪಿ..................
12 ವಚಲು...............
13 ತಂಮ..............
.. ..

41

ಅದೇ ಬಸ್ತಿಯಲ್ಲಿ ಶಾನ್ತೀಶ್ವರಬಸ್ತೀ ಮುಂದೆ ಇರುವ ಪಾದದಕಲ್ಲು

1 ಗುಣಸೇನಪಣ್ಡಿ ತಸ್ಯೆ
2 ಗುರೋಃ ಪುಷ್ಪಸೇನಸಿದ್ಧಾಂತ
3 ದೇವಸ್ಯಶ್ರೀಪಾದಂ

42

ಅದೇ ಬಸ್ತಿಯ ಪ್ರಾಕಾರದಲ್ಲಿ ವಾಯವ್ಯ ಮೂಲೆಯಲ್ಲಿ ನಟ್ಟ ಕಲ್ಲು

1 ಸ್ವಸ್ತಿಶ್ರೀಗುಣಸೇನಪಣ್ಡಿ
2 ತ ದೇವರಗಳಸಿದನಾ
3 ಗವಾವಿನಕರದೆಧ
4 ರ್ಮ್ಮ (ಸರ್ಪದ ಆಕಾರವಿಧೆ)

43

ಅದೇ ಗ್ರಾಮದ ಕೆರೆ ಏರೀ ಮೇಲಿನ ೧ನೇ ವೀರಕಲ್ಲು

1 ಶ್ರೀಸಕವರ್ಷ ೯೯೯ ನೆಯ ಪಿಂಗಳ ಸಂವತ್ಸರ
2 ಶ್ರೀ ರಾಜೇಂದ್ರ ಚೋಳಕೊಂಗಾಳ್ವಂ ರಾಜ್ಯಂ ಗಯ್ಯುತ್ತಿ...
3 ಆತನಪಟ್ಟದರಸಿ ಪದ್ಮಲದೇವಿ ಸತ್ತು......
4 ನಿಹಕಾವರದಿಂದಂ ತಾನುಂತನ್ನ ಪೆಣ್ಡು...

44

ಅದೇ ಸ್ಥಳದಲ್ಲಿ

1 .. ...ಉತ್ತಮಚೋಃ ಸೆಟ್ಟಿಸ...ಬಾಲೆಯ...
2 ...ಖಿಲ್ಗಿದಿಂದಂ.........ತಲೆಗಡಿಸಿಸತ್ತಂ ॥

45

ಅದೇ ಗ್ರಾಮದಲ್ಲಿ ಕಾರುಗೋಡು ಪಟೇಲ ವೀರರಾಜಗೌಡರ ಕಣದಲ್ಲಿ ನಟ್ಟ ವೀರಕಲ್ಲು

ಪ್ರಮಾಣ 4′ 4″ × 2′ 8″.

1 ಓನ್ನಮಃ ಸ್ವಸ್ತಿ ಸಮಸ್ತಪ್ರಶಸ್ತಿ ಸಹಿತಂಮಂಡಳೀಕ ನಾರಾಯಣನುಂಮಲೆಯಂ
2 ಬೆಂಕೊಣ್ಡಗಂಡನುಂಶ[ರ]ಣಾಗತವಜ್ರಪಂಜರರುಮಪ್ಪಶ್ರೀಪ
3 ರಿಪರದೇವ ಚೋಳದೇವರರಾಜ್ಯದಂದು[ದು]ರ್ಮ್ಮುಖಿ ಸಂವತ್ಸರದ ಚೈ
4 ತ್ರ ಶುದ್ಧಪಂಚಮಿ ಸೋಮವಾರದಂದು ಮುಳ್ಳೂರಕೋಟೆಗೆ ಬೆಳಹುನಾಡು

---

* ಈ 5 ಪಙ್ತಿಗಳು ಶಾಸನದ ಮೇಲ್ಭಾಗದಲ್ಲಿ ಬರೆಯಲ್ಪಟ್ಟಿವೆ.

5 ಗೊದ್ದುಂಬಾಡಿಮುಳವರಾದಿತ್ಯ ನಾಡಮಲ್ಲಿಕಾಜ್ಜುರ್ನನಿಡಿತಮೆಣ

6 ಸಮೊದಲಾಗಿನಾಡೆಲ್ಲನೆರದೆತ್ತಿ ಬಂದುಮುತ್ತಿ ಕೋಟೆಯಹತ್ತಿಸಿದೆ

7 ಲ್ಲಿ ಬೊಪ್ಪಗೌಡಿಯಮಲ್ಲೆಯ ಮುಳ್ಳೂರ ಕೋಟೆಯ ಕಾದು ಅಟಾಹೊಯಿ

8 ದು ವೆಂಕಧಾರದೊಳಗೆಬಿದ್ದನು ಬಿದ್ದಲ್ಲಿಗಯಾತಂಗೆ ವೀರಸೇಸೆಯಾಗಿ ಮಾಸಾ

9 ವಿಮುಖ್ಯವಾಗಿ ಊರ ಮೂನೂಹಾಳು ನೆರದಿದ್ದುರ್ ಮುಳ್ಳೂರಗದ್ದೆಯೊ

10 ಳಗೆ ಮಾಕೊವೆಯಮಂಣೊಳಗೆಗದ್ದೆ ೩ ಹಿಡಿಜೆಗಲ್ಲಲಿಗದ್ದೆ ೫ ಯಿಂತೆಂಟು

11 ಗದ್ದೆ ಬೊಪ್ಪಗೌಡಿಯ ಮಾಲ್ಯೆಯ ಮಾದ್ಯೆಯನವರು ಹೊಸಅಮಾನಿಕೆಹಿಸ
(ಕಲ್ಲಿನ ಸುತ್ತಲೂ ಬರೆದಿರುವದು)

12 ೦ಿತ ಗ ೯ ಕ್ಕೆ ಮಾಸಾವಿ ಊರುನೆರದು ಅವರಿಗೆ ಸರ್ವ್ವಬಾಧಾಪರಿಹಾರವಾಗಿಮಾಡಿದರು ಈಮರಿಯಾ
ದೆಹೀ ಸೆಂದುಬಂದದು ॥ ಈ ಕಲ್ಲುಕೊಂಗೊಳಲಿಯಬಚಾಚಾರಿಯಮಗಬೈರೋಜಿಮಾಡಿ[ದ]ಕಲ್ಲು ಶ್ರೀ
ಕೊಪಣ ತೀರ್ತ್ಥದಸೇನ ಬೋವಸೊತ್ತೆಯ ಈ ಶಾಸನದ ಅಖರವೆಬರೆದ ಮಂಗಳಮಹಾ ಶ್ರೀ ಶ್ರೀ ಶ್ರೀ

46

ಅದೇ ಹೋಬಳಿ ಮಾಲಂಬಿ ಗ್ರಾಮದ ಹಳೇಗ್ರಾಮ ನಿವೇಶನದ ಬಳಿ

ಪ್ರಮಾಣ 3′ 2″ × 2′ 8″ (ಈ ಕಲ್ಲು ೨ ತುಂಡಾಗಿಧೆ)

1 ಸ್ವಸ್ತಿ ಸೂರ್ಯ್ಯಾನ್ವಯೆ ಸುರತರುಸ್ತೂಂಬಾಯಮಾನ ಚೋಳಕು

2 ಳಗಘನಗಭಸ್ತಿಮಾಳಿಸೆಕಳ ಜನದುರಿತ ಹರಣನಿ

3 ಪುಣಕವೇರ ಕನ್ಯಕಾಸಖೀಯಮಾನ ಚೋಟಮಹಾಮಹೀ

4 ಪತಿಶ್ರೀರಾಜಕೇಸರಿವರ್ಮ್ಮರ್ ಪೆರ್ಮ್ಮನಡಿಗಳ್ ನಿಜಂಗೆ

5 ಪನಸೊಗೆಯ ಕಾಳೆಗದಲೊಟ್ಟಿ ಕೆಯ್ದುಂನೆಜಿವಿಕ್ಕುಬ

6 ರೇನೆನ್ದು ಆತನನಡಹಿದಸ್ವರ್ತ್ತರೆನ್ದು ಪಿರಿದುಂಕಾರು

7 ಣ್ಯದಿನ್ದ ಪಟ್ಟವಕಟ್ಟಿ ನಾಡಕುಡುಗೆನ್ದು ಪಞ್ಚವನ್

8 ಮಾರಾಯಗ್ಗರ್ಟ್ಟಲಾತಂಕ್ಷತ್ರಿಯಸಿಖಾಮಣಿ

9 ಕೊಂಗಾಳ್ವನೆನ್ದು ಪಟ್ಟವಕಟ್ಟಿಮಾಲವ್ವಿಯನಿತ್ತರಿ

10 ದಕ್ಕೆರ್ಗಾವುಣ್ಡರಾಚಮ್ಮನವಂಶಮೇಸಾಕ್ಷಿ ಕಣ್ಣವಂಗಲ

11 ದಳಪತ್ಯಗಾವುಣ್ಡನುಂ ಗಟಿನಿಯನನ್ನಿಯಮೇ೦ುವುಂ

12 ಕೆಟಿನ...ಚಗಾವುಣ್ಡನುಂನಲ್ಲೂರೀಟಿಯಂಗಗಾವುಣ್ಡ

13 ...ಳ್ಳೂನಾರ್ಡೆಕಲ್ನಾಡೆಪೊಱಗೆನ್ದುನುಡಿಪುಳ್ಕ........(ಮುಂದೆಕಾಣುವದಿಲ್ಲ)

47

ಅದೇ ಗ್ರಾಮದ ಹಳೇಗ್ರಾಮ ನಿವೇಶನದ ದ್ವಾರದಲ್ಲಿ

ಪ್ರಮಾಣ 1′ 10″ × 1′ 3″.

1 ಧಾತುಸಂವತ್ಸರದಆ

2 ಸ್ವೀಜಶುಧ ೫ ಲೂ ಶ್ರೀಮ

3 ತುವೆಂ[ಕ]ಟಾದ್ರಿನಾಯಕರಕೃಷ್ಣ

4 ಪ್ಪನಾಯಿಕರುಮಾಲಂಬಿರಾ

5 ಜೇಗೌಡಗೆಪಾಲಿಸಿಕೊಂಡದು

6 ಕಂದಾಯ ಗ ೧೦

7 ಹಂನೆರಡುವರಹ

8 ಂನುಪಾಲಿಸಿಕೊಂಡ

9 ದು ಇಧೇವಿ

48

ಅದೇ ಹೋಬಳಿ ಮೆಣಸದ ಹಾಳುಕೋಟೆ ಕಂದುಕದಲ್ಲಿ

1 ಸ್ವಸ್ತಿಶ್ರೀಕೊಂಗಾಳ್ವರಾಜ್ಯಂಗೆಏಕೊಮಾರಯ್ಯಸುನ್ದರ.. ಜ.........

2 ಎಡೆತುರುಕೊಳಕಟ್ಟಿಸ್ತರಲ್ಲಿ...ನಾಹಾರತುರುಹಾರನೊಟ್ಟೆ......

3 ಸಾಮಂತರ...ದಕೋ:ಗಾ...ಗೋಕಿ ಪಯನ...
4 ವಾರವೂರಾ...ಪ್ಪಟ್ಟಕೊಟ್ಟ...ದೇಣಿದೆಸೇನಿಯರ...

(ಸುನ್ದರ್ಅ ಕೊಮಾರನ್)

49

ಅದೇ ಹೋಬಳಿ ಹೊಸಹಳ್ಳಿ ಪಣೆಯಾಲದೆ ಕಟ್ಟೇಬಳಿ ನಟ್ಟ ಶಾಸನ

ಪ್ರಮಾಣ 3′ 2″ × 2′

ಇದರ ಮೇಲ್ಭಾಗದಲ್ಲಿ ಸ್ವಸ್ತಿಪ್ರಾರಂಭವಾಗಿ ೧ನೆ ಪಂಕ್ತಿ ಸ್ಪಷ್ಟವಾಗಿ ಕಾಣಿಸದಿಲ್ಲ

1 ಸ್ವಸ್ತಿಶಕವರ್ಷ ೯೯೩ ನೆಯ ಸಾ
2 ಧಾರಣಸಂವತ್ಸರದಚೈತ್ರಮಾಸ
3 ದಲಮಾವಾಸೆಯೆಂದುಶ್ರೀಮದ್ರಾಜೇ
4 ನ್ದ್ರ)ಪ್ರಿತುವಿಕೊಂಗಾಳ್ವಸುಳ್ಳಿಗೋಡಿನ
5 ಗೌರತಿಯಕೆಱೆಯಕೆಱಗಣಮ
6 ಕ್ಕಮೂಡಣಹಡುವಣಗೋಡ
7 ಬಾಳಗಾಗಿಅಯ್ವತ್ತುಖಣ್ಡುಗ
8 ಬಿಡಭೂಮಿಸುಂಹೊಷವಳ್ಳವೀ
9 ರಸಿದ್ಧೇಶ್ವರದೇವಗ್ಗ್ಂಅಚ್ಚ್ಸಾ
10 ಭೋಗಕ್ಕಂಧಾರಾಪೂರ್ವ್ವ ಕಂಬಿಟ್ಟಂ
11 ರಾ:ವಲ್ಲಭಸೆಟ್ಟ ಱಗೆಕೊಟ್ಟಗ
12 ದ್ಯಾಣಂ ೪೦ ಆಡವೆಲಂಗದ್ಯಾ
13 ಣಂ ೧॥ ತಪ್ಪಿದಂಕವಿಲೆಯನಳದಂಸ್ವದೆ
14 ತ್ತಂಪರದೆತ್ತಂವಾಯೋ:ಹರೇತವಸುಂಧರಾಂ
15 ಷಷ್ಟಿರ್ವ್ವರ್ಷಸಹಸ್ರಾಣಿವಿಷ್ಟಾಯಾಂಜಾ
ಯತೇಕ್ರಿಮಿಃ

50

ಅದೇ ಗ್ರಾಮದಲ್ಲಿ ತಿಮ್ಮಯ್ಯನ ಕೆಱೇಬಳಿ ಗದ್ದೆಯಲ್ಲಿ ನಟ್ಟ ಶಾಸನ

1 ಸ್ವಸ್ತಿಸವರ್ಷ ೯೯೩ ನೆ
2 ಸಾಧಾರಣಸಂವತ್ಸರದಚೈತ್ರ
3 ಮಾಸದಲಮೊವಾಸಿಯೆಂದುಶ್ರೀ
4 ರಾಜೇಂದ್ರಪ್ರಥುವಕೊಂಗಾಳ್ವರಾ
5 ಜ್ಯಂಗೆಯ್ಯುತ್ತಿರೆಹೊಷವಳ್ಳವೀರ
6 ಸಿದ್ಧೇಶ್ವರಮಹಾದೇ[ವ]ಗ್ಗ್ಪೊಸವಳ್ಳ
7 ಯನೀರಗಾವುಣ್ಡನಕೆಯ್ಯಲ್ಲೊಪ್ಪ
8 ಱಕೊಟ್ಟುಮಣ್ಣ ಱಕೊಣ್ಡಸತ್ತುಖ
9 ಣ್ಡಿವೆಯೆಆಡವೆಲಂಕೊಟ್ಟಂತಪ್ಪಿ
10 ದಂಕವಿಲೆಯನಳದಂ

51

ಅದೇ ಹೋಬಳಿ ದೊಡ್ಡಮಳತೆ ಗ್ರಾಮಕ್ಕೆ ಸೇರಿದೆ ಹೊನ್ನಮ್ಮನಕೆರೆ ತೂಬಿನಮೇಲೆ

1 ಶ್ರೀಮತುಪಾರ್ಥಿ[ವ]ಸಂವತ್ಸರದಪಲ್ಗುಣಸು ೧೦ ಗುರುವಾರಅನ್ನದಾನಿಅರಸಿನವರು
2 ಯಿಾತೂಬಕಟ್ಟಿಸಿದೆರುಕಟಿದೆವರುವೆಂಕಟ್ಯೆಯ್ಯಮಲ್ಲೈಯಬೊಮರಸ್ಯನಬರಹ
3 ಬಸಲಿಂಗದೇವರುನಂನಗಉಡೆನಕಾಲದಲಿಆಯಿತು

52

ಅದೇ ಹೋಬಳಿ ಗನಗೂರು ಊರುಬಾಗಿಲ ಬಳಿ

1 ....
2 ರದವೈಸಾಖಸು ೧೦ ಮಂಗಳವಾರ
3 ದಂದುತೆಂಕಗುಂಡನಾಡೆಪ್ಪತಕ್ಕಂಕಾರುಣ್ಯಂ
4 ಗೆಯ್ದು॥ - ತೊಡೆಗೆಂಡಿಲ್ಲದಿರ್ದ್ದಡೆ
5 ಹೆಣ್ಣಂಗೆಹೆಣ್ಣುಮಕ್ಕಳಿಂಗೆಸಲುವು
6 ದುಱಧೆರ್ಮ್ಮವತಪ್ಪನಡೆದಂಪಾಪವನರಕ
7 ಬಿದ್ದಗಂಗೆಯೆಕಡಿಯಲುಕವಿಲೆಯಂ
8 ಬ್ರಾಹ್ಮಣನುವಂಕೊಂದಬ್ರಂಮಾತಿಯಂಕೊಂ
ಡ
9 ಶ್ರೀಮನ್ಮಹಾಪ್ರಧಾನಪಡಿವಳಬಾನಮ್ಮರಾಜನ
ಪುತ್ರಹೆ
10 ಗ್ಗಡೆನಾಕಣಬರದೆಮಂಗಳಮಹಾಶ್ರೀ ಶ್ರೀ
11 ದವಟ್ಟವೆಸ...ಗರಾವಜ್ಜರಗಾಳಬಯ
12 ಲನಾಡಬವ್ವೋಜಗೆಯ್ದಸಾಸನ

53

ಅದೇ ಸ್ಥಳದಲ್ಲಿ

1 ....

2 ಪೃಥಿವೀರಾಜ್ಯಂಗೈಯುತ್ತಿರೆತಾಇವ

3 ....

4 ದಂಣ್ಣನಾಯಕನಿಂತನಿಬರುಮುಖ್ಯ...

5 ಕುನಾಡೆಪ್ಪತ್ತಕ್ಕಂಆಯದಾಯವ್ರೊಡೆ

6 ಯೆಪ್ಪಹೊನ್ನ ಪಮಹಣಕಾಣಕೆ

7 ...ಸಬಿಟ್ಟಂ।... ....

8 ......ಸರ್ವ್ವಾಯ............

9 ಮನುಮತಸಂವತ್ಸರದಜೇಷ್ಟ...ಸುಕ್ರವಾರ

10 ದೆಂದುಆಯದಾಯಸಹ............

11 ವಕಾರುಣ್ಯಂಗೈಯ್ದ...... ..ಕೊಂ

12 ಗಾಳ್ವದೇವ ॥

54

ಅದೇ ಹೋಬಳಿ ಗೋಣೇಮರೂರು ಗ್ರಾಮದಲ್ಲಿ ಕಂಚುವಾಳದ ಮರದ ಬಳಿ ೧ ನೇ ಶಾಸನ

(ಮೇಲುಭಾಗ ಹೋಗಿಧೆ.)

1 ....

2 ....ಮತ್ತಿಯಗ

3 ....ಕೆಱೆಯಕೆಳಗೆಗದ್ದೆಗಂಣ್ಣು

4 ...ಕ - ಕೊ ೧॥ ದೇವಿಗೆಱೆಯಕೆಳಗೆಗದೆಗಂಣ್ಣು ಆಱ

5 ...ಕೊ ೧॥ ಮಾವಿನಮುಕ್ಕವ್ರೊಳಗೆಕೊ ೧೦ ಅನ್ತುಗ ೪ ಬೆದ್ದಲುವ್ರೊ

6 ರಮೊಡಣವ್ರೋಣೆಯಿಂಬಡಗಣಕಡೆಎರಡಾರಬೆದ್ದಲು...ಕೋಪ

7 ವ್ರೊಂಣಂಗಿತಲೆಮೆಟ್ಟಿಸೆಲಕೊಂದುಗೋಪಾಳ

8 ದೇವನದೆಂಡಿನಕಾಣಿಕೆಮನೆವಣಸೊಲಗೆಬಿಟಿಯಿಂನಿಷ್ಟ್ಯಸ

9 ವ್ಯ್ವಮಾನ್ಯವಾಗಿಸ್ವರುಚಿಯಿಂದೆಕೊಟ್ಟರುಯಿಂತಪ್ಪುದಕ್ಕೆಆಮ

10 ಲ್ಲಿದೇವ ರಹರದೇವರಸರೊಪ್ಪಶ್ರೀಚೆಂನಸದಾಸಿವ

55

ಅದೇ ಸ್ಥಳದಲ್ಲಿ ೨ ನೇ ಶಾಸನ

(ಮೇಲುಭಾಗ ಕೆಳಭಾಗ ಸಹ ಹೋಗಿಧೆ)

....

1 ದೇವರಸರುಪೃಥ್ವೀರಾಜ್ಯಂಗೆಯುತ್ತಿದ್ದಲಿಯಡವು

2 ನಾಡಗಟ್ಟಬಾಡಿಯಗಡಿಯಕಾಳೆಗದಬವರದಲಿಚಿ

3 ಕ್ಕೆಯನಾಯಕಬಿದ್ದಂದುಚಿಕ್ಕೆಯನಾಯಕಸಮಕ್ಕಳಗೆತ

4 ಮಲ್ಲಿದೇವರಸರುಹರಿಹರದೇವರಸರುತಂಕನಾಡಸಮಸ್ತ-

....

56

ಅದೇ ಹೋಬಳಿ ದೊಡ್ಡಕಣಗಾಲು ಗೌಡನ ಹೊಲದಲ್ಲಿ 2 ನೇ ಕಲ್ಲು

1 ಶ್ರೀಮೂಲಸಂಗದೇಸಿಯಗಣಪುಸ್ತಕಘ

2 ಛಕೊಂಡಕುಂದಾನ್ವಯಇಂಗುಳೇಸ್ವರದಬ

3 ಳಿಯಪ- ಅದೆ- ಸುಭಚಂದ್ರದೇವರ-

4 ಪ್ರಿಯಾಗ್ರಸಿಶ್ಯರುಮಪ್ಪಪ್ರಭಾಚಂದ್ರದೇವರನಿ

5 ಸಿಧಿತಾರಣಸಂವಛರಚೈತ್ರಸುಧಪಂಚಮಿ

6 ಸುಕ್ರವಾರದೆಂದುಮುಕ್ತರಾದೆರು-

57

ಯಡವನಾಡು ಯಡೂರು ಸುಗ್ರೀದೇವರ ಗುಡಿಯಲ್ಲಿನ ಶಾಸನ-

ಪ್ರಮಾಣ 4′ 8″ × 1′ 6″

1 ಸ್ವಸ್ತಿಸಖವರ್ಷ ೧೦೧೭
2 ನೆಯಯುವಸಂವತ್ಸರ
3 ದಸ್ರಾವಣಮಾಸದಸುದಿಬಿ
4 ದಿಗೆಆದಿವಾರದಂದು
5 ಶ್ರೀಮನುಮಹಾಮ
6 ಣ್ಡಲೇಸ್ವರತ್ರಿಪುರಾ
7 ಧೀಸ್ವರಬಲೀನ್ದ್ರಕು
8 ಳಕಮಳಮಾರ್ತ್ತಣ್ಡ
9 ಚತುಮ್ರ್ಮಖಗಣ್ಡಸರ
10 ಣಾಗತವಜ್ರಪಂಜರವೈ
11 ರಿಗಜಕೇಸರಿಬಲಿಯ
12 ರಭೀಮಸಂಗ್ರಾಮರಾಮ
13 ಮಲೆಪರನಂದನವನಂ
14 ಸಂಸ್ತುತ್ಯವಂದಿಜನಂಪ
15 ರಮಣ್ಡಳಸೂಱೆಕಾಱಂ
16 ಅಯ್ಯನಂಕಕಾರಶಿ
17 ವಪಾದಸೇಖರಂಶತ್ಯರ
18 ತ್ನಾಕರಂರಿಪುಹೃದಯ
19 ಕರ್ಕ್ಕಸಂಚರಸಂಕರಕ್ಕ
20 ಸನನೇಕನಾಮಾವಳೀಮು
21 ಖ್ಯನಪ್ಪದುದ್ಧರಸಂಪಟ್ಟ
22 ಯರಸಂಗಂಜುಂಜಲದೇವಿಗಂಪು
23 ಟ್ಟಅತುಳಬಳಪರಾಕ್ರಮನಾಗಿ
24 ನವಯೌವನಾರೂಪನುಂವಿಜ
25 ಯಲಕ್ಷ್ಮೀಕಾನ್ತನುಮಾಗಿಮ
26 ಲೆಯಂಪ್ರತಿಪಾಳಿಸಿರಿ
27 ಪುಗಳಂಬೆದೆಜಿಬೆಂಕೊ
28 ಣ್ಮುಕೋಟೆಗಳಂನಿರ್ವ್ವಾಟಿಸಿವೀ
29 ರಾವತಾರಸಂಕಲಿಯುಗಾಂ

ಹಿಂಭಾಗ-

30 ತಕಂಸಂಹರಥನಾಡುನುಂ
31 ಪಾಕುವಾಡಿಯುಂನೊಡೆ
32 ಲಾಗಿಪ್ರತಿಪಾಳಿಸಿಯಾ
33 ಬ್ಬಪದಿನಯ್ದುಕುದುರೆ
34 ಯುಅಯ್ವತ್ತುಲೆಂಕರುಂಇ
35 ನ್ನೂಱಯ್ವತ್ತುಎಕ್ಕಟೆ
36 ಗರುಂನಾಲುವತ್ತಯ್ದುಕು
37 ಳಪುಟ್ಟಗೆಗಾಯದಾಳುಂಮ
38 ನೇಕಪ್ರಜೆಪರಿವಾರಬಂ
39 ಧುವರ್ಗ್ಗಮುಂತಳವರ್ಗ್ಗ
40 ಮುಂಕುಲಸ್ತ್ರೀಚಿಕಲದೇವಿ
41 ಯುಂಬೆಸಕಯ್ಯಸು..
42 ಜಲಿದೆಯಿಂರಾಜ...
43 ಕೆಱೆಯಂಕಟ್ಟಸಿ ..
44 ಯುಮನೆತ್ತಿಸಿದವ
45 ರುಬ್ರಾಹ್ಮಣರ್ಗ್ಗೆ ಚತ್ರಮಂನಿ
46 ಲಿಸಿತೂಱಗೆಟಿದ್ದಯುಮಾ
47 ಡಿಸಿಅನೇಕಧರ್ಮ್ಮಮಬೆಳೆ
48 ಗಿಶಿವಲೋಕಪ್ರಾಪ್ತನಾಗಲ್
49 ಸಹೋದರಂಜಾಜರಸಂಸ್ನೇ
50 ಹದಿಂಪರೋಕ್ಷವಿನಯಂಗೆಯ್ದು
51 ವೀರಶಾಸನವಂಬರೆಯಿಸಿ
52 ದಂಮೊಳತೆಯದುದ್ಧಮಲ್ಲಸ
53 ನ್ಧಿವಿಗ್ರಹಿಸೇನಭೋವರಾಜಿ
54 ಮಯ್ಯನಮಗಂಬಮ್ಮದೇವ
55 ನಿಂಇನ್ತುದುಧ್ಧರಸಂಮಾಡಿಸಿ
56 ದತೂಱಗೆಟಿದ್ದಯುಂಮಾಱಕೊ
57 ಣ್ಡವಂಬಾಣರಾಸಿಯುಲುಹ
58 ಸುವುಂಹಾರುವನಂಕೊಂದ
59 ಮಂಗಳಮಹಾ ಶ್ರೀ ಶ್ರೀ॥

58

ಅದೇ ನಾಡು ಕಲಕಂದೂರು ಬ್ರಹ್ಮದೇವರ ಪೀಠದಮೇಲೆ ಬರೆದಿರುವದು

1- ರೌದ್ರಿಸಂವತ್ಸರದಜ್ಯೇಷ್ಟಸುದಪಂಚಮಿಆದಿವಾರದಂದು
2- ಹುಂದ್ರ...ದೂರವಿಠಾರಿ...ಬಿಜೆಮಾಡಿಸಿದ।
3- ಶ್ರೀಮಾಣಿಕದೇವರುಮಂಗಳ
4- ಮಹಾ ಶ್ರೀ ಶ್ರೀ

59

ಅದೇ ನಾಡು ಚೌಡ್ಲುಸುಗ್ಗಿ ಗುಡಿ ಬಳಿಯ ದಾರೀಬಳಿ

1 ಸ್ವಸ್ತಿ.ಶ್ರೀಮನುಮಹಾಮಂಡಳೇಶ್ವರಂ
2 ....
3 ......ನಾರಾಯಣ.. ಣ......
4 ......ಹರಿಹರದೇವ............
5 ....
6 ....ಆಳುತ್ತಿರೆಹೇವಿಳಂ
7 ಬಿಸಂವತ್ಸರದಮಾಘಮಾಸಪೂರ್ವಪಕ್ಷಪಂ
8 ಚಮಿಅಶ್ವಿನೀನಕ್ಷ[ತ್ರ]ಗುರುವಾರದಂದುಹರಿಹ
9 ರ...ಕುಂದೂರಿಂಗೆಪೂರ್ವ್ವದಲಿಸಂ
10 ಣಂಗೆಸಲುವೆಶ್ವಾಸ್ತಿಮರಿಯಾದಿಯಕೊ
11 ಟ್ಟಕ್ರಮವೆಂತೆಂದೆಡೆಹೇಣ್ಣಿಂಗೆಹೇಣ್ಣುಮಕ್ಕ
12 ಳಿಂಗೆತೊತ್ತಿನಮಕಳಿಂಗೆಸಲುವುದುಚ
13 ವುಡ · ಮಾನೆಯೊಳುಮಾರಜನಕಾ...
14 ನೊಳತೆಯ......ಪಾರಿಸೆ.........
15 ಕುಂದೂರದಾವಮಾನೆಯೊಳುಮಾಚಿ -
16 ಕಾರಿಯುನಗಹ । ಮಾಚಜೀಯನಕಣ್ಣೈಗ
17 ಣಲೆಯಕಾವಣಪಳ್ಳಿಗುಂದೆದಆಜಣಬೆಣಚ
18 ಹೆಗಡೆಹಳ್ಳಿಯಮಾದಣಅಬಿಯೂ
19 ರಮಲಿಗೌಡಯಿಗೌಡುಗಳುಮುಖ್ಯವಾಗಿ
20 ಯಿಂತೀನಾಡುನಬರಕೆಚಂದ್ರಾದಿತ್ಯ
21 ರುಳ್ಳಂನಬರಕೊಟಸಾಸನಮರಿಯಾದಿಯಬರೆ [ದಸೇ
22 ನಬೋವಜಿನಯ್ಯಕಲ್ಲಹೊಯ್ದಮಲೋಜ..

60

ಅದೇ ನಾಡು ಹಾರೋಹಳ್ಳಿ ಗ್ರಾಮದ ಗೌಡನ ಉಂಬಳಿಗದ್ದೆ ಕಾಲವೆಯಲ್ಲಿ

1 ತೆಯಲಯ್ಯಜಾಬುಕಾಲಂಕಟ್ಟಿ...
2 ವ್ವದಿಂಬರಊಯಕೊಟ್ಟವೃಏಊತಿಯ [ರ]
3 ಸಂಗೆಬಿಟ್ಟಗ್ರಹಾರ ! ಮತ್ತಂಚ
4 ಟ್ಟಯುಂದೊರೆ ಕಬಲಹ ಕೋಜ್ಗಣೆ
5 ವಮ್ಮಂಕಾಲಂಕಟ್ಟಿಕೊಟ್ಟಂ
6 ಬಿಟ್ಟಪೊನ್ನಮಣ್ಣಿಂಗೆವಟ್ಟದಿಂ
.. ..

61

ಗಡಿನಾಡು ಹೋಬಳಿ ಗರಗಂದೂರು ಶಾನ್ತವೀರಮ್ಮನ ಮನೇದಾರಿಯಲ್ಲಿ ನಟ್ಟ ೧ ನೇ ವೀರಗಲ್ಲು

....
3 ಸ್ವಸ್ತಿಶ್ರೀಮನುಮಹಾಮಣ್ಡ
4 ಳೇಶ್ವರತ್ರಿಭುವನಮಲ್ಲವೀರ
5 ......ಮತು - ಚಂಗಾ -
6 ......ಮಹಾಮ.....
7 ...ದಿತ್ಯದೇವಗೆ...
8 ......ಣ್ಡ.. ......
9 ......ರಪ.........

62

ಅದೇ ನಾಡು ಹಾರಂಗಿ ಗ್ರಾಮಕ್ಕೆ ಈಶಾನ್ಯ ಚಿಕ್ಕಮಠದ ಬಿವಿರು ಕಾಡಿನಲ್ಲಿ

1 ಸ್ವಸ್ತಿಸಮಸ್ತಪ್ರಶಸ್ತಿ
2 ಸಹಿತಶ್ರೀಮತ್‌ಷ
3 ಣ್ಮೇದೊಕೋಕಂಕಲಿ
4 ಯುಗಬ್ರಹ್ಮಏಊದ

63

ಅದೇ ನಾಡು ತಾಕೇರಿ ಗ್ರಾಮದಲ್ಲಿ ಬಲಗೈ ಈರನ ಗದ್ದೆಯಲ್ಲಿ

1 ಸರ್ವಧಾರಿಸಂವತ್ಸರ
2 ಚೈತ್ರಬ ೫ ಆಲುಗಲು
3 ಳನಂಜರಪ್ಪಯಅಣ
4 ನವರೂಹಾನಗಲಲಿಂ
5 ಗೇಗಉಡರಿಗೆಹಾ
6 ...ಟ್ಟಗಉಡಿಕೆ

64

ಬಿಲಹ ಹೋಬಳಿ ಕಾಜೂರು ಬಸವನಗುಡಿಗೆ ಉತ್ತರದಲ್ಲಿ ಬಿದ್ದಿರುವದು

1 ಶ್ರೀಮತುಬಿಳುಗೌಡಅಣಬಗವ್ರು
2 ಡಬಯಿರು - ಕನಿಗುಯಿರಾಮನಾ
3 ಗಜ್ಯಯ
4 ಕೆಂಪಣ
5 ನಾಲ್ವರಿಗೆ
6 ಕೊಟಗ್ರಾಮ

65

ಅದೇ ಹೋಬಳಿ ಸಿರಹ ಗ್ರಾಮದ ರಾಮೇಶ್ವರ ಗುಡಿ ಮುಂದೆ

1 ಶ್ರೀಜಯಸಂವಛ
2 ರದಫಾಲ್ಗುಣಸುಧಸ
3 ಪುರ್ನ್ನವಿಬ್ರೆಹವಾರದಂ
4 ಬಿಹೊಯ್ಸಳಭುಜಬಳಶ್ರೀ
5 ವೀರಬಲ್ಲಾ[ಳ]ದೇವರಸರುಪ್ರಿ
6 ತ್ವೀರಾಜ್ಯಂಗೆಯುತ್ತಿದ್ದಲ್ಲಿಬಿಳು
7 ಹುನಾಡವಡದಶಿರಿಯರಕ
8 ಸಪ - ಗವುಡಗಳಬೀರಯ್ಯನ
9 ಮಗಮಾಯಂಣಂಗೆಸಿರಿವುರದ
10 ಮಲ್ಲಿಕರ್ಜನದೇವರಅಷ್ಟಭೋಗತೇ
11 ಜಸ್ವಾಮ್ಯನಿಧಿನಿಕ್ಷೇಪಜಲಪಸ
12 ಣಆಗಾಮಿಮುಖ್ಯವಾಗಿವ ಾ
13 ಯಂಣ್ಣಂಗೆಕಾಲುಗೆಬೆರಸಾ
14 ಗಿಧಾರೆಯ:ಯೆಱದುಕೊ
15 ಟಸಾಸನಯಿದನುಆರು
16 ಅಳಿಹಿದಡೆಗಂಗೆಯಾ
17 ತಡಿಯಲಿಕವಿಲೆಯ
18 ಕೊಂದದೋಷದಲಿಹೋಹ
19 ರುಮಂಗಳಮಹಾಶ್ರೀ
20 ಶ್ರೀ ಶ್ರೀ ಮೆಱಿವಕ್ಕ
21 ರಕಾವರು ಶ್ರೀ

66

ಅದೇ ಹೋಬಳಿ ಮೊದರವಳ್ಳಿ ಊರುಬಾಗಲಲ್ಲಿ ಹುಣಸೇಮರದ ಕೆಳಗೆ

1 ಶುಭಮಸ್ತು
2 ಶ್ರೀವತ್ಸರಮಹಂ
3 ಸಾನಾಂ । ಪರಿವಾ್ರ
4 ಜಕಸತ್ತ್ರಮಂ । ಸ್ಯೈ
5 ವಲ್ಲಾಖ್ಯಮಹಾ
6 ಯೋಗಿಂ । ಸದಾ
7 ಗ್ನಾನೈಕತತ್ಪಗಂ । ಬೇಲೂರುಕೃಷ್ಣಭೊ
8 ಪಸ್ತು । ಆಹೊಯಯತಿಕುಂಜರಂ । ಮೂದ್ರ
9 ವಳ್ಳೀಚಗ್ರಾಮಸ್ತು । ದತ್ತಂಕೃಷ್ಣಾರ್ಪಣಂ
10 ಶುಭಂ । ಕಿಮರ್ಥಂದತ್ತಮಿ ತ್ಯುಕ್ತೇ *

67

ಕೊಡ್ಲಿ ಹೋಬಳಿ ಹುಲಕೋಡು ಗ್ರಾಮಕ್ಕೆ ಪೂರ್ವ ಕನ್ನೇಶ್ವರ ದೇವರ ಗುಡಿ ಬಳಿ

1 ವಿಕಾರಿಸಂವಛರದಫಗುಣಸುಧ ೫ ಪಡವರದಿ
2 ತ್ರಿನಮೇರದೇವಣ್ಣ ನವರೂಳಿಟದಕೆಳಗೆಹೋ
3 ಗಿಅಧಲಿಹುಲುಕೋಡಚಿಕ್ಕಣ್ಣ ಯಬೆಂಮ್ಮೆ ಗೌ [ಡ
4 ನಬೀರಗಲ್ಲುಕಳಿನಬೋಜಗಡದುಶ್ರೀ
5 ಸಗೆವು ...
6 ಡಬೊ
7 ವ
8 ದೇ
9 ನ್ಮರಿಯ್ಯಂಚಿಕಣ್ಣ ಯರಿಗೆಮಂಗಳಮಅದೊರೆ

68

ಕಣಿವೆ ಹೋಬಳಿ ಹೆಗ್ಗಡಹಳ್ಳಿ ಬಸವನ ಗುಡಿಬಳಿ ೧ ನೇ ಕಲ್ಲು

1 ಶ್ರೀಸ್ವಸ್ತಿಶ್ರೀವಿಜಯಾಭ್ಯು
2 ದೆಯಶಾಲಿವಾಹನಶಕದವರು
3 ಷ ೧೬೭೨ ನೆಯ ಸಾಧಾರಣಸಂವತ್ಸರದ
4 ಮಾಘಬ ೨ ಬಾರ್ಗವ ॥ ವಾರ
5 ದೆಲ್ಲುಕುಡುಮದಮಂಜುನಾಥಸ್ವಾಮಿ
6 ಯವರಸಂನಿಧಿಯಲ್ಲುನಡವದೇವತಸೇವೆ
7 ಬಗ್ಯೆಹಾವೇರಿವೀರಪೊಡೇರು । ಸರ್ವಮಾಂನ್ಯೆ
8 ಸಂಕೇತವಾಗಿಬಿಟ್ಟಹೆಗ್ಗಡಹಳ್ಳಿಸಿರಂಗಾಲ ॥
9 ಉಭಯಗಡಿಗೆಸಲುವಉಪಗ್ರಾಮ ೬ ನು ಸಿ [ಲಾ
10 ಸಾಸನಮಾಡಿಸಿಬಿಟ್ಟುಕೊಟ್ಟದು
ಶ್ರೀ

69

ಅದೇ ಸ್ಥಳದಲ್ಲಿ ೨ ನೇ ಕಲ್ಲು

1 ಶ್ರೀಕುಡುಮದಮಂ
2 ಜುನಾಥಸ್ವಾಮಿಯ
3 ವರಸಂಕೇತ ಶ್ರೀ
†

---

* ಇಷ್ಟೇ ಬರೆದಿರುವದು.

† ಇಲ್ಲಿ ಡಮರುಗ ತ್ರಿಶೂಲ ಬರೆದಿದೆ.

70

ಅದೇ ಸ್ಥಳದಲ್ಲಿ ೩ ನೇ ಕಲ್ಲು-

1 ಸ್ವಸ್ತಿಸಮಸ್ತಭುವನಾಶ್ರಯಂಶ್ರೀ
2 ಪ್ರಿಥ್ವೀವಲ್ಲಭಂಮಹಾರಾಜಾಧಿರಾಜಪ
3 ರಮೇಸ್ವರಂಪರಮಭಟಾರಕಯ
4 ದವಕುಳಾಂಬರದ್ಯುಮಣಿಸಮ್ಯಕುತ
5 ಚೂಡಾಮಣಿಮಲರಾಜರಾಜಮ
6 ಲಪರೊಳುಗಂಡಗಂಡಭೇರುಂಡಕದನಪ್ರಚಂ
7 ಡನಸಹಾಯಸೂರಯೇಕಾಂಗವೀರಸನಿವಾರಸಿ [ದ್ಧಗಿರಿದುರ್ಗ
8 ಮಲ್ಲನುಗರರಾಯ - ರನಯ .....
....
11 ಗಂಡಶ್ರೀವಿರಹೊಯಸಣ......
....

71

ಅದೇ ಹೋಬಳಿ ಸಿರಂಗಾಲದ ಬಸವನಗುಡಿ ಸಾರಿಗೆಯಲ್ಲಿ

1 ಸ್ವಸ್ತಿಶ್ರೀಸಿರಿವಂಗಲದಮಾಚ
2 ಗಾವುಣ್ಡಂಸಿರಿಯಮತನ್ದಿವೀರ॥
3 ಮಾಚಗೊಣ್ಡನಮಗಕಾವಗೊ
4 * ಣ್ಡಕಲ್ಲನಿಱಿಸಿದಂ
5 ಮರಿಯೋಜಬಸೆದಮಂಗಳಂ

72

ಕಿಗ್ಗಟ್ನಾಡು ತಾಲ್ಲೂಕು ಬೆಟ್ಟಯತ್ತು ನಾಡಿನಲ್ಲಿ ಬಾಳಾಜಿಗ್ರಾಮದಲ್ಲಿರುವ ಕಲ್ಲು

ಪ್ರಮಾಣ 1′ 6″ × 4′ 3″

೬ ಪಂಕ್ತಿಗಳಿವೆ: ಅಕ್ಷರವೆಲ್ಲಾ ಚುಕ್ಕಿ ಚುಕ್ಕಿ ಕೆಡಿಸಿಬಿಟ್ಟಿವೆ

73

ಅದೇ ತಾಲ್ಲೂಕು ಹತ್ತುಗಟುನಾಡಿನಲ್ಲಿ ಬಾಳೆಲೆ ಗ್ರಾಮ ದೇವಸ್ಥಾನದ ಗೋಡೆಯಮೇಲೆ

1 ಪಡುಬರ ಜೋಗಿ ಸಿಲಾಗೊಲಾ
2 ಪಡುವರಾಯೊಸಿಲಾ
3 ಪಡುಬರಜೋಗಿನಮಃ॥

74

ಮಡಿಕೇರಿತಾಲ್ಲೂಕು ಹರದೂರು ಗ್ರಾಮಕ್ಕೆ ಸಮೀಪ ಕೆರಿಕಣಬ್ಬೈಲುಗಾಳಿಕಲ್ಲುಯೆಂಬ ಕಲ್ಲಿನಲ್ಲಿ

ಪ್ರಮಾಣ 2′ 10″ × 2′ 10″

ಬಲಪಾರ್ಶ್ವ

1 ಸ್ವಸ್ತಿ ಶ್ರೀ
2 ಎಱೆಯ
3 ಪನ -
4 - ದಾಹ
5 ನುರಣಾನ್ತ್ಯ
6 ವಳೆಣ್ಣ ವ
7 ಳುಸತ್ತುವ
8 ಡೆದ ಕಲ್ಲಾ
9 ಡುಂ ಇದ
10 ನಱಿವಂಗೆ
11 ಕವಿಲೆಯುಂಬಾ

ಮಧ್ಯಪಂಕ್ತಿ

12 ಣಾರಸಿಯುಂ ಅಱಿದಪಾತಕಂ

ಕೆಳಗಿನ ಪಂಕ್ತಿ

13 ಒನ್ದು ಬಾಱುಪರಿಹಾ
14 ರಂ ಮಂಗಳಮಹಾಶ್ರೀ

* ಈ ಪಙ್ತಿ ಮೇಲ್ಭಾಗದಲ್ಲಿ ಬರೆದಿದೆ.

75

ಅದೇ ತಾಲ್ಲೂಕು ಉಲುಗುಲಿಗ್ರಾಮದಲ್ಲಿ ಮುದ್ದುವೀರಣ ಪುಟ್ಟಮ್ಮನ ಕಾಫಿತೋಟದಲ್ಲಿರುವ ಕಲ್ಲು

ಪ್ರಮಾಣ 1′ 9″ x 1′ 9″

೧ ನೇ ಪಟ್ಟ

1 ಸ್ವಸ್ತಿಶ್ರೀಮನುಮಹಾಮಂಡಳೇಸ್ವರ ಚಳುಟು

2 ವಿಭಾಡ ಛಲದಂಕರಾಮ ಸತ್ಯರಾಯಸಂವ

3 ರಣಾತಿರವಜ್ರರುದಿರಮಹಿವ್ರೊಕ್ಕಸಕಾವ

4 ಶ್ರೀಮದ್ ವೀರಮುನಿವರಾದಿತ್ಯಗೋಕೂ

೨ ನೇ ಪಟ್ಟ

5 ಳದೇವಗಸರು । ರಕ್ತಾಕ್ಷಿಸಂವತ್ಸರದಕಂನ್ಯಾಮಾಸದಂದುತಂ

6 ಗುನಾಡಕಂಯುಟಿಘಳೆಯ ತುಬುಇಡಿಸಿದಲ್ಲಿಮಾಸಲಬ

7 ಣ್ಣಮ್ಮೀಲಾಳಯಮರುಳಕಾರಯೋಶಿಯಾಳುಬಿದಡೆಗರುಡು

8 ವಳತಲ್ಲಿಬಿಟ್ಟುದಾಣಿಗೆಕಾಲೆಗೆಸಂದುದುಮುಕ್ಕೂಡವೆ

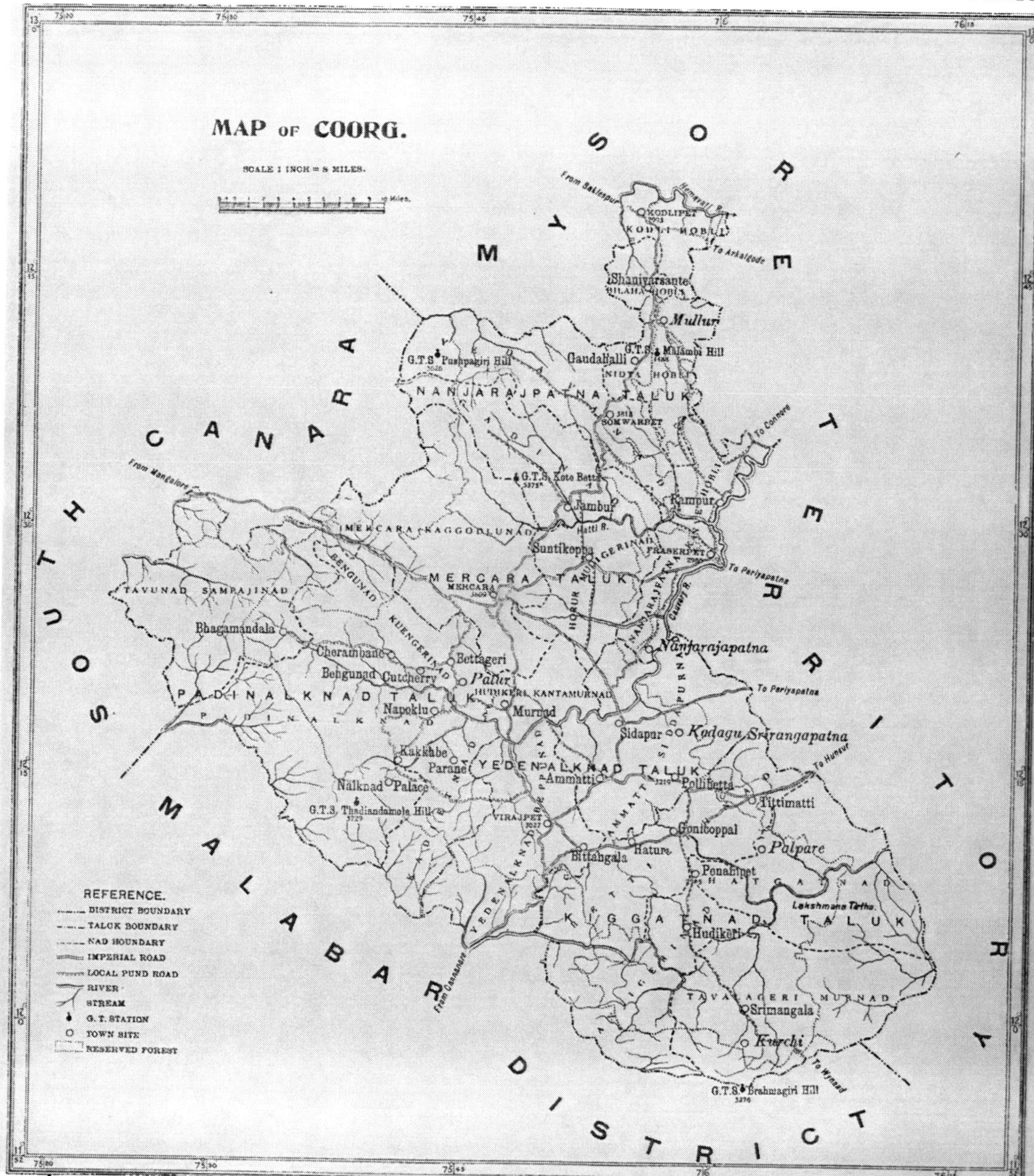

Gustav Haller.

Govt. Photozinco Office, Poona, 1914

ALPHABETICAL LIST OF PLACES WHERE THE INSCRIPTIONS WERE FOUND.

MYSORE AND COORG ARCHÆOLOGICAL SERIES

EPIGRAPHIA CARNATICA

Vol.		Published.
I.	Coorg Inscriptions[1]	1886
II.	Inscriptions at Śravaṇa Beḷgoḷa[2]	1889
III.	Inscriptions in the Mysore Disrict, Part I	1894
IV.	Inscriptions in the Mysore District, Part II	1898
V.	Inscriptions in the Hassan District	1902
VI.	Inscriptions in the Kaḍūr District	1901
VII.	Inscriptions in the Shimoga District, Part I	1902
VIII.	Inscriptions in the Shimoga District, Part II	1902
IX.	Inscriptions in the Bangalore District	1905
X.	Inscriptions in the Kolār District	1905
XI.	Inscriptions in the Chitaldroog District	1902
XII.	Inscriptions in the Tumkūr District	1904

(Government Central Book Depôt, Bangalore.)

MYSORE AND COORG FROM THE INSCRIPTIONS.

Compendium to the above, published in 1909.

(Archibald Constable & Co., London.)

[1] Revised edition, 1913.

[2] Revised edition in the Press.

APPENDIX.

Mysore and Coorg from the Inscriptions.

Emendations due to more recent discoveries, etc.

Page 3. *Nandas.*—The following may be adduced as indicating some connexion of Nandas, or rulers of Nanda descent, with the north of Mysore and other parts to the north-west. A number of leaden coins were found in 1888 at the site of Chandrāvali, an ancient city to the west of Chitaldroog. Some of these bore legends in Brāhmi characters, which have been read as *Mahārathisa Sadakana Kaḷalāya* and *Raño Muḍā Naṃdasa*, surrounding a humped bull, and having on the reverse the Buddhist symbols of a *Bōdhi* tree and a *chaityā*. The former is therefore an Ándhra coin of a Sātakarṇi, and the latter may be a Nanda coin. Another find of similar coins was made at the same place in 1909 (MAR), which also bore these legends, with the variants *Jadakana Kaḷayasa* in the first, and *Muḷā* for *Muḍā* in the second, in addition to one having the legend *Raño Chuṭukaḍḍā Naṃdasa*. With these were found, giving a clue to their period, a Roman silver *denarius* of Augustus, and a Chinese brass coin with a hole in the middle, probably belonging to 138 B.C., the time of the emperor Han Wu-ti. Coins of the same series have moreover been found at Karwar in North Kanara. Now the Sātakarṇi stone inscriptions of perhaps the 2nd century at Malavaḷḷi (Sk 263) and Banavāsi (IA, xiv, 333) give as one of his titles *Vinhukaḍḍa Chuṭukulā Nanda*, and thus seem to afford evidence of the location in some way, in that region, of Nanda rule. Even Professor Rapson read the legends on the Karwar coins at first in the same sense, but has since adopted the reading *kulānanda*, 'joy of the family,' which deprives it so far of any special historical value.

Page 8. *Mudrā Rākshasa.*—The date of this drama Professor Speyer considered should be placed many centuries earlier than is generally done. To this Mr. C. H. Tawney adds, that it is highly satisfactory to have the antiquity of this interesting play rendered so highly probable. And Mr. Vincent Smith says, it used to be dated in the 8th century, but is now ascribed by some scholars to the Gupta period, in the 5th or 6th century (Hillebrandt).

Page 10. *Punnāṭa.*—Jinasēna, who wrote his *Harivamśa* in 783, was of the Bṛihat-Punnāta-sangha.

" " *Avinīta.*—Read 'who married the Punnād king's daughter, and their son Durvvinīta united it'. . . . . .

Page 12. *Edicts* (of Aśōka).—Dr. Thomas's discovery that 256 referred to nights, and M. Sylvain Levi's new translation of *amisā* have upset the previous renderings of certain passages in the Brahmagiri and cognate edicts. Dr. Fleet now proposes the following (JRAS, 1911, p. 1098)—Thus says Dēvāṇampiya: (There are) two and-a-half years and somewhat more, during which I, who am an Upāsaka, did not display much zeal for one year. But (there is) one year, with the balance (of that period), during which I, who have betaken myself to the Sangha, have displayed much zeal: and during this time gods and men, who had not (previously) mixed in Jambudvīpa, have now been made mixed. For this is a result of zeal, and it is not to be reached by high rank (alone); for even the great heaven may be attained by a lowly person who displays zeal'. . . . . . 'And this address was delivered by him who spent 256 nights in worship'. Dr. Hultzsch translates (*id.* 1115)—'But men in Jambudvīpa who up to this time had been unassociated with the gods have (now) been made associated with the gods'. And Pandit Laddu (*id.* 1119)—'In Jambudvīpa the gods (of the well-known Hindu pantheon) who up to this time had not been associated (with men like Gautama and others) have now been made associated with them (by me through my non-sectarian zeal)'. Dr. Waddell says (AQR, January 1912, p. 105)—'Aśōka obviously intended by this reference to the gods to enforce the dogma of the higher Buddhism, that in a Buddhist country 'there is no difference between gods and men', because all are equally subject to transmigration (*cf.* Mahāyāna Texts, SBE); but the existence of the gods is here accepted by Aśōka, whose favourite title was 'The Beloved of the Gods'. Dr. Thomas writes (JRAS, 1912, p. 480)—'M. Levi's convincing interpretation of *amisā* has been generally accepted, and the resultant meaning that "those men in Jambudvīpa who had 'had unmixing gods' have been mixed with the gods" appears inevitable. But the practical import is far from clear, and I am unable to solve the problem. That the gods mentioned are real gods (see Fleet and Hultzsch above) and not kings, as M. Levi suggested, and that the *munisā* are ordinary men and not deified teachers, as is proposed by Pandit Laddu, is the most natural interpretation. We must remember that the result described had been attained—and not by greatness, but by energy—in little more than a year. Are we to understand a conversion of people who previously did not recognize the Brahmanical gods? In any case the result is a curious outcome of Aśōka's first work as a zealous Buddhist. But for the laity, even among the Buddhists, heaven is the goal in prospect as appears later in this very edict, and also in Rock Edict vi. Asōka is himself *dēvānāmpriya*. Prof. Venis (in letter to Dr. Hultzsch, quoted JRAS 1913, p. 652) says—'If plain folk are to understand Dēvānāmpriya when he says that a new condition of things had been so rapidly brought about in Jambudvīpa by his religious zeal, they must be shown some outward physical fact or sign which they could at once accept as the intelligible or usual attendant of religious zeal.' Dr. H. adds—'This postulate is complied with if we assume that the 'gods' (*dēvā*) of the Rūpnāth edict are identical with the *divyāni rūpāni*, etc., of the fourth rock edict, and that in both cases Aśōka wished to remind his subjects of certain religious shows at which he had exhibited to them *in effigie* the gods whose abodes they would be able to reach by the zealous practice of *dhamma*'. In regard to the 256, Dr. Fleet (*id.* 656), writes—'We know that Aśōka was anointed as king when 218 years had elapsed, *i.e.*, at some time in the year 219 current after the death of Buddha, and that he then reigned for 37 years: this carries us on to some point in the year 219+37 = 256 current; and giving a year the figures of which are the same with those of the nights which are mentioned in the record. The topic of the record is zeal or energy in the practice of morality and religion; and the record expands the dying speech of Buddha, whose last words were—'Work out your salvation by diligence.' Taken with the other points, the agreement in the numbers—256 nights and 256 years—indicates a conclusion which seems irresistible: namely, that, after reigning for 37 years, Aśōka, in the course of the 256th year after the death of Buddha, abdicated and passed into religious retirement on the hill Suvarnagiri; that the address published in the record was delivered by him on the 256th night after that event; that it was delivered on that particular occasion because he then fulfilled in worship at night in his retirement a number of nights equal to the number of years which in the meantime had been completed since the death of Buddha; and that it contains his last pronouncement, if not actually his dying words.'

Page 14. *For* 'he sent' *read* 'under him were sent'. . . .

" " (Note)—*Read* 'Māmūlanār's verses in the *Aganānūru*, and he is of the'. . . .

" 15. *Sivakhada-Nāgasiri.*—According to Rapson this is the name of the Prince associated with the Queen in the donation. Her name is not given. But from an inscription at Kanheri is said to be Nāgamulanikā.

Page 19. There is an inscription of a Bāṇa king Aggapa-Rāju, of 968 A.D., in the Nellore district (iii, 1201).

Page 20. *The Chōḷa king.*—Before this *insert*—'The Nolamba king Mahēndra (c. 878) is called *Mahābali-kula-vidhvamsanam*, or destroyer of the Mahābali family (EI, x, 65).

Page 21. *Aśōka sent*—Read 'under Aśōka was sent'.

" 25. Māndhātṛivarmmā's father was Kumāravarmmā. Mṛigēsavarmmā's queen was Prabhāvati of the Kaikēya family, and mother of Ravivarmmā (MAR 1911).

Page 31. *Sister*—add 'Ālabbe' (Sh 64).

" 32. *Or law of adoption*—Substitute note—Dattaka is mentioned by Vatsyāyana, author of the *Kāma-sūtra*, as having written a separate work on one branch (named *Vaiśka*) of the subject, at the instance of the dancing girls of Pātaliputra. Dattaka may be placed in perhaps the first century A.D. (JRAS 1911, p. 183). Dattaka appears in Kannada as Jattaka. Thus the Hoysala prince Ereyanga is described (Ak 102a) as *abalā-Jattakan*, or a Jattaka to the weaker sex.

Page 33. *Appogāl village*—add "The Tamil chronicle attributes to him another grant at Tagadūr in 288 to Brāhmans for the worship of Mūlasthān Īsvara" (see IA, i, 361).

Page 34. *End of para.* 2—add "A grant by him to a Buddhist has been obtained at Melekōte, Tumkūr tāluq (MAR 1910).

Page 35. *Outside customs*—add "A grant of his 25th year has been found" (MAR 1911).

" 35. *End of para.*—continue—He married the daughter of Skandavarmmā, the Rāja of Punnāḍ. This is of course the Punnāta in the south-west of Mysore to which reference has been made before, in connection with the Jain migration under Bhadrabāhu. (Substitute for next para.)—

Durvvinīta, his son by the Punnāḍ Rāja's daughter, succeeded him in c. 482, although his father, acting on the advice of his own guru, had set him aside (from the succession) in favour of another son. But Lakshmī (the goddess of sovereignty) came to him of her own accord and embraced his broad chest (Bn 141, Mi 110, DB 68). His supersession at first is confirmed by the interesting old Siragunda stone inscription (Cm 50), which states that Nirvvinīta's (*i.e.* Avinīta's) younger son obtained the Koṅgaṇi crown. This he did, it adds, from Kāḍuveṭṭi (a common name for the Pallava king) and the Vallava (Ballaha or Rāshṭrakūṭa) king[1]. But we are informed in Nr 35 that Durvvinīta captured Kāḍuveṭṭi on the field of battle and placed his own daughter's son Jayasimha-Vallabha on his hereditary throne. This is the name of the Chalukya prince who by defeating the Rāshṭrakūṭas laid the foundation of the Chalukya power in the South. It may perhaps be inferred therefore that Durvvinīta had entered into alliance with the Chalukyas and given his daughter in marriage to the representative of that family, though this is not actually mentioned anywhere.

Durvvinīta was distinguished for his literary ability. For we are told that he wrote a commentary on the fifteenth *sarga* of the *Kirātārjuniya*, a Sanskrit poem by Bhāravi. This *sarga* is full of verbal puzzles and riddles. One stanza contains no consonant but *n*, with a single *t* at the end; in another, each half-line read backwards is similar to the other half (see IGI, ii, 240; JRAS 1911, 187). We are also informed (Tm 23, and grant of his 40th year lately found, MAR 1912) that he was himself the author of a *Śabdāvatāra* (the name of a work always attributed to the Jain grammarian Pūjyapāda [2]), and of a version in Sanskrit of the *Vaḍḍakathā*, which from Tm 23 apparently means the *Bṛihatkathā*, a work known in oriental literature as having been written in the Paiśāchi dialect[3]. He is no doubt the Durvvinīta named in Nṛipatunga's *Kavirāja-mārgga* as one of the distinguished early Kannaḍa authors.

Page 36. *Omit* lines 1–5, him . . . Bhadrabāhu. Also 12–17, Another . . . Nirvvinīta.

„ „ *End of para.*—add "One has been lately found of his 40th year (MAR 1912)."

„ 41. *End of second para.*—Add 'which was maintained by Kambharasa (IA xviii, 313). He fell in a battle against Vallaha at Kāgimogeyūr, in the Tumkūr country (MAR 1910).'

Page 42. *Pṛithuvipati.*—add 'His name may have been Diṇḍika.' *On the throne*—add–' in 817.' *Pallavādhiraja's daughter*—continue 'and gave his own daughter Jāyabbe, the younger sister of Nītimārgga, to Nolambādhirāja.' *To footnote* add SII ii, 381.

Page 45. *The exact date of which event is not known*—substitute—"the date of which event is 869".

„ 47. *Thirty-two Thousand* (para. 3) continue "A grant in the reign of Rakkasa-Ganga has been found at Haḷe Būdanūr, Mandya tāluq, without date. But on another side of the same stone is one of Rājēndra-Chōḷa's 12th year. Nāgavarmmā, the author of *Chhandōmbudhi*, says that Rakkasa-Ganga was his king. This has been omitted for some reason by Mr. Kittel in his edition of the work".

Page 49. *In table.*—After *Harivarmmā*, 247–266, add "[2] and footnote", "In the Tamil chronicle 288 is given as a date in his reign". After *Mādhava* III, 357–370, add "[3] and footnote." "At this point, between Mādhava III and Avinīta, the Tamil chronicle inserts a Diṇḍikara-Rāja or Hariśchandra, who ruled for only a short time". After *Avinīta*, continue "c. 430–482 (1. 2) Kali-Ganga, Nirvvinīta (1. 3)m. Punnāḍ princess". After *Durvvinīta* continue "c. 482–522. ." and omit 1. 2.

Page 50. *In table.*—For '670,' against Bhūvikrama and Sivamāra I substitute '679.' *Under Prithivipati* I, insert "? Diṇḍika". *After Rājamalla Satyavākya* I—add '817–828' . . '*After Nītimārgga* I,' add '—869'.

Page 55. *Omit* 'the younger sister of Noḷambādhirāja', and *after Jāyabbe* insert "the younger sister of Nītimārgga."

Page 56.—*Fighting with the Ganga king*—add 'He is said to have destroyed the Mahābali family (the Bāṇas), and hence was called Mahābali-kula-vidhvamsanam' (EI x, 65). *End of para.*—add 'He apparently had a younger brother (Mb 38), the Noḷambādhirāja-Nolipayya ruling in 897 (Mi 52), who had a son Ankayya (Mi 27). *Para.* 3—omit 'Noḷipayya'; '897 in Mi 52'; 'and Ankayya.'

---

[1] An interesting parallel to this occurrence took place some centuries later, when the Ganga king Śivamāra-Saigoṭṭa on his release from captivity, was crowned with their own hands by Gōvinda-Prabhūtavarsha, the Rāshṭrakūṭa king, and Nandivarmmā, the Pallava king (Yd 60, Nl 60).

[2] Thus we have in Nr 40 the following verse :—

nyāsam Jainēndra-sañjñam sakala-budha-nutaṃ Pāṇinīyasya bhūyō- |
nyāsam Śabdāvatāraṃ manuja-tati-hitaṃ Vaidya-śāstraṃ cha kṛitvā ||
yas Tatvārtthasya ṭīkāṃ vyarachayad iha tāṃ bhāty asau Pūjyapāda- |
svāmī bhūpāla-vandyaḥ sva-para-hita-vachah pūrnna-dṛig-bōdha-vṛittaḥ ||

Perhaps Pūjyapāda may have been Durvvinīta's preceptor, but this is not so stated.

[3] It is strange that in a Sanskrit sentence the above Prākrit word should be used in designating a work which has a recognized Sanskrit title. The actual name in Tm 23 is *Bṛihatvṛithaḥ*, but this seems to be a mistake of the engraver.

Page 57. *After para.* 2 insert 'The following is a tentative table of the Noḷambas, with dates obtained from inscriptions :—

Mangala
Noḷambādhirāja
praised by the Karṇāṭas
|
1. Simhapōta, Singapōta
Kali-Noḷambādi-arasa
fought for Ganga king Śivamāra II agst. Duggamāra, his rival for the throne.
|
2. Chārupoṇnera c. 780
Paramēsvara-Pallavādhirāja
in time of Rāshṭrakūṭa king Jagattunga-Prabhūtavarsha (Gōvinda II).
|
3. Polalchōra c. 825
Pallavamalla, Noḷambādhirāja
m. Jāyabbe, dr. of Ganga king Satyavākya I, and yr. sister of Nītimārgga I.

4. Vīra-Mahēndra, Mayinda 878–895
Noḷamba-Nārāyaṇa
Mahābali-kula-vidhvamsanam
m. 1. Ganga princess Gāmabbe
2. Kadamba princess Dīvalabbe

5. Noḷambādhirāja-Noḷipayya 897
|
Ankayya.

(Children of 4:)

by 1.
6. Ayyapa 918–929
Noḷambādhirāja-Naṇṇiga, Naṇṇigāśraya
m. Ganga princess Pollabbe

by 2.
Pallavendra-Iriva-Noḷamba

(Children of 6:)

7. Aṇṇiga, Aṇṇayya 931–940
Bira-Noḷamba
m. Chaluki princess Attiyabbe
|
Iruḷa 929

8. Dilīpayya, Dilīparasa 943–956
Iriva-Noḷamba
Noḷambādhirāja Noḷapayya
Iriva-Noḷambādhirāja-Nuḷipayya
|
9. Naṇṇi-Noḷamba 975

Page 66. For '*Pulikēsi I*' read 'Pulikēsi II.'

„ 67. Under '*Dantidurga*' in the table, add Sāhasatunga.

„ 74. Vikrama, given in the table, has dropped out here in printing. After '*Iriva Nolambādhirāja*', l. 1, read 'Vikrama Tribhuvanamalla, the son of Satyāsraya's son Daśavarmma, succeeded his uncle (Dg. 1), and dispersed the hosts of his enemies. Sk 287, Sb 281, 471 are of his reign'. For '*Satyāsraya's*', l. 5, read 'Vikrama's'.

Page 130. Note—add 'The Bēḍas are said in Manucci to leap on to the quarters of the horse behind and cut off the nose of the horseman. This mode of attack is paralleled by that of the wild Irish at the end of the 14th century, as described in Froissart's Chronicle, where it is said that they leap from the ground behind a horseman and embrace the rider so tightly that he can in no way get rid of them, and cut his throat'.

Page 131. For '*There are no inscriptions of his time*' read 'Bn 118 is of his time'.

„ 133. Add note to l. 11—'But the Seven Kombus mentioned in Sk 136 of 1068 may perhaps refer to the Coorgs'.

Page 134. In table, under '10. *Vīra-Rāja*'—for 'died 1862' read 'died 1859'. In l. 4 from bottom—for '1738' read '1788'.

Page 135, para. 2—For '*first Linga-Rāja*' read 'second Linga-Rāja'.

„ 136. End of para. 2—read 'He died in London in Sept. 1859. His body was temporarily placed in the catacombs at Kensal Green Cemetery, and the next year sent to India for interment'.

Page 143. l. 21. For '*Panchava mahārāya*' read 'Manija.'

l. 25 For '*when—the latter*' read 'he sent word to Panchavan-mahārāya, who'.

Page 145. For last two lines, read 'originally founded and endowed by the Kongālva king Rājādhirāja in the name of his mother, and recovered the grants, which are still continued. The Vijayanagar king Harihara II at the same time made a grant of Muḷḷur-nād to Gonka-Raḍḍi-nāyaka, who had been noticed (for his bravery) by his general Guṇḍappa-daṇṇāyaka (Cg 39)'.

Page 146. For l. 13–17 substitute ' Avinīta married the daughter of Skandavarmmā, the Rāja of Punnāḍ, and their son was Durvvinīta, who reigned from c. 482 to 522.

Page 153. Add to footnote ' Padinālkunāḍ is mentioned in 1277 and 1295, in the time of the Hoysalas (Ch 65, 44) '.

Page 161. Read ' bearer of the Hadapa (or betel bag) '.

Page 176. L. 9 from bottom, read ' abduction of a gurū's wife and the murder of Brāhmans '.

„ 178. For ' *mana* (maunds) ' read ' *māna* (a half seer) '.

„ 196. *Dattaka-sūtra*—See correction above to p. 32.

„ 197. For ' (Kolhapur &c.) ' read ' (Karahāṭa or Karhāḍ in Satāra District). l. 22 insert ' and that Prabhāchandra composed the *Nyāyakumuda-chandrōdaya*, a Nyāsa on Śākaṭāyana's sūtras '—and omit this passage from l. 18–19.

Page 201. For ' Umēśadatta ' read ' Harihara-sūri '.

„ 203. Add note to l. 11–' A grant of the 4th century by the Ganga king Mādhava III to a Buddhist named Buddhisatva has been obtained at Melekōṭe, Tumkūr District (MAR 1910).

Page 205. L. 17–Insert ' (see the beginning of Ck 137).

„ 207. End of para. 2. add ' (Sr 86) '. See also remarks now on Cg 8 and 9.

INDEX TO INTRODUCTION.

List of Public Institutions, Libraries, etc., to which copies of Archæological Survey Reports are regularly supplied.

I.—COUNTRIES OUTSIDE INDIA.

UNITED KINGDOM.

Aberdeen University Library, Aberdeen.
Royal Library, Windsor Castle, Berks.
Birmingham University Library.
Bendall Library, Cambridge.
Cambridge University Library, Cambridge.
National Library of Ireland, Leinster House, Kildare Street, Dublin.
Royal Irish Academy, 19, Dawson Street, Dublin.
Trinity College Library, Dublin.
Advocates' Library, Edinburgh.
University Library, Edinburgh.
Royal Society, Edinburgh.
Royal Scottish Museum, Edinburgh.
Society of Antiquaries of Scotland, National Museum of Antiquities, Queen Street, Edinburgh.
Glasgow University Library, Glasgow.
British Museum Library, Great Russell Street, Bloomsbury, London. W.C.
Folklore Society, 11, Old Square Lincoln's Inn, London, W.C.
India Office Library, London, S.W.
Imperial Institute, London.
Library of the Oriental Department of the British Museum, London, W.C.
London Library, St. James Square, London, S.W.
London University Library, Imperial Institute, London, S.W.
National Art Library, South Kensington Museum, London.
Royal Academy of Arts, Burlington House, Piccadilly, London, W.
Royal Anthropological Institute of Great Britain and Ireland, 50, Great Russell Street, London, W.C.
Royal Asiatic Society, 22, Albemarle Street, London, W.
Royal Colonial Institute, Northumberland Avenue, London, W.C.
Royal Institute of British Architects, 9, Conduit Street, Hanover Square, London, W.
Royal Society, Burlington House, Piccadilly, London, W.
Society of Antiquaries of London, Burlington House, Piccadilly, London, W.
Society for the Protection of Ancient Buildings, 10, Buckingham Street, Adelphi, London, W.C.
Society for the Promotion of Hellenic Studies, London.
Bodleian Library, Oxford.
Indian Institute, Oxford.

FRANCE.

Bibliothéque Nationale, Paris.
Bibliothéque J. Doucet 19, Rue Spontine in Paris.
Directeur Général de l'Union Coloniale Francaise, 44, Chaussé d'Antin, Paris.
The Ecole speciale des Langues Orientales, Vivantas, Paris.
Institut de France, Paris.
Institut Ethnogrophique International de Paris, 28, Rue Bonaparte, Paris.
Musée Guimet, 7, Place d'léna, Paris.
Revue Archéologique, 28, Rue Bonaparte. Paris.
Société Asiatique, 1, Rue de Seine, Paris.
University of Lyons.

GERMANY.

Königliches Museumfür Völkerkunde, Berlin.
Königliche Preussische Akademie der Wissenschaften, Berlin.
Royal Library, Berlin.
Königliche Gesellschaft der Wissenschaften zu Göttingen, Göttingen, Germany.
Bibliothek der Deutschen Morgenlandischen Gesellschaft, Halle (Saale) Germany.
Royal Library, Munich, Bavaria.

AUSTRIA.

Hungarian Academy, Buda-Pesth.
Imperial Academy of Sciences, Vienna.

ITALY.

R. Biblioteca Nazionale, Centrale di Firenze, Italy.
Societá Asiatio Italiana, Firenze, Italy.
Secretary Rivista di Storia Antica, Padova, Italy.
American School of Classical Studies at Rome.
Biblioteca Nazionale, Vittorio Emanuele, Rome.
British School at Rome, Palazza Odescalchi, Piazza S. S. Apostoli, Rome.

HOLLAND.

Koninklijke Akademie van Wetenschappen te Amsterdam, Holland.
Koninklijk Instituut van Nederlandsch Indië, The Hague, Holland.

RUSSIA.

Imperial Academy of Sciences (for the Asiatic Museum), St. Petersburg, Russia.

DENMARK.

National Museum, Copenhagen, Denmark.
Royal Library, Copenhagen, Denmark.

BELGIUM.

Academie Royale d'Archeologie de Belgique, Anvers.

SWEDEN.

University Library, Upsala.

NORWAY.

University Library, Christiana.

GREECE.

British School at Athens, Greece
La Société Archeologique d'Athènes, Athèns.

JAPAN.

President, Asiatic Society of Japan, Tokio.

China.

North China Branch of the Royal Asiatic Society, Shanghai.

America.

Field Museum of Natural History, Chicago, U.S.A.
American Oriental Society, 235, Bishop Street, New Haven, Conn., U.S.A.
Free Library of Philadelphia, U.S.A.
Library of Congress, Washington, U.S.A.
Secretary, National Museum, Washington, U.S.A.
Smithsonian Institution, Washington, D.C., U.S.A.
The American Philosophical Society, 104, South Fifth Street, Philadelphia, U.S.A.

Siam.

Vajiranana National Library, Bangkok.

British Colonies.

Royal Asiatic Society, Ceylon Branch, Colombo.
The Museum, Canterbury, New Zealand.
Melbourne Library, Melbourne, Australia.
Victoria Public Library, Perth, Western Australia.
Literary and Historical Society, Quebec, Canada.
University Library, Sydney, New South Wales.
Straits Branch, Royal Asiatic Society, Singapore.

Foreign Colonies.

Bataviaasch Genootschap van Kunsten en Wetenschappen, Batavia.
De l'Institut Francais d'Archèologie Orientale du Caire, Cairo, Egypt.
Museum of Arabic Art, Cairo, Egypt.
De l'Ecole Francaise d'Extreme Orient, Hanoi, Indo-China.
Ethnological Survey for the Philliphine Islands, Department of Interior, Manila.

II.—INDIA.

(1) Imperial.

Imperial Library, Calcutta.
Indian Museum, Calcutta.
Department of Education Library, Delhi.
Central Library, Army Headquarters, Simla.

(2) Provincial.

Madras.

The Government College, Kumbakonam.
Christian College Library, Madras.
Government Central Museum, Madras.
Pachaiyappa's College, Madras.
Presidency College, Madras.
Public Library, Madras.
School of Art, Madras.
Secretariat Library, Fort St. George.
University Library, Madras.
St. Aloysius College, Mangalore.
Noble College, Masulipatam.
The Sanskrit College, Mylapore.
The Government College, Rajahmundry.
The Teachers' College, Saidapet, Chingleput district.
St. Joseph's College, Trichinopoly.
S.P.G. College, Trichinopoly.
Maharaja's College, Trivandrum.
The Sanskrit College, Tiruvadi.
Maharaja's College, Vizianagram.
Telugu Academy, Pudupet, Madras.

Bombay.

Gujarat College, Ahmedabad.
Bombay Branch of the Royal Asiatic Society, Town Hall, Bombay.
Elphinstone College, Bombay.
Prince of Wales Museum, Bombay.
St. Xavier's College, Bombay.
Secretariat Library, Bombay.
School of Art, Bombay.
University Library, Bombay.
Wilson College, Bombay.
The College of Science, Poona.
Deccan College, Poona.
Fergusson College, Poona.

Bengal.

Wesleyan Mission College, Bankura.
Barisal Public Library, Barisal.
Burdwan Raj Public Library, Burdwan.
Asiatic Society of Bengal, 57, Park Street, Calcutta.
Bangabasi College Calcutta.
Bengal Chamber of Commerce, Calcutta.
Bangiya Sahitya Parishad Sabha, Calcutta.
Bethune College, Calcutta.
Calcutta Historical Society, Calcutta.
Calcutta University Institute, College Square, Calcutta.
Chaitanya Library, 4-1, Beadon Street, Calcutta.
Church Mission Society, Calcutta.
Economic Museum, Calcutta.
Editor, Bengal Past and Present, Kidderpore Vicarage, Calcutta.
Goethals' Indian Library, 30, Park Street, Calcutta.
Government School of Art, Calcutta.
Library of the United Service Club, Calcutta.
L.M.S. College, Bhowanipur, Calcutta.
Mahabodhi Society, Baniapooker Lane, Calcutta.
Metropolitan Institution, Calcutta.
Presidency College Library, 1, College Square, Calcutta.
Sanskrit College Library, 1, College Square, Calcutta.
Scottish Churches College, Calcutta.
Secretariat Library, Writers' Buildings, Calcutta.
University Library, The Senate House, Calcutta.
Hoogly College, Chinsura.
Chittagong College.
Beer Chandra Public Library at Comilla.
Dacca College.
Northbrook Hall Library, Dacca.
Provincial Library, Dacca.
Jaganath College, Dacca.
Krishnagar College, Krishnagar.
Daulatpur Hindu Academy, Khulna.
Midnapur College, Midnapur.
Narail Victoria College, Narail.
Rajshahi College, Rajshahi.
Varendra Research Society, Rajshahi.
Serampore College, Serampore.
Civil Engineering College, Sibpur.

Bihar and Orissa.

Bihar National College, Bankipore.
Bihar and Orissa Secretariat Library.
Bihar School of Engineering, Bankipore.
Patna College, Bankipore.
Ravenshaw College, Cuttack.
St. Columba's College, Hazaribagh.

United Provinces.

Agra College, Agra.
Palace Library of the Most Revd. the Archbishop at Agra.
St. John's College, Agra.
Lyall Library, Aligarh.
M.A.O. College Library, Aligarh.
Christian College, Allahabad.
Muir Central College, Allahabad.
Panini Office, Allahabad.
Public Library, Allahabad.
Secretariat Library, Public Works Department, Allahabad.
University Library, Allahabad.
Carmichael Library, Benares.
Central Hindu College, Benares.
Queen's College, Benares.
Sanskrit College, Benares.
Christ's Church College, Cawnpore.
Canning College, Lucknow.
Provincial Museum Library, Lucknow.
Public Library, Lucknow.
Lyall Library, Meerut.
Archæological Museum, Muttra.
Thomason College, Roorkee.

Punjab.

Khalsa College, Amritsar.
Aitchison College, Lahore.
Central Training College, Lahore.
Dyal Singh College, Lahore.
Dayanand Anglo-Vedic College, Lahore.
Forman Christian College, Lahore.
Government College Library, Lahore.
Islamia College, Lahore.
Museum Library, Lahore.
Punjab Historical Society, Lahore.
Punjab Public Library, Lahore.
Secretariat Library, Public Works Department, Lahore.
University Library, Lahore.

Delhi.

The Museum, Delhi.
Public Library, Delhi.
St. Stephen's College, Delhi.

North-west Frontier Province.

Peshawar Museum, Peshawar.
Secretariat Library, Peshawar.

Burma.

Myanma Awia Club, Kyaiklat, Pyapon District.
Mandalay Public Library, Mandalay.
Buddhist Library, Nathinggyaung, Bassein District.
Buddhist Propaganda Society, Pegu.
Young Men's Buddhist Association, Pegu.
Baptist College, Rangoon.
Bernard Free Library, Rangoon.
Burma Research Society, Rangoon.
Cedi Yengana Association Library, Shwe Dagon Pagoda, Rangoon.
Phayre Museum, Rangoon.
Rangoon College, Rangoon.
Rangoon Literary Society, Rangoon.
Secretariat Library, Rangoon.
Soolay Pagoda Library, Rangoon.
Teachers' Institute, Rangoon.
Trustees of the Shwe Dagon Pagoda, Rangoon.
Young Men's Buddhist Association, Rangoon.

Assam.

Cotton Library, Dhubri.
Cotton College, Gauhati.
Curzon Hall Library, Gauhati.
Government Library, Shillong.
Secretariat Library, Shillong.
Victoria Jubilee Library, Tezpur.

Central Provinces.

Public Library of Amraoti Town.
High School Committee, Balaghat.
Government College, Jubbulpore.
Training College, Jubbulpore.
Jagannath High School, Mandla.
Hislop College, Nagpur.
Morris College, Nagpur.
Museum Library, Nagpur.
Secretariat Library, Nagpur.
Victoria Technical Institute Library, Nagpur.
Public Library, Saugor.
Victoria Library, Seoni.

(3) Native States.

Mysore.

Central College, Bangalore.
Indian Institute of Science, Bangalore.
Chief Commissioner of Coorg's Library, Bangalore.
Maharaja's College, Mysore.

Hyderabad.

Resident's Library, Hyderabad.
Nizam's State Library, Hyderabad.
Nizam's College Library, Hyderabad.

Central India.

Rajkumar College, Indore.
Dhar Museum Library, Dhar.
Library of the Agent to the Governor-General, Indore.

Rajaputana.

College Library, Ajmer.
Rajaputana Museum, Ajmer.
Library of the Chief Commissioner and Agent to the Governor-General, Ajmere.

Baroda.

Library of the Resident at Baroda.
Baroda Museum.

Kathiawar.

Sir Bhagwatsingji Library, Gondal (Kathiawar).
Watson Museum of Antiquities, Rajkot.

Travancore.

Travancore Darbar.

Gwalior.

Gwalior Darbar.

Chamba.

Bhuri Singh Museum, Chamba.